Vendor Questions

Here is a list of questions to ask the vendor during an interview:

1. How many years have you been in business? (If the person is just starting out, that is not necessarily a problem. Check if the vendor has a strong education or has experience with another company doing the same type of work.)

2. How many years have you been in this location?

3. Are you insured with a liability policy with a minimum of $1 million worth of coverage? (If so, you would like to be put on the insurance certificate as an additional insured. If not, find another vendor.)

4. What happens in case of equipment breakdown? (If it's not already on-site, backup equipment should be available to be delivered to the site immediately in case of an emergency.)

5. In case of an illness, who will take the place of a vendor?

6. When do you need a final count? (This question is for caterers.)

7. Who are three clients whom I may contact who had a similar event to mine in the last year? (If you are booking someone to handle a wedding, their experience doing a corporate holiday party is not going to give you an apples-to-apples comparison. You want referrals with like parties.)

8. What are your professional affiliations?

9. How do I make my final payment? Cash? Personal check? Bank check? Credit card? (Do not pay in cash until the event is over to your satisfaction. Otherwise, pay by check or credit card.)

10. How long before the event may I cancel without penalty? (The farther away you are from the event when you cancel, the less in cancellation penalties you should be charged.)

Budget Breakdown

When planning a typical party budget, you can expect the percentage of expenses to breakdown in the following manner. Your budget may vary due to your preferences.

Item	Percent of Total Budget
Printed pieces: Invitations, thank-you notes, programs, place cards	3 percent
Decorations: Balloons, flowers, banners, props, linens	15 percent
Food and beverages including servers	40 percent
Entertainment, activities	20 percent
Prizes, gifts, favors	3 percent
Rental items	14 percent
Miscellaneous	5 percent

The Five W's of Invitations

The following details should be included in every invitation you send out:

1. Who is throwing the party? Write out the full names of the hosts.
2. What type of party is it? Formal or casual, cocktail or dinner, theme or scheme. Prepare your guests for what they should expect the minute they walk in the door.
3. When is the party? Make sure you tell the day, date, and start and finish times of the event.
4. Where is the party? Give the address, directions, and a map if necessary.
5. Why is the party being held? State the occasion (birthday, anniversary, bon voyage, new baby, etc.) and honoree's name, if applicable.
6. Your how-to's should include how to respond, the dress code, and what to bring if it's a potluck event. Also, include phone number for emergency situations.

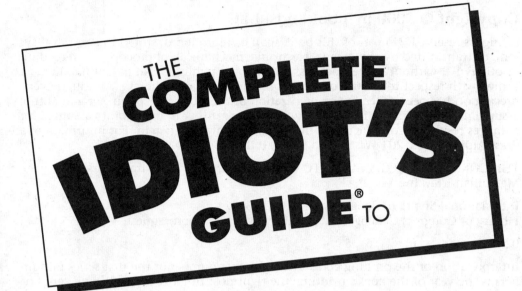

THE COMPLETE IDIOT'S GUIDE® TO

Throwing a Great Party

by Phyllis Cambria and Patty Sachs

Produced by BookEnds, LLC

alpha
books

Macmillan USA, Inc.
201 West 103rd Street
Indianapolis, IN 46290

A Pearson Education Company

International Standard Book Number: 0-02-863974-x
Library of Congress Catalog Card Number: Available upon request.

02 01 00   8 7 6 5 4 3 2 1

Interpretation of the printing code: The rightmost number of the first series of numbers is the year of the book's printing; the rightmost number of the second series of numbers is the number of the book's printing. For example, a printing code of 00-1 shows that the first printing occurred in 2000.

Printed in the United States of America

Publisher
Marie Butler-Knight

Product Manager
Phil Kitchel

Managing Editor
Cari Luna

Acquisitions Editor
Amy Zavatto

Development Editor
BookEnds, LLC

Production Editor
Billy Fields

Copy Editor
Amy Borrelli

Illustrator
Brian Moyer

Cover Designers
Mike Freeland
Kevin Spear

Book Designers
Scott Cook and Amy Adams of DesignLab

Indexer
Lisa Wilson

Layout/Proofreading
Darin Crone
Mary Hunt
Joe Millay
Gloria Schurick

Contents at a Glance

Contents

xi

Foreword

Where was *The Complete Idiot's Guide to Throwing a Great Party* when I gave my first get-together! I could have used the expert help from authors Phyllis Cambria and Patty Sachs. Now it's all here—everything you need to know about hosting parties—in one complete reference guide.

In a simple and easy-to-follow format, party pros Cambria and Sachs invite even first-timers to host a party with "Festive Fundamentals." They offer all the basics for a guaranteed successful event, even if you're a nervous novice. The authors cover everything from awesome invitations to zippy cleanup, in a breezy, well-written style that makes this great resource fun and easy to use. They even wrap up the party information like a present, by providing sections on "Going Pro" for those who want to make party-hosting a profession.

The Complete Idiot's Guide to Throwing a Great Party is chock-full of practical party-planning tips. The sidebars are especially helpful, with lots of fast and easy ideas. Watch for quickies like "Chips and Tips" that offer general party tips and information, "Party Pitfalls" that provide warnings to watch out for, "Festive Facts" with entertaining anecdotes, and "Shindig Sayings" to help you understand popular party terms. And if you just want to cut to the chase and get to the basics for throwing a successful party, check out "The Least You Need to Know" for the nitty-gritty.

You'll find help with everything having to do with parties—planning the guest list, choosing a theme, partying without going to the poorhouse, inviting invitations, setting the stage, tasty refreshments, and helpful how-to hostess tips. The authors cover all kinds of party themes from cocktail parties to black-tie affairs, from seasonal celebrations to life's big events—for all ages and occasions. They teach us how to wind up the party gracefully when it's time for the guests to go home. And they're right there with tips on how to clean up the post-party confetti and clutter.

If that's not enough, the book contains a bonus section with Party-Planning Worksheets, offering projected budgets, party planning, and vendor guidelines. You'll find product and service resources, including reference materials, wonderful Web sites, and information on how to contact the authors. And if you need help with beverage selection, you'll find tips on how to choose and serve a variety of wines.

Finally, if you just need an excuse for a party, check out the Calendar of U.S. Holidays that offers suggestions for a full year of party options. You can celebrate Elvis Presley's birthday, Winnie the Pooh Day, National Earmuff Day, Sadie Hawkins Day, Underdog Day, and my favorite—National Dessert Day.

So what are you waiting for? You don't need an excuse to host a party, now that Cambria and Sachs are here. They've done most of the work for you, and you'll find it all in their Party Central guidebook: *The Complete Idiot's Guide to Throwing a Great Party!*

Penny Warner is the author of over 30 books, including *Kids' Pick-A-Party, Kids' Party Games and Activities, Slumber Parties, Storybook Parties, Baby Birthday Parties,* and *The Best Party Book.*

Penny Warner

Penny Warner has sold over 30 books for parents and kids, featuring ideas on parties, games, activities, snacks, and child development. Warner has appeared numerous times on San Francisco Bay Area and national television, presenting party tips for adults and children. She lives in Danville, CA, with her husband and has two grown children.

Introduction

Notes from the Authors

A note from Phyllis:

A few years ago, after almost 20 years as a professional event coordinator and part-time freelance writer, I had decided to test the book-publishing waters. However, whenever I felt I had a great idea for a book, I'd do some research and find that a certain other planner, Patty Sachs, already had the same idea and had written a book about it. If I read an article in the newspaper about party planning, Patty Sachs was often quoted. Whenever I'd talk with other coordinators around the country, Patty's name would come up in the conversation.

Finally, out of curiosity (and mild envy), I bought one of her books and learned why she was so successful. Her ideas are extremely clever and she writes books that are fun to read. Happily, her philosophy about throwing a great party matches mine, and it's the same philosophy you'll find in this book:

- ➤ Plan early.
- ➤ Themes are great.
- ➤ The party starts with the invitation.
- ➤ Follow through with all you do.
- ➤ Have as much fun planning it as you do hosting it.
- ➤ Show your guests how happy you are to have them there by choosing something special and personal to give them.
- ➤ Have a schedule of activities ready, but don't play traffic cop by insisting that guests follow it exactly.
- ➤ Serve interesting, delicious, plentiful, and appropriate food and drinks.
- ➤ Thank everyone who was a part of the event.

Over the last few years, I continued planning a wide variety of events in homes, for corporations, and for nonprofit organizations. I spoke about party planning around the country, I won numerous awards for my work, and my ideas were often featured in magazines. However, whenever someone would ask me if I had written a book, I'd say, "No, but you should check out Patty Sachs. She's written a bunch of them and I agree with everything she says."

A couple of years ago, when I first signed on to the Internet, I was astounded and delighted with all the resources that were available to me. And I felt that it was finally my turn to give something back to all the people who helped me over the years, including those anonymous millions who posted information on the Web. I decided the best way to return the favor was to answer questions for folks who needed help with something I knew about: party planning. So several times a week I'd answer party-planning questions on various message boards across the Web.

One day, a request for assistance came from another member of a party planners group trying to find a resource for a product she was seeking. The person turned out to be Patty Sachs. I was so excited! Not only was I very familiar with a manufacturer I could recommend, but I was going to be able to "meet" her and to help someone that I admired so much. I sent the information, she replied "Thank you," and that was the end of that.

Later I got a note from Patty saying, "Who are you? You have all these great ideas. Why haven't I heard of you before? Why don't you write a book?"

I wrote back and in a short time, Patty and I realized that not only did we have a lot in common and a comparable work ethic and philosophy, we also had a very similar writing style. She asked me to collaborate with her on a number of projects. The partnership has worked so well, we formed our own company, Party Plans Plus. When the proposal to write *The Complete Idiot's Guide to Throwing a Great Party* was presented to Patty, she agreed to do it, but only if I would join her, and I jumped at the chance. We are thrilled to share the knowledge that took us years to acquire, and to give you the tools to produce a party you and your friends will remember for a lifetime.

Here is what Patty has to say:

Yep, that's how it happened. I have a few more decades of producing parties than Phyllis, since I was born on my mother's birthday—and the story goes that that was the first of a lifetime of "Patty" events. The teacher in me surfaced after a few years of professional planning, when I started writing party guides, articles, and books.

The philosophy that Phyllis and I share is just that—to share. I am often asked, "Why do you give away all your trade secrets? Pretty soon no one will need your party-planning services." I just smile and say, "That's actually my goal. I'd like for everyone who wants to throw a party to have the gumption and the confidence to go right ahead and do it."

I think books like this one are the safety net that party hosts need to go out on the wire. As they say, "Knowledge is power." So the information we share with you here will give you the party power you need to produce a memorable and successful event.

From the moment the party-throwing inspiration hits you, you will be able to open this book for ground-floor party-planning guidance. From there, the steps and directions for creating everything from invitations to thank-you notes are there for you to explore, adapt, and follow. We have searched through our memory banks and file cabinets for those ideas that are tried and true. We also let our imaginations wander to bring you some of our brilliant (we modestly agree on that) brainstorms that are guaranteed to dazzle your guests.

During this project we have been e-mailing our "high fives" to each other as each chapter unfolded with our cooperative efforts. We've given you hundreds of ideas that are easy enough for the newest host to attempt, intriguing enough for the neighborhood Martha Stewart, or inventive enough for the party pro who is looking to add a couple of tricks to his or her arsenal.

Our wish for you is the success that you are striving for, whether your goal is to plan an impromptu baseball-game-watching gathering, entertain gourmet-style, produce a birthday banquet, or throw an all-out blast for your neighborhood or family reunion.

Every day holds a reason to celebrate ... so start today!

How to Use This Book

This book is carefully organized to present the tools and techniques you can use to plan the perfect party. We've broken it down into the basics so that you can see how to plan any party. We've also given you full party plans with all the details, from the invitations to the food to how to decorate, making it easy for you.

Part 1, "Festive Fundamentals," gives you all the basics of planning a party. It breaks down the party into where, who, what, where, why, and how.

Part 2, "To Party Means to Plan," might be the most important factor of throwing a successful party. To ensure that your guests will want to come back for more, you need to be careful when planning everything, from the budget to the theme to your guest list.

Part 3, "The Hostess with the Mostess ..." is key to any party. This part will show you how to be the perfect host, stock a bar, and keep everything running smoothly while you find the time to enjoy yourself.

Part 4, "Classic Occasions," is all about those times when you need to host the most basic party. Whether it's cocktails, a business dinner, or a formal black-tie gala, you'll get tips on everything from what to serve to how to serve it.

Part 5, "Seasonal Celebrations," will give you ideas on throwing a terrific holiday party any time of the year. This part doesn't just give you tips for the most popular holidays, but looks at ways to make Mother's Day, Father's Day, and even Valentine's Day special for everyone.

Part 6, "Life's Big Events," takes a look at all of life's most-important milestones and shows how you, as the host, can make them even more memorable.

Part 7, "The Party's Ooooo-ver," looks at all of those things you'll need to do to get your house back in order, get your guests off safely, and collect all those party souvenirs and photos for yourself and to share with your guests.

You'll also get a number of appendixes that include party-planning worksheets, a resource list, a wine guide, a calendar of American holidays, an anniversary gift list, and a glossary of those all-important party words.

Extras

Each chapter covers everything you will need to know in terms of planning your party. However, while writing the book we came across a number of fun facts, tidbits, and related topics that we thought might be interesting to you. These have been placed in different boxes within each chapter:

Festive Facts

When planning a party, the fun usually comes from the unexpected. For that reason we've put together many unexpected or interesting and fun facts related to the topic at hand.

Party Pitfall

Anytime you are planning a party, you are bound to run across something that will make your life harder. We've made an attempt here to warn you before disaster strikes.

Shindig Sayings

These terms and definitions are all part of the world of party planning. They will help you understand what people are talking about when you are planning your big event.

Chips and Tips

These little tips will make not just your party planning but your life outside the party easier. Be sure to read them and learn something new!

Acknowledgments

We would like to thank our editor, Jessica Faust, for putting up with two often-pooped party people and seeing our vision.

Acknowledgments for Phyllis Cambria:

I would like to thank my husband, Doug, for his patience and support; my family for their understanding while I undertook another "Phyllis project;" my parents, Pat and Jerry Mangino, for being the original party people; my "partyner," Patty Sachs, for seeking me out to join her and for all the giggles and great ideas; Bobby Rodriguez for letting me learn the event business with him; Elaine Micelli Vasquez for giving me my first writing job; my friends at the South Florida-Caribbean Chapter of the International Special Events Society for always being willing to share information; and Jeff Breslauer for his friendship, encouragement, help, and "filling in the blanks."

Acknowledgments for Patty Sachs:

There's too little space here for me to give proper and heartfelt thanks to Phyllis, my "partyner" in this project. She put her heart and soul, days and nights, and wit and wisdom into the writing of this book. She carried me through from start to finish, even though she had signed on to only "travel the road, sharin' the load." In only a dozen hours in person and hundreds of hours on the 'Net, I have gained a respect for her ethics and integrity. She's become my perfect party-planning pal! (Yeah, we talk like that.)

About writing this book, my brother and agent, Terry, said, "You should do that;" my mom, Elsie, (as always) said, "You can do that;" and my kids, Frank, Cathy, and Deena, said, "Oh no! She's doing it again!" I especially loved hearing my darling grandgirls, Jasmine, Mackenzie, Aysia, and Sophia, say, "Why's Grandma doing that?" Ah, then there's my newest grandgirly, Carly Jade, who would have said (if she could talk), "I just have to smile, and she always stops doing that." I celebrate and cherish them all.

Trademarks

Part 1

Festive Fundamentals

Throwing a party can be one of the most stressful events in life. You worry that everyone is having fun, the food tastes right, the entertainment is good enough, and even whether anyone will show up.

Relax! Planning a party should be enjoyable—even fun. In this part of the book, you'll learn the absolute basics for throwing a great party—everything from planning your guest list to choosing and hiring consultants. So whether you are planning a friend's birthday or just gathering old friends together, hold your glass high and say, "Cheers, I can do this."

Chapter 1

Home Is
Where the
Party Is

In This Chapter

➤ Making your home ready for a party

➤ Preparing the party food

➤ Reasons to throw a party

➤ Planning your party

There are so many different excuses you could make to not have a party: You don't know who to invite, you don't have the room, it will take too long to plan, you have nothing to celebrate, or even that you just don't know how to cook. Relax! Planning and throwing a party should be fun and exciting … and easy.

In this chapter, you'll learn that the best way to throw a party is in your own home, and sometimes the best kind of party is one that just happens. You don't have to be celebrating a milestone event, and you don't even need to have more than two people. A party is a feeling, and a special way to celebrate that feeling. So sit back and learn how to turn your small apartment or house into Party Central and to throw the party of a lifetime.

Taking the Party Home

When planning a party, one of the first great worries is where the party should be. Well, that's easy—at home, of course. You probably think you don't have enough room, right? Wrong! While most homes aren't set up for ballroom dancing or hula hoop contests, there are ways to adjust and arrange the space to be more party-ready and they're all outlined in Chapter 10, "Setting Up Your Space."

What if you want to go beyond just chips, dips, and the stereo? What if you really want to go whole hog to make a theme-party extravaganza? You probably need to rent a space for that, right? Wrong again! Whether you want to set up your dining room as a disco or turn your rec room into a recording studio, you can do it.

Given a generous lead time, the proper materials, and some help from talented hands, you can accomplish these decoration dreams with relative ease. Unlike a rented party site, where rules and limitations can cause you deadline stress, an at-home party gives you 24-hour access to your party site—meaning that these preparty setups can be almost stress-free.

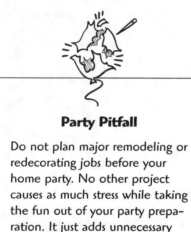

Party Pitfall

Do not plan major remodeling or redecorating jobs before your home party. No other project causes as much stress while taking the fun out of your party preparation. It just adds unnecessary pressure to the party process.

Shindig Sayings

An **on-site caterer** provides food for party guests at a hotel, banquet hall, restaurant, or private club.

Home Cooking

So now that you know where the party is going to be held, the next step is to plan the rest. Neglecting the details about food, drink, and even decorations could be the biggest mistake you make, so plan well.

Serving refreshments that are appropriate to your tastes, budget, and the event is another perk of entertaining at home. Unlike most banquet centers, restaurants, or hotel catering departments, you can select a menu from your favorite cookbooks, magazines, newspapers, or Web sites. There is no limit to the types of food and beverages you can serve in your own home.

If you plan a party with an *on-site caterer,* you will need an accurate head count so they know how many guests to serve. When you plan a party at home, you need only be prepared for your best guess, according to your invitation responses.

Hiring a caterer to come into your home is much different because you can find one with specialties that match your party's needs.

If a caterer isn't for you, organize an old-fashioned potluck get-together. Ask all your guests to bring a dish to share. Just make sure you find out what people are bringing so you don't end up with a table full of chocolate chip cookies.

When none of these options appeals to you, there are always the old standbys—fill bowls full of pretzels, chips, and dips, or order take-out. Too often we get wrapped up in the food, and we forget that a party is really just an excuse for friends to gather and have fun.

Timing Is Everything

A party at home means that you are under no time constraints. No one is going to tell when to start or when the fun is over. You don't have to watch the clock and sweat per-hour site fees. You also don't have to rush your guests out to make room for the next gang of revelers.

Let's Get Together

The reasons for getting together are as many and varied as there are hosts with an imagination and a willingness to entertain. The simplest reason (the first time you balance your checkbook) could spur you on to planning a large bash with dozens of guests, while an extra-special occasion (a silver wedding anniversary) might inspire you to arrange only a small, intimate gathering for a few dear people.

The real secret to success is to plan your work and work your plan. Do it right, from concept to conclusion, and you can have as much fun planning the party as you have at the party.

Milestone events like birthdays, anniversaries, graduations, weddings, and retirements are generally viewed as party-giving opportunities. Those are the most natural times to concoct celebrations, and they usually involve making more complex plans and inviting larger numbers of guests. If your house or apartment can accommodate the group, it makes good sense to consider having it there.

Party Pitfall

When planning a party, be sure to look into municipal ordinances or your community or condo association rules. Are there any rules regarding noise or party times? You don't want to plan your party to begin at 8 P.M. if your association rules say there can be no parties after 9 P.M.!

Chips and Tips

Invite one or two friends to join you as co-hosts. It not only divides the workload, it also reduces the expense, and best of all, it turns the planning process into a party-before-the-party.

Planned in a Minute ... or a Month

Think about the best party you have ever attended. Do you know if it was planned in minutes or in months? Does it matter?

It doesn't take a lot to qualify as a party. Take good company plus some tasty food and drink, and maybe add some entertainment. Voilá! You have a party! Doesn't that sound easy?

Well, it can be a piece of cake or it can be a major production—that's your choice. Obviously, the farther ahead you start planning your event, the more elaborate you can make it. That is a bonus benefit of extra lead time.

Your decision to have a party can be made months, even years, in advance. Parties can be painstakingly planned down to the finest detail—or arranged on a whim to invite folks over for that same night!

Sometimes the rush to hold a spur-of-the-moment celebration inspires instances of ingeniousness that turn out to be incredibly successful and even unforgettable. Don't let a little thing like lack of time stop you.

Festive Facts

Recently a woman who had missed her 45th class reunion called a classmate who had attended and asked her to recap the event.

While talking, they decided it would be fun to invite a few other people and share in all the stories. They made calls to a few others who, in turn, made a few calls. Before the day was out, 15 women were set to attend a potluck luncheon just two days later.

With just a brainstorm and a few phone calls, this special gathering turned out to be sentimental, hilarious, and unforgettable.

As Long As We're Here

There is often a time when you either have a small group of people in your home, or you are out with them, and the idea to have a party at your place is born.

If you are like most people, your food supply will not be adequate for a big gang. You can ask the more creative chefs to work with what's in your pantry, you can call for takeout, send some folks to the market, or, if the friends live close by, you can send everyone home to raid their own refrigerators. Remember, while food is important, fun and fellowship come first.

Once you have your improvised party buffet and bar tables set up with whatever you decide to serve, the party will likely move into full swing. Everyone is already in a festive mood from getting the grub together.

Imagine the stories that will stem from your hodgepodge home party. Without weeks of worry and woe, you have earned the "Best Host of a Last-Minute Party" award.

Chips and Tips

Have a bunch of leftover mismatched items from a number of parties? Set them out along with a collection of decorative party props. Call it a *Sanford and Son* celebration—the original trash tycoons!

And It's Good for You

Mental health experts all agree that celebration is good for you. It makes sense. Whenever you gather with others to pay tribute to someone or to just be together, your sense of well-being gets a boost.

Holidays and milestone occasions need not be the only times your family and friends gather. You can open your home to them for reasons real or invented.

Good for a Child's Heart

Children thrive at parties when adults are there to pay special attention to them. The impromptu celebration to acknowledge an accomplishment of a child is worth 10 times the labor that goes into producing it. Auditioned for the play, but didn't get the part? He deserves a party just for trying out. Passed an exam to bring a C up to a B? This definitely calls for a party.

Festive Facts

A 13-year-old boy hated every minute that he had his braces on. Once they were finally removed, he decided to throw a huge party in honor of his "new teeth." His smile was from ear to ear as he enjoyed a menu of his "before braces" favorite foods—popcorn, caramel, and peanut butter.

So often these small but significant victories are overlooked when, with just a little effort, you can give your child the best gift of all—a lift in self-esteem. To put a smile on a child's face, there are no better words than "congratulations," "great job," or "I'm proud of you." A paper crown, a few balloons, a frozen pizza, and a plate of cookies are all you really need to make a party that will be remembered forever.

As you read on, you will learn all the tactics and strategies to simplify and enhance your home parties. You'll develop the confidence to look for new reasons to celebrate. When you are appointed, by yourself or by others, to meet a party challenge, you will share in the great rewards of hosting a houseful. You will experience the thrill of watching people you care about relax and enjoy themselves. They'll feel the stress of their lives melt in the embrace of your celebration. Those you pay tribute to will feel bathed in the warmth of your welcome. Follow your urge to wine and dine. Each time you plan an event or give folks an opportunity to celebrate life, you will not only make merry with them, but you will be one step closer to being a real party pro.

The Least You Need to Know

➤ Having a party at home gives you a wider selection of foods to serve.

➤ Utilize the yard, patio, garage, or deck to make your party space bigger.

➤ Get the help of your guests when a spontaneous party is planned.

➤ Celebrations are good for your heart and your soul.

Chapter 2

People Make the Party

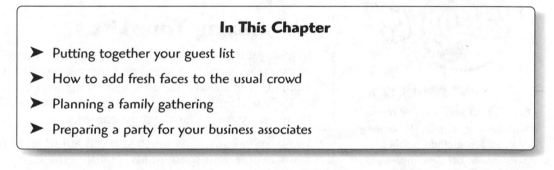

In This Chapter

➤ Putting together your guest list

➤ How to add fresh faces to the usual crowd

➤ Planning a family gathering

➤ Preparing a party for your business associates

Who you invite to your party is often the most difficult part of planning the whole event. Your guest list is determined by many things, with the reason for the event or occasion being the most important. You generally include mostly family and dear friends to a birthday, anniversary, or wedding party. This list is the easiest to prepare. When you are planning an event like a graduation or retirement party, however, the scope of guests broadens to include neighbors, schoolmates, and work associates.

The decisions whether to invite this person or that can be difficult when your space and budget are limited. Everyone cannot be invited. Instead of being afraid you might commit social suicide, read on to discover a few guidelines to follow when you set your invitation list.

The Pulse of the Party

Your guests do not show up at your party just to see your home, eat your food, or drink your beverages. Although that is part of why they accept your invitation, the biggest motivation is to be with you and your other guests. This is true whether it is a

Chips and Tips

Throw a party where each regular member of the group *is* asked to bring someone new to freshen up the collection of faces.

Chips and Tips

Check with your caterer to find ways to save money. Big money savers often include holding the party on an off day—mid-week or a Sunday afternoon—and serving just hors d'oeuvres, or not serving alcohol.

special celebration or just a small get-together. People, their personalities, their differences, and their similarities are the magic ingredient of a wonderful party. How they interact to enjoy themselves is the real success element for your event.

In the initial planning stages of your party you will always have a set guest list in your mind—those nearest and dearest to you.

When it is possible, though, it is a good strategy to bring in a few new faces to add a different dimension to your established party cast.

Whether you are adding new faces or just inviting the same old crowd, the guests are what really make the party.

Organizing Your List

In an ideal world we would always be able to invite everyone we want to a party, and they would all get along. Unfortunately, we don't live in an ideal world, and when planning a guest list there are a number of things every party planner must consider.

You have to know how much you can afford and how many people your space holds. Probably the most difficult thing you'll have to do though, is *not* invite people.

Here are some quick and easy tips for facing those guest list challenges.

Less Means More

When you have a large guest list and your budget is small, it is a good idea to cut down on elaborate plans to be able to include more people. The budget for a five-course steak dinner for a dozen guests, for instance, may be stretched to feed chicken casserole to 25.

When throwing a party in your home, remember that being able to invite all those whom you wish to share your special day with is far more important than serving fancy foods and beverages.

Making the Cut

When making a guest list, it is imperative to know how to make cuts. It just isn't always possible to invite everyone you want. True, there are times when the list is not negotiable—everyone on it is a "must." However, those times are generally few and far between. For the most part, you are given the chance to review a list and make decisions based on how many people you can reasonably have at your party.

Unfortunately, there will also be times when the guest of honor will provide you with a guest list. For crowd control, suggest a maximum amount. Even the most gracious host must draw the line somewhere, so be realistic about your budget and home's limits.

If the roster is left up to you, begin by listing the guest of honor, immediate family, and a few of his or her closest friends. Then, if you have the option, start adding in other friends, followed by more distant relatives, and so on.

Another option to the growing guest list is an open house. An open house is when you set a time for your party and people are free to come and go as they please. One of the biggest advantages of an open house is that not all of the guests are usually there at one time, so you can often stretch the list.

If you are concerned about your open house getting out of hand, you might want to send guests invitations that stagger the party's hours. However, be sure that the same or comparable refreshments are available throughout the entire event. This will help avoid some people feeling as if they were invited to dinner, while others were invited only for dessert.

Party Pitfall

The idea, in theory, behind an open house is that guests will come and go throughout the course of the party. However, sometimes the bulk of the guests show up at the same time. Or, they are having such a good time, they don't want to leave. This can really wreak havoc on your plans to control the number of guests at your party, so don't over-invite.

There's One in Every Bunch

Do you have someone on your family list that stands out as a troublemaker, the proverbial "bad apple"? This is the person who doesn't think anything is done right. With some family feuds, you may have one guest threaten not to attend if a certain other person is invited.

Do not fall into this blackmail bin. As the host you have the right to do as you please—it is your party. Even though it might be difficult, invite whom you want.

There are ways around these social landmines. To begin with, you need to "know thy enemy"—that is, if you are prepared going into it, you can take steps to diffuse the situation before it becomes a problem.

Ask for help from the party spoiler, the one who does nothing but criticize. Tell him or her that his or her help will make the party a success.

This personal involvement will invariably distract him or her. After all, who wants to malign an event you had a hand in planning?

For the Hatfield and McCoy elements, invite both and give them the option to attend. Be honest with them. Explain that you would love to have them in attendance; however, you will not tolerate any open hostility. Ask them to make an effort to bury the hatchet—preferably not in each other's heads—and attend. Remind them how important they are to the guest of honor; stroke their egos. Then give them the option to decide.

Chips and Tips

If at all possible, separate the warring factions by distance (place them in separate rooms) or time (give them different arrival and departure times). You also might want to assign one or two other guests to chaperone the guests and act as a buffer should any interchanges occur. (A first aid kit and 911 on speed dial are probably not bad ideas, either.)

Party Pitfall

Double-check your guest list with another close friend to prevent forgetting anyone.

For the guest who is there only to eat the food and watch the game, take him out of the picture … literally. Set up a TV in another room, as far away from the party as possible, and put the couch potato in there. Give him food and beverages and tell him he can keep the door shut so no one will disturb him.

He gets to watch the game; you lose the bump on the log and a major distraction.

As you can see, whatever the negative situation, it's possible to turn it into a positive.

Gathering the People Together

There are dozens of ways you can prepare a guest list and plan a party. You could choose to throw a bash for friends only, a family reunion of sorts, or include business associates. Whichever way you choose to go, the list will still take planning and preparation.

You Gotta Have Friends

Good friends don't need a reason to have a party. Being together while doing anything is fun, relaxing, and—for the most part—nurturing to the relationships. That is one of the most rewarding parts of friendship.

When you host a party for your close friends, you have the best of all worlds. You know all about these people. You can anticipate their likes and dislikes, indulge their foibles and fantasies, and help them achieve their goals and ambitions. With all of this inside knowledge, you can plan a party that fits this group like a gala glove.

The list is easy. Except for an occasional addition of friends of friends, it is set in "plaster of party." A gala or wacky invitation builds the event anticipation, and word of mouth will get this invitation out on the "friend network" within hours.

It's a Family Affair

Hosting a party for your family is probably the easiest of all scenarios. Forgiving and understanding all your shortcomings, emergencies, and phobias, your family members will either pitch in to help or simply accept your oversights.

You might have fallen into the family pattern of doing every party the same way. Why not be totally individual with your next one? Dare to be different. Throw off tradition now and then and surprise your kinfolk.

Send an invitation to each member of the family, one to the parents and one to each child. That special touch will get the youngsters enthused about attending another one of those "family" deals.

There are many ways to do it. Put together a theme party, surprise them with a distant relative, make it a formal dinner instead of a barbecue, or hire some entertainment. Have fun and turn your ho-hum party into a home run.

Chips and Tips

Occasionally, if room permits, allow teenaged children to bring a friend. This is the age when any time away from friends is almost torture for a kid.

Mixing Business with Pleasure

As we get older, we often make friends with the people we work with. We find ourselves socializing with them, not only during our lunch hour, but also in the evenings and on weekends.

These friendships are sometimes different than the friends we made through other routes. When fellow employees take time to enjoy each other outside the workspace, it is often relaxing and helps to raise morale. These get-togethers sometimes occur even more regularly than get-togethers with friends or family.

Entertaining business friends and associates should be done thoughtfully and carefully. Remember, you don't want any of these people to remember that you stripped on the dining room table after throwing back a few too many.

Party Pitfall

Choose how you plan to entertain co-workers carefully. While these occasions may seem social, there are sometimes road hazards to be aware of. In a business relationship, your co-worker today may be your boss tomorrow. Likewise, someone who works for you might one day leapfrog past you.

13

Have fun, of course. But be aware. Plan this event as carefully as you might plan a business presentation.

Unless you are the boss, it is rare that a work-related party would be held at your home. If this situation does arise, ask to have a committee work with you. This will allow a number of key people to have input toward the event.

Chips and Tips

When you are the low person on the totem pole and you would like to move up the ladder, this type of social event can work in your favor. If it's unlikely that you will be given extra responsibilities at the office, putting together an exceptional event will enable others to see you as more responsible or socially capable than you are currently viewed.

Chips and Tips

Dollar stores often sell dozens of items like plastic chairs, dishes, cups, and utensils that can be personalized by painting the child's name on them to use and then take as favors.

Have the first committee meeting at your home so the group can survey your surroundings and make suggestions that fit the space. As host, you will likely be in charge of the committee. This is a chance to take a leadership role and make sure each committee member shines. They, in turn, will allow you to shine as well.

Kids Are Guests, Too

Whether you have children or not, there will be times when kids are in your home for a party. If you plan for your home to be party central for a group of tots or teens, there are certain preparations that must be made.

The first consideration is often food. Make different food and beverage choices for the children than you would for the adults.

Get input from the parents or try to blend popular junk food with appealing but healthy choices; that way, the parents won't panic and the kids won't balk at what is being served. Just make it a kid-friendly menu.

It is a big challenge to keep toddlers and preschoolers amused, happy, and safe. To enable you and your guests to socialize, recruit older kids to help with the youngsters by paying them to baby-sit.

If the entertainment on hand isn't suitable for your young guests, ask parents to bring a child's favorite toys or videos with them.

Remember, entertainment planned for young guests must be suited to their age and the space you have for them. There are dozens of books and Web sites that offer ideas and directions for games and activities designed to occupy kids of all ages.

Groups and Troops

If you or one of your family members belong to an organized group or team, there is a good chance that you will get your turn to host an event.

When it comes time to gather at your home, the plans can be easy and uncomplicated. Since these events are usually very short in duration, they often require providing little more than pizza and beer, wine, or soda. It can even be a potluck supper where all you supply are the drinks and dishes.

It is also possible that you could be called upon to entertain in a more formal way, perhaps for a recognition dinner or a going-away tribute. You, then, will often find yourself working with a committee or cohost at these events.

There are also those get-togethers that are very impromptu. For instance, an important but unexpected game victory makes a big celebration mandatory. So stock up on party goods to keep on hand and have some take-out menus handy for hosting the home team.

Party Pitfall

Depending upon their age, children have a short attention span. It is better to have a large variety of amusements that will keep them constantly entertained.

Party of Pastimes and Passions

Regularly scheduled meeting times are ideal for taking turns to entertain, especially to share an interest or intrigue. If you are a collector, crafter, or hobbyist, you most likely socialize with fellow enthusiasts to enjoy the activity that binds you together as a group.

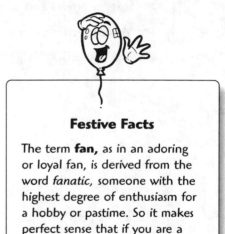

Festive Facts

The term **fan,** as in an adoring or loyal fan, is derived from the word *fanatic*, someone with the highest degree of enthusiasm for a hobby or pastime. So it makes perfect sense that if you are a fan of a sport, you are also a fanatic.

Avid adorers of food or wine, culinary arts, flower arranging, book clubs, or home decorating hold high-tone parties at which they partake in their common delights. If you have a gathering for your in-common companions, the path is quite clear—just plan to please yourself, and you will probably please them all.

Blending Different Groups

When you pay tribute to a person, all the important people in his or her life will want to be there—friends, family, and school- and workmates. The family and friends will not always know each other, and business associates will often be unfamiliar to both. To help turn strangers into friends, print up name tags color-coded to reflect different relationships: family, friend, co-worker, classmate and so on. Be sure to include a more detailed explanation of the guest's relationship to the honored guest. For example: "JOHN SMITH, Jack's next-door neighbor" or "JANE NELSON, Jack's sister."

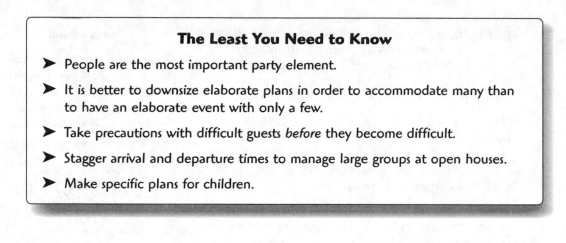

The Least You Need to Know

➤ People are the most important party element.

➤ It is better to downsize elaborate plans in order to accommodate many than to have an elaborate event with only a few.

➤ Take precautions with difficult guests *before* they become difficult.

➤ Stagger arrival and departure times to manage large groups at open houses.

➤ Make specific plans for children.

Chapter 3

Here's the Plan

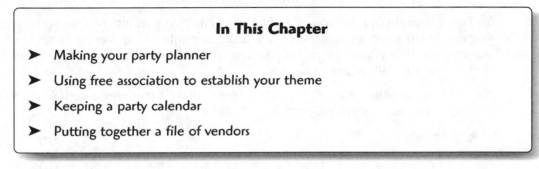

In This Chapter

➤ Making your party planner

➤ Using free association to establish your theme

➤ Keeping a party calendar

➤ Putting together a file of vendors

Now that you've figured out why you're having the party, it's time to sit down and plan it from start to finish—every detail down to the toothpicks. By planning even the smallest details, you can set your occasion apart from one that later brings about an "I seem to recall that party" response.

When planning a party, your main objective is a smoothly produced event that gives your guests a feeling of comfort and welcome, and that the party was planned just for them. In this chapter you'll learn how to establish the perfect party plan.

You Could Write a Book

In the process of planning your party, you'll find it very helpful to write a book outlining every facet of your event. This will be an organized, complete record of every step taken on the way to your incredible event. It will be invaluable not only for this party, but for those you plan in the future. You will be able to look back and recognize the do's and don'ts (hopefully not too many don'ts) of throwing a smashingly successful party.

Chips and Tips

Check an office supply store for festive colored binders and index cards to help set your party mood while you plan.

To put together your party planner, you need a three-ring binder with lined paper, category dividers, clear plastic sleeves, and a zipper pocket for pencils, pens, and a calculator. You will also need a pack of 3" × 5" lined index cards to make a festivity file. Both the notebook and file will play an important part in your party plans and will be referenced throughout this chapter.

While small, impromptu gatherings will probably not need many pages—in fact, maybe just one or two—your planner and file are still invaluable resources. Even if it's just your guest list, menu, chores, contacts and shopping list, a party organizer notebook will help keep you on track.

To begin your event plan, you must first draw an overall picture of your party. Then you can begin zeroing in on tasks like making any contacts or commitments. Not until you see the vision of your entertaining endeavor can you decide what your budget and time allowance might be.

To fill in all elements of your event masterpiece, make a section for each of the following basic categories in the planner and file:

➤ Calendar

➤ The Five *W*s

➤ Theme

➤ Printed Pieces (invitations, place cards, programs, menus)

➤ Food and Beverage (menus, recipes, shopping list)

➤ Site Preparation (decorations, rentals, yard spray)

➤ Entertainment and Activities

➤ Gifts, Prizes, and Favors

➤ Master Budget and Shopping List

Now that you have built the categories into your planner, we'll take a close look at what should go into each category.

Let Me Count the Days

One of the first sheets in your planner will be a calendar and a timeline. List on your timeline items such as: three weeks before, mail invitations; one week before, give head count to caterer and so on. Then transfer all of that to your calendar to serve as a reminder when items are expected or needed to be done.

The Five Ws

Establishing the why, when, who, where, and what of your party is the very first step in party planning. If you've already gotten this far, you probably know why—a birthday or some other special occasion. Now it is time to determine the when, who, where, and what.

Since you know why already, it is likely that you probably have a pretty good handle on when. The day is often determined by a special occasion date, holiday, or a season. Getting more specific and selecting exact dates and times may depend on the guest of honor's and host's schedules, or on the availability of a party site. You also might want to consider the schedule of key guests whose presence is vital to the party's success.

Planning where, who, and what are variables that depend on each host.

Who's There?

So with your absolutes in mind, let's plan the ideal guest list. Depending on the event, the numbers will likely vary. All names should include their address, phone number, and e-mail address.

Where Are We Going?

Where the party is held is not just important to the party planning, but also to the guest list.

In Chapter 10, "Setting Up Your Space," you will find creative solutions to space limitations, but adjustments to your guest list might need to be made depending upon the space you have.

If you choose to rent a space, note the address, the contact, and any important details like maximum capacity and payment due dates.

Chips and Tips

If your at-home party can't stretch to accommodate the "must haves" on your list, perhaps you can hold the party at a friend's home or plan an open house where people will come and go.

What's That?

Now that you know why, when, who, and where, it is time to take a look at what kind of party it will be. This is usually easy to decide once you have identified who your guests are and how much space you have.

If you don't have a party theme in mind, read Chapter 6, "The Theme Says It All," to get ideas on choosing the perfect theme for your event. Once you've decided, add that to your book. Remember if there are others affected, whose feedback is important, get them involved in the process. One good way is to invite them in for a *brainstorming* party or set up a conference call or on-line chat.

Congratulations! You now have all the basic elements of your party pinned down. Outline each one in the first section of your planner. This is the overall party picture.

A Theme Come True

Your next step in your planner is establishing all of your theme or scheme details. For some of the more general themes, the list of "gotta haves" is easy to make. Some are easy, while others take a little more imagination to come up with just the right ideas.

Free Association Planning

When planning your theme, make up free association lists of any persons, places, things, or events that relate to the theme in any way. At this point, don't edit your thinking. As you fine-tune your plans later, you can address feasibility and cost. Right now, just think, write, and have fun!

Once the list has been established, you can sort through it to settle on your main party aspects. Don't rule out any good, but potentially "too expensive," idea yet. Chapter 7, "Banking on a Budget," holds some budget-reining strategies for you.

Festive Facts

Margaret Mitchell, author of *Gone with the Wind,* never thought she was a very good writer and had no intention of even showing her novel to a publisher. Until one fateful day when a "friend" told her that she agreed with Margaret and that she thought Margaret was wasting her time even trying to write. This made Margaret furious and had her marching, manuscript in hand, down to a Georgia hotel where Macmillan editor Harold Latham was staying. And the rest, as they say, is history.

Party Theme: Gone with the Wind

Here is an example of a free association form for a *Gone with the Wind* party. It is unlikely that they will be able to utilize every idea, but they will be able to pick and choose to come up with a great theme party.

Food and Beverage:

Mint julep, lemonade, bourbon, branch water, fried chicken, sweet potato pie, hush puppies, black-eyed peas, collard greens, red-eye gravy, catfish, crawfish, iced tea, corn, fried green tomatoes, pralines, praline cookies, Mississippi mud pie, peanut butter cookies, watermelon, buttermilk, ham, grits, okra, shrimp gumbo, dirty rice, corn fritters, rabbit stew, pheasant, possum, quail, …

Entertainment:

Fiddle, guitar, accordion, spoons, banjo, jazz, Dixieland, Cajun-Zydeco, washboard, square dance, Virginia reel, yodelers, barbershop quartet, gospel, county fair, *Gone with the Wind*, Margaret Mitchell, Civil War re-enactments, fox hunt, steeplechase, quilting bee, …

Chips and Tips

Once your start listing items, you may need to substitute one idea for another to stay on track, so keep this list in your notebook.

Decor:

Tara, magnolias, Atlanta, jasmine, jonquils, antebellum clothes, Confederate and Union flags and uniforms, cotton, velvet drapes, Spanish moss, mansions, fireflies, hoop skirts, oil lamps, horses, foxes, …

Miscellaneous:

GWTW cast, "I don't know nothin' about birthin' babies," "As God as my witness, I'll never go hungry again," "I'll think about that tomorrow," "Frankly, my dear, I don't give a damn," …

Then pull out the components you want to focus on and break down and list estimated prices. This will help you to determine your budget.

Party-Planning-at-a-Glance Worksheet

Copy this sheet to help you record your own party ideas.

Party-Planning-at-a-Glance Worksheet

Occasion: _____

Date _____ Time _____

# of Guests _____ (Are these friends, family or other?)

_____

Hosts: _____

Guest(s) of Honor: _____

_____

Special Date _____ (actual date of anniversary, birthday, etc. if different)

Location (if other than home): _____

_____

Theme or Motif: _____

Invitation Ideas: _____

_____

Food Ideas: _____

_____

Beverage Ideas: _____

_____

Rental equipment needed: _____

_____

Activities and game ideas: _____

_____

_____

_____

Entertainment or talent needed: _____

_____

_____

Favors/gifts needed and ideas: _____

_____

_____

Photography/Videography: _____

Room Decorations:

_____

_____

_____

Table Decorations: _____

_____

Special Details (place cards, name tags, napkin holders):

_____

_____

Servers or Helpers: _____

_____

Special Preparations:

_____

_____

The Printed Word

Invitations, programs, menus, place cards, and thank-you notes play a great role in producing a complete party plan. Add maps, game instructions, song sheets, or weekend itineraries and you've come up with quite a number of items that need to be printed. Whether you choose to do it yourself or do it professionally, you need to keep track of it in your planner.

The items you store in this section (in plastic sleeves) are samples, artwork, proofs, receipts, and completed order forms for everything.

Delicious Details

If you are the chef du jour or hiring a caterer, your food and beverage pages should consist of menus, recipes, shopping lists, and costs. Notes about past parties will be helpful, so jot those down.

Plan your bar (see Chapter 9, "Tiny Bubbles: Stocking Your Bar,") and estimate drink prices. Check on what equipment you'll need to rent or buy. Also include fees for servers or bartenders.

Potluck Pleasures

If applicable, put your potluck party assignment sheets and menu plans in the food-and-beverage

Chips and Tips

Anytime you come home from a party, jot down what you loved and what you didn't think worked well. This will help you plan your future parties.

section as well. Note food items promised. Give guests ideas as to what to bring that will be compatible with other dishes. This detail is extremely important to avoid duplication or missed dishes from your meal.

Festive Facts

One very clever host decided to assign potluck items according to last name initials of her guests. Unfortunately, it never crossed the host's mind that the majority of the guests, all family members, were Smiths. It was a bitter-"sweet" surprise to have each Smith show up with dessert. Assign items very carefully to avoid this.

Include all paper goods and linen costs along with food and beverage costs, rentals, and staff fees, and add to the master budget sheet.

Spruce Up the Site

Preparing your site includes everything from decorations to extra toilets. When filling out your planner, include all decoration ideas and rentals, such as extra lighting, flowers, props, and even clean-up crews.

Chips and Tips

Before you start planning and shopping for your decorations, make an inventory list of everything that you already have that might be useable. Consult with your most creative thinker (second most, if you are No. 1) to come up with innovative ways to integrate them into your plan.

Tally up all the costs for site preparation and add them to your master budget.

Send in the Clowns, the Band, the Fun

Thought we'd never get to the fun part, huh? Well, true, the enjoyment that entertainment and activities add to an event is substantial. If you don't know any performers, get referrals for reliable entertainment or talent agencies. They will be able to help you find and *book* talent. Check videotapes of likely performers and then see them in action before you hire them.

In addition to musicians and DJs, talent agencies also can help you book concessions, games, face painters, fortune-tellers, magicians, caricaturists, or other variety artists.

Collect cards from photographers and videographers whose work you like as well. Good performers, videographers and photographers usually work every weekend, so sign your contracts as soon as possible to ensure you'll get the people you want.

File all paperwork in your party planner under entertainment and activities and adjust your budget accordingly.

Something to Take Home

The best party hosts send their guests home with a memento or prize to make the party last a little bit longer. They can be trivial trinkets or total treasures. Check catalogs and search discount stores for likely items and store ideas in your planner.

Use the gifts, prizes, and favors section to save photos of your favorite finds labeled with source name, contact number and all costs. Plan to receive your items at least three weeks before your event to allow time for returns and *rainchecks*. If there is imprinting, engraving, or hand lettering, schedule your orders for delivery four weeks in advance in case reprints are needed.

Add up the cost of your gifts, prizes, and favors and post them on the master budget sheet.

Contacts, Contracts, and Costs

Chapter 5, "When It's Time to Go Pro" goes into contract details. Just be sure to read and ask questions before you sign on the dotted line. If you feel more comfortable, have your attorney review it. Remember, without a signed contract, you have no guarantees or recourse. Keep all contracts in your planner.

Double-check with all vendors two weeks in advance of the event, and then again a few days before. Make certain you have contact numbers to reach your vendors during nonbusiness hours. Likewise, give your vendor every phone number possible to contact you should the need arise.

Shindig Sayings

To **book** talent means that you have signed a contract that they will perform at your event.

When a catalog item or an item on sale is not available when you place your order, you often will receive a **raincheck**. That means when the stock has been replenished, you will automatically be sent the item.

Party Pitfall

The average household plumbing often will back up when used to excess, or when foreign items are thrown in a toilet. So when hosting a large outdoor party, rent a portable toilet to accommodate the overflow, so to speak, of rest room activity.

Chips and Tips

To avoid stress, rent or borrow a cell phone for the few days before a big event so that anyone can contact you to solve a last-minute problem.

Chips and Tips

Give a copy of the party schedule to principals such as the DJ, caterer, any entertainers, video cameraman, and photographer so that they are all on site and in sync for a flawless festive flow.

All references, estimates, bids, contracts, and work-sheets should be kept in the appropriate section of your planner and fees recorded on the master budget sheet.

The Minute-by-Minute Waltz

As the party plans progress, the schedule for the event itself will come into focus. A minute-by-minute schedule will keep the party on track and assure that no detail is left unattended. Nothing will be overlooked with an air-tight schedule that regulates the flow of the party to be steady and pleasant for the guests. Party pauses can be deadly, times when nothing seems to be happening or something is happening too slowly. All of this is prevented with a "minute-by-minute waltz" dance card.

➤ Did you thank the guests? Yes, at 8:45, according to the schedule.

➤ What about handing out the favors? Sure did. At 11:00 sharp.

➤ I'll bet we forgot to get a photo of Grandma and Grandpa. No, between 10:00 and 11:00 all the family photos were taken.

So, be sure to set aside time during your preparations to make a printed schedule for your party.

Remember, this schedule is supposed to work for you, not against you. As long as you have hit the really important items, if your guests are having fun with sing-alongs, don't jump in and say, "Stop singing. We have to play charades now!" Play host, not traffic cop.

What's in the Cards for Us?

Remember that pack of 3" × 5" cards you were instructed to buy at the beginning of the chapter? These are your party people cards. In other words, these should contain all the pertinent contact information and any details you might need on vendors or suppliers. This way, you can slip a mini-party planner in your pocket or purse to make calls without dragging around your notebook.

The Least You Need to Know

➤ A party planner is invaluable to any host.

➤ Use a free association worksheet to help establish your party's theme.

➤ Include vendor's comments and dates of conversations in your party planner and contact cards.

➤ See performers in action before hiring them.

➤ Get signed itemized contracts from vendors.

Chapter 4

Party Pooling: Sharing a Celebration

In This Chapter

➤ Co-hosting is the simplest form of party pooling

➤ Create a party pool for neighbors, family, friends

➤ Build your own member party directory

➤ Raise money for your neighborhood or club

➤ Ease party-planning stress with a party pool

In this era of two-career families and single parenting, there is a genuine shortage of leisure time. Young families struggle to get their day-to-day money and time commitments met, and still enjoy leisure activities with each other. While we're living longer and celebrating more, we also have less time to prepare for it. This pressure could easily take all the fun out of partying.

Party pooling, even in its simplest form, can prevent that from ever happening. Truth is, the act of sharing time, goods, and talents actually allows us to benefit from and support the trend toward busy, productive family life along with the explosive celebration industry. Throwing a party can be as easy as pie—or cake—à la mode.

Won't You Join Me?

The most basic *party pooling* is co-hosting. A successful system is one where each co-host invites his or her quota of guests and shares the work and expense. Such events are often planned as social paybacks, that is where the co-hosts invite guests who have entertained them By putting their heads, hands, and pocketbooks together, the participants of this mini-pool can produce a party where the result will not only be two or three times better for each co-host but at an investment that is one-third to one-half what would have been spent in solo-hosting.

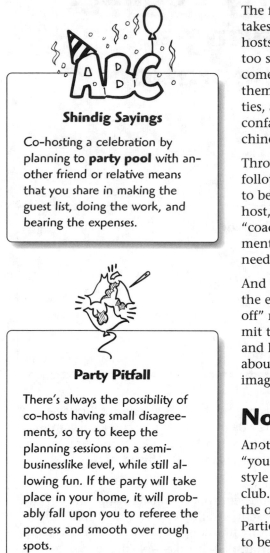

Shindig Sayings

Co-hosting a celebration by planning to **party pool** with another friend or relative means that you share in making the guest list, doing the work, and bearing the expenses.

Party Pitfall

There's always the possibility of co-hosts having small disagreements, so try to keep the planning sessions on a semi-businesslike level, while still allowing fun. If the party will take place in your home, it will probably fall upon you to referee the process and smooth over rough spots.

The first step to co-hosting is the idea meeting that takes place, preferably in the home of one of the hosts. Over brunch, lunch, or dessert (hey, it's never too soon to start the party), the team brainstorms to come up with the master plan. At this gathering, the theme, if any, is established. Often all the details, duties, and costs are discussed as well. The goal of the confab is to start turning the wheels of the party machine and building the excitement.

Throughout the pre-party planning stages, you will be following checklists and double-checking task progress to be sure no detail is overlooked. If you are the home host, you will quite likely be the "task master" or "coach." A notebook for tracking all of these assignments is a requirement; just as every good coach needs a playbook, you need your notebook.

And what better time to rehash the party and recount the events than at the final meeting, the "party payoff" meeting. This is the time when all members submit their receipts to be tallied, the total is divided, and hosts are paid. If you have enjoyed the jokes about ladies at lunch dividing up the bill, you can imagine the scenario at this final fling.

Now It's My Turn

Another way of getting help for your party is with the "you help me and I'll help you" party pool. With this style of party pooling you form a celebration co-op club. Whenever someone in the club throws a party, the other members, or *S.W.A.P.* (Special Workers at Parties) team, chip in to help. The club doesn't need to be anything official, it is really just a few folks who like to throw parties and dislike being overwhelmed by the day-of-the-event workload.

With this reciprocal plan, the host does all the up-front organization and the S.W.A.P. team runs the gala. There generally is no exchange of money, unless a helper has made a purchase for the host. The secret to the success of this scheme is for members of the team to clear their party schedule with other team members. Two events on one night could be a party plight that could swamp the S.W.A.P. team.

Celebration Committees

Clubs, neighborhoods, businesses, teams, schools, and church organizations are all groups who routinely throw parties the cooperative way. From the ground-floor plans to the parting word, all duties are shared in an equitable way, according to each participant's resources or available time.

Shindig Sayings

A **S.W.A.P.** team are the members of your party-pooling group who show up at your party ready to work. While they know they are there to help with any of the needed duties they are also prepared to join in the fun.

Festive Facts

When a hurricane left a Florida neighborhood without electricity, residents feared their food would go bad in their freezers. Instead of letting that happen, all the neighbors got together and just cooked up everything that had thawed out and gobbled up all the frozen desserts. Without air conditioning, the neighbors enjoyed a cool evening breeze as they continued to turn a horrible situation into one that was bearable—in fact, it was fun.

Fund-raising events are a perfect example of occasions when everyone pitches in to make the function a huge success. A shared workload is an easier workload.

Diving Into the Primary Party Pool

As friends and neighbors, we join forces to drive our kids to school, team up to baby-sit for each other, and pitch in when it's painting or moving time. Like farmers who help each other to raise barns or bring in the crops, we continuously try to help others succeed.

However, when it comes to planning and throwing a party, the advantages of pooling exceed saving money and time. There is also the benefit of having additional creative abilities, enthusiasm, and energy to contribute to the party picture.

Let's say you want to throw a very special bash for your son's high school graduation. Unfortunately, once you start putting together a long guest list, start planning the many details and establishing a budget, it's likely you will be discouraged and decide to celebrate with your immediate family on a small scale instead.

Chips and Tips

For basic co-hosting, you can tap into resources found in your personal address book, but for more elaborate affairs, a full-fledged party pool will keep you from drowning in duties.

However, as a member of a party pool, you don't have to give up your dreams of paying tribute to your son's success, because you will have the resources of your party pool to keep you afloat.

With party pooling, a host can double the quality of his party without spending an extra dollar or undertaking an excessive amount of work. You will get the job done in grand style by sharing talents, equipment, labor, and resources of your party pool. Everyone wades into the winnings.

In addition to reduced stress, the benefits of being in a party pool include saving both time, in searching for party goods and suppliers, and money, for purchase or rental of items. Just think, with the money you save, you can practice the two-party system—one on Friday and one on Saturday.

Building Your Pool

Someone has to put time and energy into organizing the pool and maintaining it. If it's too much work for you, start the pool and recruit another participant to share the responsibility. As you progress in the project, more help will surface. Once the party pool is filled and ready for activity, the member rewards will come floating in.

Once built, your pool can be run in one of these ways.

1. Put together a directory of all party-pool members and their potential pool contributions (time, talent, equipment). Simply print and distribute a small directory for the members (fellow employees, relatives, neighbors, association members) to use in arranging their own pooling activities.

2. Create a system where credits are earned and spent by printing a directory and setting up a record-keeping system tracking all party-pool activity, such as what has been used by whom. This method, while a little complicated, will help eliminate any squabbles over who is always using the folding chairs and who never helps others.

Your Party Directory

Regardless of which plan you are going to follow, the next step in your party pool is producing an official directory that lists information collected from each participant. Next to each member's name, you will note his or her available contributions in goods or services. As a cross reference, items and services are listed categorically with member's name. Below is a list of the goods and services you might want to seek out.

Chips and Tips

Decorations and props created for other events are excellent pool items. A treasure chest, for instance, can be used for pirate, Renaissance, medieval, or Peter Pan parties.

Catering:

➤ Cooking/baking
➤ Barbecuing
➤ Bartending/serving
➤ Cake decorating
➤ Candy making

Creative arts:

➤ Costume design
➤ Crafts
➤ Face painting
➤ Floral arranging
➤ Sewing

Equipment:

➤ Catering equipment
➤ Tables and chairs
➤ Costumes
➤ Ice chests
➤ Lights
➤ Linens
➤ Plants
➤ Tents

Graphic and visual arts:

➤ Calligraphy
➤ Desktop publishing
➤ Photography/ videography
➤ Printing
➤ Web site design

Professional services:

➤ Accounting/bookkeeping
➤ Cosmetology
➤ Fund-raising
➤ Legal services
➤ Party/event planning
➤ Personal services (errands, shopping, gift wrapping, baby-sitting, pet-sitting, coat check)
➤ Secretarial (word processing, research, filing, addressing, typing, telephones, collating, copying)

Performing arts:

➤ Acting/music/singing
➤ Dancing/choreography
➤ Clown
➤ Disc jockey
➤ Juggling
➤ Magic
➤ Mime
➤ Psychic services (handwriting, palm reading, tea-leaf reading)
➤ Puppetry
➤ Stand-up comedy

Technical support:

➤ Carpentry
➤ Construction
➤ Electricity
➤ Landscaping
➤ Lighting/Sound
➤ Plumbing
➤ Pyrotechnics

Transportation:

➤ Automobile

➤ Boat

➤ Miscellaneous (sleigh rides, snow-mobiles, hay wagon, carriages, child-size train)

Each member should also list any limitations or preferences:

➤ Smoking/non-smoking

➤ Religious restrictions

➤ Available days and times

➤ Location restrictions

Now that you have the member forms completed, the information verified, and a list compiled for the official directory, you have created a party pool. Only members will have access to the directory (unless you are planning a fund-raiser and want additional exposure to pump up the funds). Once the directories have been printed and distributed, get ready for the big splash made by those diving into your party pool.

Party Pool by the Rules

The rules for this pool do not prohibit horseplay, yelling, glass containers, or pets. Nor are the hours restricting. In fact, the more of the above, the better the party. However, there are a few rules to observe.

In Plan No. 1, making arrangements to utilize another's equipment and skills is between the individuals. No record will be kept of the activity. It is each member's job to keep track of his own participation and if unable to comply, just say no.

Chips and Tips

When members are willing to share a skill or talent that is in their actual line of work, their commitment (per occasion) should be limited to an hour or two gratis and perhaps, at a discount after that.

Festive Facts

When planning a hockey banquet, the moms tapped into their party pool for almost all of their supplies, decorations, and entertainment. This stretched their event budget to include a ticket to an NHL game for each member of the team.

Plan No. 2 involves a simple bookkeeping system in which all uses of services or equipment are recorded. Each member receives credits or debits to his account. Members may charge small fees if they feel it necessary, for material or maintenance expenses.

Paying Off the Pool

Party pooling can expand your resources immensely with a surge of expertise and support. The party pool concept brings to its members an enthusiasm and anticipation that may start them on a whirl of home entertaining.

With the shared-hosting options covered in this chapter, from the most basic to the very complex, you can have a team to help you succeed with a splash. When you jump into your party pool, you'll never again get in over your head.

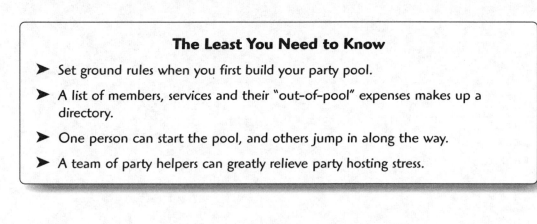

The Least You Need to Know

➤ Set ground rules when you first build your party pool.

➤ A list of members, services and their "out-of-pool" expenses makes up a directory.

➤ One person can start the pool, and others jump in along the way.

➤ A team of party helpers can greatly relieve party hosting stress.

Chapter 5

When It's Time to Go Pro

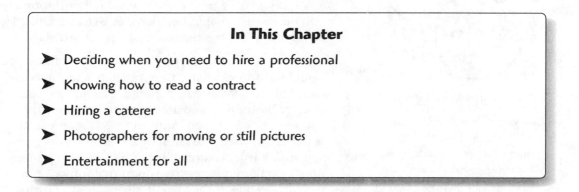

In This Chapter

➤ Deciding when you need to hire a professional

➤ Knowing how to read a contract

➤ Hiring a caterer

➤ Photographers for moving or still pictures

➤ Entertainment for all

Just by reading this book you will hone your party skills and gain confidence to throw any party you choose. However, there may be times when you feel the need to get expert help in planning, catering, decorating, entertainment, or photographing your special event. You might make this decision because you don't have the time to do the work yourself, or you just need an expert to make sure everything is done right.

When hiring an expert, your first option is to seek the recommendations of friends and family. Find out the names of suppliers they have hired or seen in action. Unfortunately, though, that isn't always going to be possible, but when it isn't, your only resource is the phone book or Internet. You will want to have the right questions ready, so that in your search you can make the perfect choice of a reputable, experienced, and suitable party professional.

Going Pro with Style

You've been planning your party for months, but realize that you need someone to oversee the actual event, make the food, entertain your guests, or just take photographs. The question isn't how to find these people, but how to find the *proper* people for your party.

The best way to find the right professional is through word of mouth. Ask friends, family, or co-workers—anyone you trust for recommendations on the right professional for you.

If you've asked around and you still come up blank, there are some ways you can find vendors to work with. First, try contacting professional associations that potential suppliers may belong to. Most have a standard of professional practice to ensure that you are dealing with an event professional.

Chips and Tips

Call your favorite restaurant to see if you might be able to get someone to freelance for you. Often your regular waitperson will be free to help you at your party.

In Appendix B, "Party-Planning Product and Service Resources," you'll find a resource list full of information on professional associations, as well as qualified books and Web sites that might help you get started.

Once you have identified a professional you think you would like to work with, the next step is to interview each potential vendor in person, preferably at their place of business. If you are trying to set up an appointment and the vendor resists meeting in person, you might as well cross him or her off your list. Something fishy is probably going on. A true professional won't mind meeting you in their office or at the party venue. If they won't meet you, it's possible the vendor is running a fly-by-night operation.

Here is a list of questions to ask the vendor during an interview:

1. How many years have you been in business? (If the person is just starting out, that is not necessarily a problem. Check if the vendor has a strong education or has similar work experience with another company.)

2. How many years have you been at this location?

3. Are you insured with a liability policy with a minimum of $1 million worth of coverage? (If so, you would like to be put on the insurance certificate as an additional insured. If not, find another vendor.)

4. What happens in case of equipment breakdown? (If it's not already on-site, backup equipment should be available to be delivered to the site immediately in case of an emergency.)

5. In case of an illness, who will take the place of a vendor?

6. When do you need a final count? (This question is for caterers.)

7. Who are three clients whom I may contact who have had a similar event to mine in the last year? (If you are booking someone to handle a wedding, their experience doing a corporate holiday party is not going to give you an apples-to-apples comparison. You want referrals with like parties.)

8. What are your professional affiliations?

9. How do I make my final payment? Cash? Personal check? Bank check? Credit card? (Do not pay in cash until the event is over to your satisfaction. Otherwise, pay by check or credit card.)

10. How long before the event may I cancel without penalty? (The farther away you are from the event when you cancel, the less in penalties you should be charged.

Oftentimes, vendors will supply you with letters of recommendation. Do not allow these letters to substitute for calling referrals directly. By getting personal with someone, you are much more likely to get the real scoop.

And finally—and most importantly—request a printed bid or estimate. The promptness, thoroughness, or professionalism with which they respond is your first clue to their business expertise and performance.

Signing a Consultant on the Dotted Line

Special event coordinator, party planner, event specialist, wedding consultant—whatever you call him or her, this is the person you will hire to be your party "safety net." Jump in and enjoy, because this professional will see to it that everything will be planned the way you want it.

Your planner could assist you with your entire event or just one or more portions of it. It is even possible to hire an *on-site manager* who will, after one or two consultation meetings, show up on the big day and coordinate the event from setup to teardown.

A professional consultant will work with vendors of your choosing or make recommendations from her known "performers" to make up the ideal team for your needs. There are big advantages to working with a coordinator's preferred suppliers, those

Shindig Sayings

An **on-site manager** is someone who will show up on the day of your event to coordinate and oversee everything from the setup to the teardown and cleanup.

with whom there is an established long-term relationship.

While the fee you pay a planner, by the job or by the hour, may seem high, the services he or she offers are invaluable. In fact, since planners often receive professional discounts not available to the consumer, his or her fee might be absorbed in the savings you make using the discount. Plus, since the planner works at this every day, he or she has access to unique, hard-to-find resources and suppliers that will add unforgettable touches to your event.

An experienced planner will help implement the details, protect your interests, and determine the timing needed to make your event pull together, without flaw. For example, he or she will contract and reconfirm deliveries and setups to make sure that every piece of the party design is put in place. Good news! A planner's job can also include cleaning up at party's end, when you are too pooped to "un-party." This type of careful and comprehensive coordination, along with expert scheduling, gives you the luxury of enjoying your party—as much or more than your guests.

Whose party is this, anyway? It is important that you find a coordinator who shares your vision and will enhance and implement it rather than impose his or her own concept. The ideal planning partner will offer creative ideas that will help you stay within your budget or perhaps be more imaginative, and at the same time, strive to lead you to your desired party plan.

In other words, get a complete list of what, when, and how your plan will be carried out and exactly what and when you will be expected to pay. If you are hiring the planner for just parts of your event, you must get a list of details that will be your responsibility to complete. Leave none of this to doubt.

A Catered Affair

When your event calls for something far more substantial or elaborate than chips and dip, and your cooking skills are more along the lines of opening a can and heating the contents thoroughly, you might want to consider hiring a caterer.

Even if you are a fantastic cook, there may be occasions when hiring a professional is a good idea. Are you feeding the masses, and are your cooking facilities limited? Perhaps the menu is complicated and you would be too busy preparing and serving the meal. Whatever your reason—necessity or luxury—hiring a catering service might be just the needed ingredient for your party's success.

For larger parties, many caterers bring full kitchens equipped to prepare elaborate menus for you and your guests. If your party is smaller, your caterer might even prepare food in your kitchen, but for the most part, will bring it ready-to-serve. Some set up kitchens in tractor trailers, while others create a kitchen under a tent in your yard. There will be times the caterer will commandeer your garage, or simply pull up into your driveway with a real chuck wagon and serve up a feast for your cowhands.

Chips and Tips

You can get a referral to find a caterer from the National Association of Catering Executives 708-480-9080 or www.nace.net.

Should you need to rent items like dishes, glasses, and flatware, you may want to make a trip to the rental store to get into the swing of planning your party. Good party-rental stores will offer a wide variety of styles to suit your style, tastes, and theme of your event.

Festive Facts

While a cowboy was out on the trail driving cattle, his world revolved around the chuck wagon. Made from a Civil War army-surplus wagon, the chuck wagon was built to hold food and other supplies for the cowboys. Driven by the cook, the chuck wagon traveled in front of cowboys and carried not only their food, but also cooking supplies and even extra guns, personal items, or musical instruments.

However, if you are short on time or are not sure what you want, your caterer, with care and expertise, will make choices that will be superb. In order to keep up with competition, successful caterers are prepared to set up incredibly beautiful tables with yours, theirs, or rented linens and serving containers. Many keep warehouses of their own stock to only be used at parties they cater.

Whether you decide to do the cooking yourself or have food simply delivered, one of the best investments you can make for your party's success is to hire a wait staff for last-minute preparations. They will also serve the food, clear dishes during the party, and be in charge of postparty cleanup. Most caterers will be happy to send experienced servers to do their miracles, but there's nothing wrong in hiring your own children or those of your friends.

Shindig Sayings

An **open or hosted bar** means that guests are not expected to pay for any of the drinks available at the bar. An open bar can last the duration of the night, or for a set time period.

Chips and Tips

Caterers, like most vendors, have their specialties. When calling, make sure to ask what it is. The answer could rescue you from hiring the wrong company for your needs.

Chips and Tips

You can find a list of photographers from the International Freelance Photographers Association (www.aipress.com).

Total bar setup is another party service that your caterer can provide. This may be as uncomplicated as sending over a portable bar and bartender and using your liquor, or as complete as allowing you to use their stock for a by-the-drink price at an *open or hosted bar* (guests can order any drink available in the bar selection) during a set time period.

Once you've had a chance to review your caterer's menus and have settled on something (or at least narrowed it down), ask for a food tasting of all the dishes. While you are at it, ask if you may peek into an event comparable to yours, to see a sample of his or her work in action.

It is always a good idea to determine whether or not the staff will be the "*first line*" or will "*add-on*" help be used. In some cases you might want to meet with the person who will be in charge of your party, since this isn't always the boss.

Say "Cheese"

What is worse than not taking photographs of your wonderful party? Well, how about taking tons of incredible photos but, unfortunately, your camera jammed somewhere around Photo No. 4 and the rest are ruined? That, dear host, is the reason for Party Rule No. 1: Hire a professional to document your once-in-a-lifetime special occasions.

Sure, your best friend might be a master at taking great shots with his Brownie, instant, or disposable camera, but for images that are first-rate, whether candid or well-posed, be sure to include a professional photographer in your budget.

A professional photographer will not only know all the ins and outs of lighting, shadows, film exposures, settings, composition, and making people relaxed and looking their best, but will also know the tricks and tactics used in developing film that will result in photos destined to be cherished heirlooms.

Remember, quality photographers carry a variety of cameras with them to capture the best images. Plus, they usually have the backup equipment to ensure that you will have pictures of your event despite camera failure.

As with any other professional, choose a photographer who has experience in the type of work you want. If your party is casual and free-flowing, you will be looking for good, semi-posed group shots. In this case, a serious portrait photographer may not have the personality to get guests to act and interact comfortably. Costume parties require a prom or wedding photographer to get those posed yet relaxed shots, and for a family portrait it takes yet another expertise. Skim through sample albums to find the type of photos you would like to have.

Instead of just looking through photo albums, why not ask to visit your photographer during an event shoot, to observe his style and methods? Take special care to note if he or his equipment is obtrusive. Was he dressed appropriately? Did his subjects seem relaxed, and did they smile easily for the photographer? And whatever you do, don't let anything be a substitute for getting personal recommendations from past clients. These people can be your very best source of information.

And before signing any contract, make sure that you like the photographer. It is going to be awfully hard to smile if you bristle at everything he says or every joke he makes.

While you might find a professional photographer essential to your needs, do provide your guests with disposable cameras to take the casual, informal shots. This will guarantee that you see what is happening in every corner of the party, even when you weren't there. To ensure that guests get the point of the cameras, leave a camera on the table with a note attached which reads: "Take your turn at snapping photos of the guests at the table and other Kodak moments."

Just because you are supplying cameras, don't rely on these to be your only photographs. Remember, when you are making memories of a lifetime, always choose a professional.

Shindig Sayings

A **first line** staff member is someone who works for the caterer on a regular basis and knows the caterer's needs and expectations, while an **add-on** is someone who is used by this caterer on only an occasional basis or who may never have worked for this caterer before.

Party Pitfall

When looking through a photographer's album, be wary of blurry shots or shots where the subjects don't look happy. Taking a great picture means a lot more than just finding a great pose.

Festive Facts

Fred was hosting a family reunion at his house and wanted to capture all those generations on film. To do so, he hired a photographer for family-group photos, strictly based on the man's work samples. Unfortunately, when the photos came back, they were nothing like those seen in the albums. Had he checked customer feedback first, he would have learned that the studio office was always in chaos and that most photos were delayed for weeks, or worse yet, lost forever. And he wouldn't have lost a precious keepsake of the reunion.

They're Moving Pictures, So Move!

What a professional photographer accomplishes with still shots, a trained *videographer* can achieve with video images. Their editing skills can produce a tight collection of video images that tell the story of your party in an interesting manner.

The rules of hiring a videographer are almost the same as hiring a photographer. They also have specialty areas, whether it's weddings, graduations, or children, so be sure to view several reels of their work at events similar to your own. Make certain, too, that you check their references and have a rapport with the videographer. If he or she doesn't make you feel relaxed, the images he or she shoots will show it.

And just as you might with a photographer, it is important to see the videographer in action. Attend one or more functions similar to yours. Even if these are private parties, you can sometimes inconspicuously attend and observe.

When checking over your contract, be sure to note who will be taking the video. Is it the person you actually met with or an assistant? This could make all the difference in what your final video looks like, and is definitely worth noting in the contract.

Chips and Tips

Some photographers will come to your event, take the photos, and leave the film for you to develop. The savings in this agreement over purchasing prints is considerable.

Design Team

Your dream is to transform your home into the Taj Mahal. Chances are you won't find all the materials you need to accomplish that at your local party store. That's where an event designer comes in. A good designer will turn your dream into a visual reality. Like a set designer for a play or movie, an event designer will build props and supply furnishings to capture the mood and theme you desire. Good designers are also masters of illusion. They can create items using lightweight and portable materials that will turn canvas into marble and Styrofoam into stone, all so realistic looking you would have to touch them to realize they weren't real.

Designers will work with all the members of your party team to create plans for every aspect of the party, from the sign-in tables to the buffet tables, from the dining room to the powder room. These talented artists are limited only by your budget and imagination. However, even with a limited budget, the right designer will know where and how to spend the allotted dollars to achieve the best effect for your vision.

Event designers often have specialties. While there are a number of people who have a wide range of designs, you will more likely find that some specialize in wedding designs, while still another does business theater or bar/bat mitzvahs. If possible, ask to see not only the sketches and notes for an event similar to yours, but also photos of how the plan turned into the final party design.

If you have limited size, time, or budget constraints, your designer or planner can also arrange for less-elaborate effects which will be centered around the dining and buffet tables. Different themes will be achieved through the use of table settings, linens, chair covers, centerpieces, and miscellaneous themed pieces.

Shindig Sayings

Unlike a photographer who uses still images, a **videographer** uses moving pictures to tell a story. He or she usually has the skill to not only film the event, but edit the tape to a more interesting format and length than you would be able to do.

Party Pitfall

To avoid guests walking off with disposable cameras at the end of the party, set out a basket bearing a sign, "Leave cameras here," near the exit as a reminder.

Chips and Tips

Many professional videographers are members of the Wedding & Event and Videographers Association International (www.weva.com).

Chips and Tips

If you are having trouble verbalizing your vision, try to share pictures cut from magazines or clipped in books that have the feel of the effect you are hoping to achieve.

Chips and Tips

Contact the American Rental Association (www.ARARental.org or 1-800-334-2177) for their member's stores in your area.

Another option for the budget conscious is a qualified balloon artist. The balloon industry has come a long way from blowing up some balloons and hanging them from the ceiling, or filling up a bunch of balloons with helium and placing them helter-skelter around the room. Today's balloon artists take classes, belong to associations, and even go to conferences where other artists from around the world gather to exchange ideas and designs.

Using a variety of products, balloon artists can build walls of color, write out messages, drape a ceiling, create sculptures made up entirely of latex and Mylar balloons, or arrange for hundreds of balloons to drop at a given time on your guests' heads.

The right designer can help make all your party fantasies come true, at a budget you can afford. Just make sure to check any references that might be made available to you.

If You Can't Buy It ... Rent It

There undoubtedly will be times when you will host a party that has more than eight or twelve guests—the standard size for dinner place settings. When those times occur, head to your local rental store. There you will find a wide variety of dishes, glasses, serving pieces, silverware, and even linens that will fit any table size. And speaking of tables, rental stores also carry different-sized tables and carry chairs—folding or padded, metal or wood. Many rental businesses even carry child-sized table and chair sets.

A good rental store is the place to find things like tents, candlesticks, portable bars, chafing dishes, punch bowls ... anything you would need to pull off a special event.

Even with a signed contract, it is always a good idea to call the rental store a week before the event, just to ensure that they are aware of the delivery and all the items contracted for.

Let Me Entertain You

The party is set, the guests have arrived, they are dazzled by the decor, and their mouths are watering at the first taste of the exceptional cuisine—and the party just flops. Why? Because at a party for young business professionals, you chose to ask your cousin to play "Lady of Spain" on his accordion while your niece tap dances.

You've probably been to many parties where your host feels that his CD collection, no matter how sparse, is sufficient entertainment. How many minutes was it before you "remembered" that your grandmother was in a coma and you had to run?

The type of entertainment planned for a party doesn't have to be elaborate, but it should be appropriate to the event. For instance, you wouldn't plan a Mexican fiesta with an Israeli dance troupe. By the same token, you shouldn't bring in a rap group to entertain a group of senior citizens. Choose the entertainment type to suit your theme, guest list, and surroundings.

Party Pitfall

When your rental items are picked up, or delivered, do not sign the acceptance receipt until you have counted and examined each item. If there are missing, damaged, or permanently stained items, you need to mark it down on your receipt. Otherwise, you will be charged substantial replacement fees after the event.

Chips and Tips

Save money by asking friends to bring their favorite CDs. That will help ensure that you are always playing music at least one of them likes.

Besides music, try thinking of other forms of entertainment. You might hire celebrity look-alikes for a movie-theme event. How about sketch artists or caricaturists for an art theme? Highland dancers would be good for a St. Patrick's Day party, while a New Orleans-style jazz band would be just right for a Mardi Gras gathering.

Since it's difficult to find the exact entertainers you need from the phone book, work with a reliable talent agent, or let your event planner obtain the proper performers for you.

Before You Sign on the Dotted Line

Before you sign any contract, make sure it contains these provisions and that you understand all aspects of the contract. If necessary, have your attorney review any paperwork.

These provisions should appear on all contracts:

➤ The types of services rendered

➤ Times of arrival and departure

➤ Event date, time and location

➤ Set-up and tear down schedule, if applicable

➤ Fee-payment schedule including overtime fees

➤ Cancellation policies

➤ Liability insurance in place for a minimum of $1 million naming you as an additional insured for the duration of your event

➤ Contact information during and after business hours

➤ Sales tax, if any

➤ Additional labor or equipment fees

➤ Inclement weather provisions, if applicable

➤ Power, lighting, gas and/or water requirements, if applicable

➤ Set up and clean-up fees, if applicable

➤ Meals provided and break schedules, if applicable

➤ Dressing area, if necessary

➤ Attire, if applicable

➤ Back-up equipment, if applicable

➤ Who is responsible for obtaining and paying for any permits, if necessary

Look for these additional items on an event planners contract.

➤ Liability—if decor items are rented or owned by planner, who is contracting with vendors (you or the planner)

➤ Who is responsible for negotiating all vendor contracts—you or the planner

➤ Who will pay the vendors—you or the planner, per-hour or per-job cost

➤ Replacement fee on lost or damaged rental items

When hiring a caterer, check the contract for these additional types of services rendered:

➤ Liability— or replacement fees if items are rented

➤ Trash-disposal provisions

➤ Disposal of leftovers

➤ Per-person or per-job cost

When hiring a photographer, look for these additional clauses in your contract:

➤ The number of photos taken

➤ Per-hour, per-photo, or per-job cost

➤ Cost of photo duplication

➤ Types and sizes of final photographs

➤ Special effects on photos

➤ Due date of final album

➤ Who owns the proof sheets, negatives or proof photos

➤ Photo copyrights

When hiring a videographer, look for these additional clauses to your contract:

➤ How many hours of raw footage will be shot

➤ Per-hour, per-job cost

➤ Cost of videotape duplication

➤ Format of final product

➤ Special effects on the final edited reel

➤ Due date of final edited reel

➤ Who owns the raw footage

➤ Copyrights

If hiring a decor designer, look for these additional provisions to the standard contract:

➤ If decor items are rented or owned

➤ Replacement fee on lost or damaged rental items

The Least You Need to Know

➤ Never hire someone unless you've had a chance to interview him or her in person first.

➤ When hiring a caterer, be sure you get a chance to sample every item from the menu before signing the contract.

➤ Always make sure to see samples of any professional's work before finalizing an agreement and ask for referrals of clients who have had events similar to yours.

➤ Be sure to call all professionals a week before the event to confirm details.

Part 2

To Party Means to Plan

Wouldn't it be great if you could throw the best party anyone has ever seen without doing any work? Sure it would be great, but then everyone would be doing it. Throwing a great party means working at it. You need to plan a theme, set your budget (and stick to it), and, of course, invite your guests.

Many people shy away from throwing parties because planning them seems like too much work. Now it is your turn to move out of the ranks of the party fearful to the party fearless. Read on to discover how easy it can be to stock a bar, what it takes to make fancy and fun invitations, and how to make even the smallest apartment large enough to hold a bash your guests will never forget.

Chapter 6

The Theme Says It All

In This Chapter

➤ Determining a theme

➤ Looking at your home's decor to establish a theme

➤ Hobbies make great theme parties

➤ Following your theme through from the invitations to the good-byes

---

Birthday or anniversary, barbecue or tea party, formal or casual—whatever the celebration or its style, adding a theme can add excitement and personality to your parties. A theme adds a dimension to events that most gatherings lack. It brings up the level of interest and unites the guests before the day of the party with a common excitement.

In this chapter you'll learn how to give a boring, everyday party pizzazz just by adding a theme. You'll learn how to excite your guests with theme invitations, decorations, and even food.

Is a Theme Necessary?

Is a theme necessary for you to host a successful celebration? Perhaps not. Desirable? Let's explore that. Here are two party examples—you choose the party to which you would prefer to go.

1. **Party 1**

   You go to your mailbox and find a store-bought party invitation. It's a standard greeting card with a balloon design imprinted on the front. You open it, and handwritten in the very small spaces provided, it says: "We're Having a Party!" It gives the names of the host, address, phone number, and date.

   Handwritten on the back of the card (because there is no proper place provided to write it), it reads: "We want to show off the videos of our trip to China. Hope you can make it. Dress is casual. Buffet and cocktails will be served."

   Ho-hum.

2. **Party 2**

   Your doorbell rings. When you open the door, your letter carrier hands you a cardboard mailer (a Chinese take-out box). The carton, trimmed with large Chinese lettering, has on it a shiny red label in the shape of a dragon that bears your name and address. You open it and there you find a fortune cookie, tea bag, and a colorful paper fan along with an invitation printed on a postcard of the Great Wall of China. The invitation reads: "Join us for video highlights of our journey to the mysterious Orient, along with cocktails and a *Szechwan, Mandarin,* and *Cantonese* buffet supper. We begin our journey down the Yangtzee River at 8 P.M. on Saturday, January 20, 2001. Call 989-555-2938 by January 10 to reserve your place in our pagoda. Mandarin garments encouraged. Bill and Nancy Smith."

   Now, which party would you rather attend?

   The first example is the way we are usually invited to parties. It's functional … but boring. From the invitation, you know you will spend an evening watching home movies from your friend's recent trip. These occasions have a boredom stigma and are often successful as a cure for insomnia.

   The second one immediately tells you this is going to be an interesting party. In fact, if the party lives up to the magic of the invitation, it's going to be unforgettable. This has to be more than a boring evening watching home movies. A party like this will not only be memorable, but possibly educational and definitely exciting.

Shindig Sayings

Many of the foods in **Mandarin** cuisine are wheat, instead of rice-based, consisting of dumplings, breads, and noodles. The food is mild in taste.

Cantonese food is the mildest and most common kind of Chinese food.

Szechwan food is liberal in the use of garlic, scallions, and chilies on chicken, pork, and seafood.

Now, isn't that the way you'd want your guests to look forward to all of your parties?

In the case of the second party, your friends have not only sent out a unique invitation, but have chosen to wrap the entire party around a Chinese theme. It makes perfect sense. The films are of their trip to China, they probably have brought back interesting souvenirs, and it's an easy theme to carry through. Why not make the experience of watching the video as exciting for their friends as taking the trip was for them?

Sometimes choosing a theme is not as obvious, and you will be required to use a little creative imagination when coming up with your theme.

Let the Occasion Set the Theme

Chances are, you have already held a number of parties with simple themes. Have you ever purchased birthday party goods imprinted with "Over the Hill," or a golf design, or scenes from a nursery rhyme? Those are themes.

You can make any holiday event extraordinary by expanding on a theme. For example, "Trim a Tree" or "Carve a Pumpkin" are very common themes for Christmas and Halloween. However, you can make a simple holiday party unique by taking the typical holiday and adding a twist—"Pilgrim's Turkey Trot" or "Stars and Stripes Triathlon." By giving these holidays another added dimension—ragtime dancing and sports—you have made a mundane holiday memorable.

Sometimes if you just move the routine date of an event, it is enough to create a festive atmosphere that brands it truly special. If you want, host a "Christmas in July," or in May have an "Every Night Is New Year's Eve" theme party for a person who adores the holiday season.

You see, you don't have to create something new, you just have to move it out of context to make it reappear in an exciting way.

Kids' Play

Kids' parties are usually theme-related. In fact, there is a huge industry devoted to designing preprinted party goods of a favorite cartoon or comic character, sports, dolls, space travel, or other child-friendly subjects. It is so easy to buy these products. Just go into the store or an online vendor and pick out every item that's in a particular line.

The problem is that while such party goods are festive, they are also perhaps too familiar or common for some people.

Crafty parents will often produce extremely individualized themes for their children's parties by creating their own invitations, decorations, costumes, favors, and fun foods. When this is the case, the whole family often joins in to make a party of preparing for the party.

There is nothing wrong in buying prepackaged theme designs. They can be very helpful if you feel your skills are lacking or you're just short of time. However, with very little effort, you can still make these party packages more personal and unique.

Parties by Design

Why should the kids get to have all the fun? There's no reason that big kids can't hold a theme party with a little more adult pizzazz—not when there are so many ways of shaking things up and coming up with a fabulous bash. Shouldn't a 60th anniversary party, planned for a couple who were wed during the big band era, swing? Or how about basing a graduation celebration for a finance student around the trappings of big business and Wall Street?

You can invent your theme by looking around your surroundings. This is particularly effective when you are starting out because it means you don't have to fight your decor—you work with it. It's very difficult to hold a *Lost in Space* party when you are surrounded by furniture that looks as if it belongs in a ranch house in Texas. You can do it, of course, but it takes a lot more work and money to transform it. Why fight it? Look at your furniture. Even if it's a mishmash, chances are there is at least one style that stands out. Let the design decide the feeling for the event, then all you have to do is create a theme to suit the occasion and the surroundings.

Festive Facts

An eager hostess invited her guests to celebrate her new washing machine at an impromptu all-white dinner party. Within hours she had tumbled together a menu, table decor, and party favors for her "blanc" bash. Getting into the spirit, the guests dressed in white and brought small gifts like detergent, bleach, and softeners, for the new "occupant."

It's a Grand Old Flag

Is your decor Early American? You can plan a colonial party featuring Yankee pot roast and flags on display to honor Betsy Ross, the creator of the first American flag. Then hold a rousing sing-along of patriotic songs. If it's not a general celebration but a milestone birthday, give the theme a patriotic plug such as "He's a Grand Old Man."

Festive Facts

In June 1776, Betsy Ross was a brave widow struggling to run her own upholstery business. Upholsterers in colonial America not only worked on furniture, but did all manner of sewing work, which included making flags. According to accounts given by Betsy Ross, General Washington came to her home and showed her a rough design of the flag that included a six-pointed star. Betsy, a standout with the scissors, demonstrated how to cut a five-pointed star in a single snip. Impressed, George Washington entrusted Betsy with making our first flag.

Futuristic Festivities

Is your furniture style high-tech? If so, a futuristic celebration would be more appropriate. Show off all your technological devices and set them up against your chrome and glass furniture. You and your guests can play virtual or video games. Serve freeze-dried cuisine, like the meals eaten by astronauts, or have guests place their dinner orders online or via a fax. This atmosphere would be ideal for a graduation, retirement, engagement, or going-away party with the title, "Here's to Your Future." High-tech styles also work well with "Man of the New Millennium" or *Star Trek* theme parties.

Using Your Surroundings

Wicker and rattan furniture will set the scene for a luau, beach party, or some oriental themes.

Shindig Sayings

A **smorgasbord** is a Scandinavian buffet offering a variety of hot and cold foods.

Likewise, a Danish Modern setting calls for a *smorgasbord,* while an English Tudor is perfect for either a formal dinner with Beef Wellington or set up as a lively pub complete with fish and chips and dart games.

If your home is made up of a wide variety of differing styles too numerous to define, then use this to your advantage. Create a "Pieces of My Life" party and tag each item that has a great story: "Found at Goodwill thrift shop for $5 a week after I left home" or "Picked out of my neighbor's garbage late one night." Neither you nor your guests will ever again look at your furnishings without smiling at the memories.

If you want to narrow your eclectic surroundings down further, look around your home and see if there is one focal point that draws everyone's attention. Is your living room dominated by a grand piano? A concert, cabaret, or piano bar party is the perfect choice. Use sheet music, books, or musical instruments to accent this theme.

When there is an important event happening, does everyone come to your place to watch your large-screen TV? You can be the producer of a theme party around a televised event like the Academy Awards, the Grammys, or the Superbowl. Let the focal point of your home be the kick-off point for a black-tie-and-gown awards soiree or a sports spuds-and-suds day.

As you can see, any type of surroundings or focal point can be made to work to your advantage and turned into a theme.

Home Is Where I Hang My Hat

If looking at the inside of your home doesn't inspire you, look outside.

Live in an apartment building? You can pretend it is a high-rise penthouse. Get a friend to act as a door attendant outside your building to greet and usher in your guests. Make it a very chic and avant-garde event set in New York's *SoHo*. Or pretend you live in the notorious Dakota apartments across the street from Central Park and home to the late John Lennon and the site of *Rosemary's Baby*. Consider the possibilities. What other stories can that building tell? Uptown or downtown, this theme will give your parties a new lease.

Festive Facts

SoHo is a New York City neighborhood named after its location, **SO**uth of **HO**uston Street. SoHo is famous for the old industrial buildings that grace its streets and for the shops, galleries, and artists who reside there.

Do you live out on the farm or in the country? You can have a party at your homestead that will allow for some real stretching out. Outdoor locations lend themselves to casual themes like:

➤ "Westward Ho" (urban cowboy, Tex-Mex, cattle drive, barbecue)

➤ "State Fair" (if your friends can fruits, raise animals, grow vegetables—any activities you'd find at a State Fair—show them off at this party)

➤ "Take a Break by the Lake" (terrific for having everyone come over for a dip in your own private swimming hole)

Guests can enjoy everything from volleyball to horseback riding in wide-open spaces. If you are lucky enough to live in the country, let it be the scheme for your theme.

Love Will Keep Us Together

There is really no limit to taking a typical celebration and giving it some sizzle. When it comes to anniversary parties, there is a good plan for any year, from the first to the 75th. You might pick the couple's wedding song as the central theme or trace their life together via several song titles: "We've Only Just Begun," "She's Having My Baby," "Sunrise, Sunset," "Love Will Keep Us Together," and "I Would Still Choose You."

Here are some ways to choose your themes based on personal information about the happy couple.

1. Select the ballads of a favorite singer of the celebrating couple, or pick the music of a particular era that is meaningful to your guests of honor. Romance, nostalgia, and sentiment can be created by playing "their song."

2. Where did they meet? For a 50th anniversary couple, replicate their favorite restaurant and the meal they enjoyed on their first date. Print a menu from that year with authentic prices, charge the guests for their dinner, and present the cash to the couple for a special meal—at today's prices.

Chips and Tips

If you are throwing a party for someone, you most likely know them very well; however, if you don't, contact his or her family or best friends to ask them about the habits and haunts of the guest of honor to help you with your theme selection.

Couples about to be married or wed from a few years to several decades will be thrilled with such thoughtful celebrations and will cherish the memories through their lifetime together.

Leisure Pursuits

Symbols of hobbies, pastimes, and talents are great bases for a theme party. Have you been collecting comic books for a lifetime? Then why not hold a superhero party? (You will be surprised at how many adult men will be attracted to this theme.) This is a party strong in primary colors and whimsy (see Chapter 23, "From Tots to Teens—Total Party Plans").

Your passion for gardening will bloom in a "Ladies for Lunch" garden party. Use homegrown flowers, plants, and produce (see Chapter 18, "Spring Flings").

Chips and Tips

Go to secondhand stores or garage sales to buy copies of old books. Use them as favors or decorations.

Chips and Tips

The most important rule for deciding upon a theme is to consider the guest of honor and his or her personality, interests, talents, pastimes, and goals. You'll find the ideal theme for celebrating a person, and there is no better honor.

Is he hot-wired to ESPN's all-sports coverage? Then a gridiron idea is the perfect party plan (see Chapter 23).

By the Book

When you walk into your friend's home and it's filled floor to ceiling with books, you've got your theme right there. If novels are to his liking, scan his bookshelves for likely inspiration. Perhaps he has the entire *Hardy Boys* or John Grisham collection? It doesn't take a detective to analyze the evidence that he would love being feted at a mystery party.

Check out their bookshelves and see if you can determine a pattern.

1. *Gone with the Wind* fan? This theme begs for mint juleps, fresh flowers, fried chicken, and southern hospitality. Your guests will gather on the verandah and party as if there's no tomorrow (see Chapter 19, "The Heat Is On").

2. Would she die for *Dracula?* Ghastly friends will "suck up" to you for an invitation to celebrate your "ghost of honor" (see Chapter 20, "Fall Festivities").

Getting the idea? There are almost as many themes as there are book titles.

Couch Potato Chips

Just like a book party, you can easily make the same plans for the couch potato and his favorite TV shows, or the film fan and her selection of video picks. Familiarize yourself with your friend's habits and hobbies for clues to the theme party that would be a good fit.

Pastime Parties

Virtually any hobby can be adapted to a theme party. Bugs, bats, or birds—whatever your friend's pastime pursuits, you can create a theme that showcases what he or she loves.

A Combination of Sights and Delights

For people who love to travel or someone with strong ethnic ties, theme parties with an international flair are the ticket. However, to give a generic international subject a twist, you can combine themes to create other variations. For example, if you choose a gambling theme, add some international adventure by setting the casino in Monte Carlo.

1. A beach party is invariably fun, but it takes on a down under dimension when you "put another shrimp on the *barbie*" for an Australian soiree. G'day, mates!

2. A trip into The Twilight Zone can be your party theme with the addition of fortune-tellers; palm, tarot-card, and tea-leaf readers; handwriting analysts; and psychic messages from beyond.

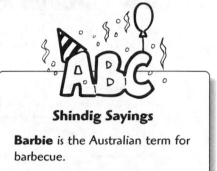

Shindig Sayings

Barbie is the Australian term for barbecue.

Pack your party plan and treat your worldly (and otherworldly) guests to an imaginary trip. No matter what your destination, your guests will love you for going that extra mile.

Time Tunnel

If you are brainstorming ideas, don't forget to look back in time to celebrate past eras. There were cakewalks and ice cream socials at the turn of the twentieth century. The 1920s brought prohibition, flappers, and bathtub gin. The "B-Boys"—Beach Boys and The Beatles—epitomize the styles of the '60s. Take a trip down nostalgia lane. Each decade is a source of theme inspiration.

Alternately, you can zoom ahead into the space age, with themes following leaders like *Star Wars, Star Trek,* and true-life space exploration.

Make Mine with a Twist

Although not really themes, serving styles can be the basis of a party theme. Clam bakes, barbecues, tailgates, potlucks, fish fries, or fondue cooking are among the ways of serving that are quite social and theme inspiring.

Several strategies are also party basics that can be built on. These include scavenger hunts, progressive parties, ongoing parties (like dining or tasting clubs), surprise parties, and housewarming parties. Here, too, you can blend a personalized theme with the strategy for a super event.

Set the scavenger hunt into a Halloween theme where guests have to trick or treat for treasures on their list. Or put the fondue party in a Swiss setting for a tasty trip theme.

Get creative. Explore every avenue available to look for theme inspiration.

Follow Through in All You Do

Finally, if you're still stuck, you can find multiple resources and books for total party plans. For instance, if you're online, check out www.PartyPlansPlus.com for a wide range of events planned from the invitation to the souvenirs.

The key to a successful theme celebration is to follow through. Start with the invitation and make sure you follow the theme with your choices of decor, menu, entertainment, prizes, and souvenirs.

The Least You Need to Know

➤ A party with a theme gives all of the guests something in common long before they arrive at the party.

➤ Theme parties give you a path to follow and narrow your choices to make planning simple.

➤ A theme can be based on almost anything: hobbies, collections, the site, talents, interests, or occupations.

➤ For best results, incorporate the theme into every element of the party.

Chapter 7

Banking on a Budget

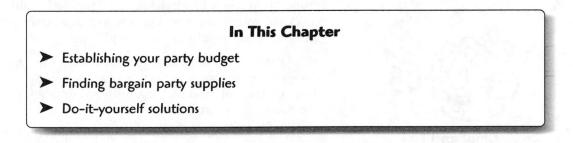

In This Chapter

➤ Establishing your party budget

➤ Finding bargain party supplies

➤ Do-it-yourself solutions

Throwing a party doesn't mean you have to throw your budget out of whack. Although it does require spending some money, it shouldn't mean spending your kid's college funds or your dream vacation savings. That would take a lot of the enjoyment out of planning a party. And we all know that the first rule of throwing a party is for the host to enjoy it!

So, get out your pencil and sharpen it to a fine point while we show you how to prepare a party budget with some clever cost-cutting and money-saving maneuvers.

Rule of Thumb

The party budget rule of thumb is that there is no set rule. Parties and budgets are as individual as the people who throw them. While one host routinely spends $500 on a casual get-together, another might not spend that amount on a year's worth of entertaining. The good news is that, with a little creativity and flexibility, you can spend as much or as little as you can afford and still achieve an outstanding outcome.

Chips and Tips

To save time and error in your master plans, consider using one of the software management programs to track budget items, actual costs, and reminders for special deadlines. Staying on top of expenditures and timelines will prevent party pitfalls.

Chips and Tips

When you are stumped for a product, service, or vendor resource, give your local party store a call for help. A good store will have a file of "festive folks" and will happily share their leads. Don't, however, forget to get other references.

One of the first things you'll need to consider is the type of party you are having and who will be attending. Casual gatherings with close friends and family usually don't require a large outlay. While formal parties with new acquaintances or business associates may mean you'll want to show off a little more.

Time and Money

Say you have a family birthday and you know that inviting folks over for a barbecue is the easiest and least-expensive way for you to entertain. Since this is a special celebration, however, you want to make it a little more elaborate. You start to think you'll add a few decorations, some simple activities, and perhaps light entertainment to make it more festive. You think, "That won't break the bank." Then after a little checking, you discover that things cost more than you imagined and the tally is mounting.

All of these extras will mean spending more time and money to make things perfect. If your life is busy, time is money, so finding bargains for your fabulous fete could cost a fortune.

So decide if you can afford to hire someone to do it all for you, or if time is tight, will shopping for plates in three stores be worth the dollar or two you'll save.

Distributing the Dollars

Depending upon your personal preferences, your budget allocations will vary. For some hosts, the food is paramount, while for others it's the entertainment. Decide what's important to you and plan your budget accordingly.

The following percentages represent a typical distribution of dollars for a party. Yours may vary depending on tastes, preferences, and flexibility.

Beware of Budget Busters

Just when you think you have it all decided and everything is within your budget, the unexpected expense will crop up to throw your budget for a loophole. When this happens (sorry, but it is "when" and not "if"), you will need to have plans B and C ready.

Some examples of *Murphy's Law* budget busters include sales tax, miscalculating postage, unplanned shipping costs, and rush charges for last-minute items you decide you "must" have.

Item	Percentage of Total Budget
Printed pieces: Invitations, thank-you notes, programs, place cards	3 percent
Decorations: Balloons, flowers, banners, props, linens	15 percent
Food and beverages including labor	40 percent
Entertainment, activities	20 percent
Prizes, gifts, favors	3 percent
Rental items	14 percent
Miscellaneous	5 percent

Chic but Cheap Solutions

The best way to save money on your budget is to go cheap. Whether you are hunting for bargain basement prices, scouring garage sales, or just digging in your own basement, you'll find things you can use for your party, before you go and spend thousands of dollars on things like decorations or entertainment.

Bargain Basement Bonanzas

The art of bargain hunting will be a boon to some party hosts. You can search for close-out and discount items, and holiday sale items ranging from dollar-a-yard linens for your elegant table to the penny-a-piece party favors that fill goody bags for your guests.

When purchasing any holiday sale merchandise, think about what it can be used for other occasions during the year. For instance, red items can be used for Christmas, Valentine's Day and patriotic holidays. Think ahead. Buy great items when you can at a good price and save all year.

Chips and Tips

While your goals will dictate how you divvy up your festivity funds, the most important thing to remember is that you can't spend the same buck twice, so keep an eye on the limits. Once you have listed all of your potential expenses on your master budget sheet, decide how you will mete out your money. Alter the budget, and adjust your party pocketbook accordingly.

Hunting Those Bargains

Tracking down illusive party penny savers takes time, but here are some great places to start your search besides local party goods suppliers. Check rental stores for sale of used but good items, thrift shops, discount clubs, flea markets, and garage sales. Or search the Web and check out auctions (www.eBay.com is great) and online merchants such as www.GreatEntertaining.com.

Attack bargain chasing as diligently as you would job hunting. The money you save will be like finding a second income source.

Festive Facts

A hostess in search of a tropical drink glass called the local liquor distributor in desperation. She needed 200 for a champagne taste party, but with a beer budget. The manager had 400 lovely glasses bearing a full-color parrot insignia and only a tiny logo. He sold them all to her at 10 cents each. He even threw in the huge parrot signs that matched. A creative search paid off in ... well, parrots!

Do It Yourself

Sometimes it is better and cheaper to do it yourself. Cooking up a batch of your favorite chili is going to save money over buying a dozen cans, and it will be far more tasty. A quick trip to the farmers' market to gather bunches of flowers and greens will blossom into savings when you arrange them simply yourself.

Another do-it-yourself winner is to enlist the services (and talents) of amateur entertainers and musicians that will work for free or reasonable rates. Many college or high school drama, choral, or orchestra groups will perform at your party for just a donation to their trip or uniform funds. This pleasant entertainment adds a bright touch to your home party.

A Borrower Be

One of the best ways to stretch your savings is through party pooling as discussed in Chapter 4, "Party Pooling: Sharing a Celebration." When you borrow party basics like twinkle lights, tables, chairs, coat racks, linens, serving pieces, or a helium tank, you will drastically reduce your party payouts.

When entertaining the same guests over and again, learn to recycle props. A treasure chest can be used for a pirate party, tropical theme, Peter Pan or "we treasure you" events.

Occasionally your local theater group, department store, supermarket, video store, or movie theater will let you rent or borrow props. Make friends with managers of stores you frequent. Often displays, posters, props, and decorations from store promotions will be yours for the taking.

Chips and Tips

When considering a menu, check recipes closely. If you are going to need to buy a number of specialty ingredients that you won't use again or will go bad before you can use them another time, check out if buying the dish premade might be a more budget-friendly alternative in the long run.

Buried Treasures

Speaking of treasure chests, the most valuable savings may be buried in your cupboards, garage, attic, basement, and closets. Explore these areas with an open mind for unique items that can be used or adapted to fit your party scheme.

Getting Crafty

If you are artistic and crafty, you can save lots of money by using your creations to enhance your party decor. The methods practiced in craft circles are many and varied; the arts-and-craft stores are a mass of possibilities. Crafting can result in party invitations, decorations, costumes, table decor, gifts, and favors. Almost every facet of your party can be coordinated through the world of glue guns, rubber stamps, stencils, beads, feathers, sequins, stickers, Styrofoam, paints, and glitter. All of these can be used to turn trash to treasure.

Party Pitfall

Audition all entertainment, particularly low-cost or free. Set up an opportunity to listen to your nephew's "nice little band" during rehearsal to make sure they are skilled enough and appropriate. Sometimes you just can't afford "free" entertainment.

Head to the library, check the Internet, or do some channel-surfing on your television. There are dozens of programs on local cable access, Discovery, Home & Garden Television, and Lifetime channels. Crafting is an easy way to safe money while creating one-of-a-kind effects that show your artistic talents.

Bring Your Own

B.Y.O.E. (Bring Your Own Everything) would be a very good way to save scads of money on your event, but it may be a little drastic and is definitely a tactless hosting method.

However, potluck can extend to more than just hot dishes or gelatin molds. Guests may be asked to provide paper and plastic food service items, centerpieces or room decorations. The organization of games and activities is a contribution that will help the host immensely. Start your party planning by making a list of those chores you will gladly part with. Then when a guest asks, "Is there anything I can do to help?" You'll be ready.

The Early Bird Beats the Budget

Ordering certain items early also will enable you to take advantage of sales and special promotions, and you won't have to pay additional fees for rush processing or mailing.

One of the biggest unexpected expenses is that of paying top dollar for something because it's ordered at the last minute. This happens when you either forget to buy or reserve something, or you think of something brilliant in the final hours before the event. This is mostly true when the item needs to be shipped or personalized with engraving or imprinting. Whatever the cause, those deadline disasters will eat into your party budget like the guests at the fresh jumbo-shrimp display.

So, if you get that sudden lightning bolt of inspiration for a fantastic addition to your party, try to control your enthusiasm long enough to determine if it will affect the overall party success and how it will affect your budget.

Party Pitfall

A host found an online merchant for 10 outdoor torches at a savings of $2 each over his local party store. To receive them by ground shipping in 5 to 7 days would have cost $8. This still would have saved him $12. However, since he needed them rushed to him in two days, he not only would have been charged $8 more for rush shipping, the merchant also would have charged $10 more for rush handling. In the end it would have cost him $6 more to order them online.

Unless the detail is going to add a big scoop of à la mode to your party pie, pass on the idea.

The budget-balancing act for your party doesn't mean you have to walk a tightrope or act like a tightwad. Plan carefully and, of course, use this book as a safety net.

The Least You Need to Know

➤ There is no rule of thumb other than your personal preferences.

➤ Look for hidden expenses whenever you plan a party.

➤ Decide what's important to you and plan your budget accordingly.

➤ Shop year-round for party supplies.

➤ Party bargains are easy to find if you always have your eyes peeled.

Chapter 8

The Honour of Your Company ...

In This Chapter

➤ Including all the necessary details in your invitation

➤ Putting together a formal invitation

➤ Creating funky envelopes

➤ Matching your invitation to your party's theme

➤ Using the Internet to invite your guests

Since the invitation is the first time your guests will get to see what type of event you are hosting, it is the most important first ingredient to your party's success. In this chapter you'll learn how you can create inviting invitations. Perfect attendance is almost guaranteed as your peruse these invitation inspirations.

Invitation Imperatives

A good invitation is just like a good news story: Its first goal is to cover the five *W*s of who, what, when, where, and why, along with how-tos and other party imperatives.

You'll want to answer these questions in the invitation.

1. Who is throwing the party? Write out the full names of the hosts.

2. What type of party is it? Formal or casual, cocktail or dinner, theme or scheme. Prepare your guests for what they should expect the minute they walk in the door.

3. When is the party? Make sure you tell the day, date, and start and finish times of the event.

4. Where is the party? Give the address, directions, and a map if necessary.

5. Why is the party being held? State the occasion (birthday, anniversary, bon voyage, new baby, etc.) and honoree's name, if applicable.

6. Your how-tos should include how to respond, the dress code, and what to bring if it's a potluck event. Also include a phone number for responses.

Festive Facts

Just recently a stressed-out hostess inadvertently omitted the date from her invitation. This meant that every invited guest was required to call to find out when the event was to be held. Her faux pas may have qualified her as the only hapless hostess in history to receive a prompt 100 percent response.

Shindig Sayings

A **self-mailer** is an invitation printed on heavy stock and folded either in half or in thirds, affixed with a seal, addressed, stamped, and mailed. This can be done to conserve envelopes or as part of the design plan.

Make sure you have someone else review your invitation before sending it out. This will ensure you have included all the necessary information.

Formal or Funky

Your invitation is a forecast of things to come, so make it as accurate as you can by designing it to match your party atmosphere.

An invitation to a very casual affair can be a hand-printed note copied on attractive stationery and sent as a *self-mailer*. Find a pre-printed paper that matches your theme.

For an elegant occasion such as a wedding or formal sit-down dinner, you might consider more elaborate invitations. Whichever invitation you chose, make sure it reflects your style of the event.

A Formal Flare

For elegant events, you'll find numerous sample books of imprinted materials through your printer, card shop, stationery supplier or on-line.

If ordering from a book isn't your style, you can design formal invitations yourself using a desktop-publishing program and quality invitation stock available from specialty-paper companies or office supply stores. Or work with artists from a full-service print shop.

Once you've chosen and proofread your invitations, simply address, stamp and mail.

Creative Casual

For a party that isn't so formal, you have the advantage of being able to use your imagination. Remember, sometimes it isn't so much what you say but how you say it.

For an informal celebration, not only can your invitation be imaginative, you are not limited to sending it in an envelope. In fact, almost any non-flammable, nonbreakable object can go directly through the mail if it has a clearly printed label attached and the correct postage affixed. When in doubt, take your proposed container to the post office to be inspected and approved. Don't spend the time and effort preparing a bunch of creative cards if they can't be mailed.

Handmade envelopes to match your theme will add to the appeal of your invitation. The list of materials that can be used to construct your envelope is almost limitless. They include wallpaper, gift wrap, newspaper, magazine covers, fabric, or even children's artwork.

Message in a Bottle

A handcrafted "Message in a Bottle" invitation would be captivating for even more than just island or tropical parties. Trinkets and symbols of your party theme can accompany the see-through invitation on its journey into your guests' mailboxes.

Party Pitfall

Reply envelopes should always carry the correct postage. It's inappropriate to ask your guests to pay for the return of the response card.

Chips and Tips

Invitations that are 5" to 11½" long, 3½" to 6⅛" high, and ⁷⁄₁₀₀₀" to ¼" thick and weigh 1 ounce or under require one first-class postage stamp. Mail that is larger or smaller than these dimensions, or heavier than 1 ounce, should be taken to the post office to determine proper postage.

Party Pitfall

Proper invitations of any kind should never go through a postage meter.

73

To achieve the effect, recycle a plastic soda, water, or juice bottle. With a bit of crafting and some inexpensive supplies, you can produce an invitation that will get your guests hopping—island hopping, that is.

You also can send invitations in recycled cardboard paper towel tubes, corrugated cartons, plastic bags or cookie tins, to name a few.

Once you have settled on the product of your whimsy, be sure to send yourself a prototype. The sample invitation should be constructed in the exact way as those you are making for your guests so that you can test its travel time and condition upon arrival.

Innovative and Inventive Invitations

Once you've decided to go with a theme for your next event, it's important you start with the invitation.

Later in the book, in Chapters 17 through 23, you'll see a number of innovative invitation ideas that are matched to themes. Have fun. Let your invitation be the start of the party ... weeks before its scheduled to begin.

A(verage) to Z(any) Invitation Gimmicks

Once you've determined that you are going to send out a funky invitation, it's important to expand your creativity to the wording. After all, sending a packet of salsa is great, but also loses its flavor if your wording is formal.

Here's a sample of items you can use to attach to your invitation and their related catchphrases. Keep in mind that groaning is good for you.

> ➤ **Eraser:** "Correct me if I'm wrong ..."
> ➤ **Gum:** "We want 'chew' to come ..."
> ➤ **Horoscope:** "The stars say there's a party in your future ..."
> ➤ **Zipper:** "Zip your lip—it's a surprise ..."

Chips and Tips

Always include an invitation addressed to yourself with the batch to establish that they were posted, the promptness of receipt, and as a souvenir for your party scrapbook.

Party Pitfall

Do not sprinkle confetti, especially the metallic kind, into your invitation envelope. However festive, they are very unwelcome when they fall into a computer keyboard or carpeting.

Check out inexpensive small toys generally used as prizes in cereal, candy boxes, or in souvenir bags for a child's party as likely items to attach to your invitation.

Respond By ...

Most invitations require an *RSVP* or "respond by." While more formal invitations often include a card that needs to be sent back to the host, casual RSVPs can be done by phone.

Spreading the Word

The most popular way to send in invitation is through the mail. However, it is important to make sure you mail it out early enough to ensure that people have enough time to hire babysitters, plan costumes, or just get excited. We've put together a list of mailing tips:

➤ **Milestone occasions:** (weddings, special anniversaries, or milestone birthdays): Send invitations out four to six weeks before the event.

➤ **Theme or costume parties:** Mail the invitations at least four weeks ahead.

➤ **Holiday parties:** Invite your guests four to six weeks ahead of the party date, especially if your party is on a Saturday night.

➤ **Casual get-togethers or informal parties:** Depending on your timeline, invitations can be presented just prior to the party (make a phone call for a same day or next-day event), up to three weeks in advance.

Aside from sending written invitations, you can use other ways to get the word out about your next party. Some ideas are more suited for your party's style than others, so take care in selecting the appropriate method.

By Word of Mouth

You and your friends are sitting around the office having lunch, trying to figure out what to do for the weekend. Suddenly you say, "Hey, why doesn't everyone come to my place after work on Friday? Bring your swimsuit. We can order in some pizzas." This is an impromptu invitation meant for those within earshot.

Shindig Sayings

RSVP stands for *repondez, s'il vous plait* in French ("please respond"). This means that whether guests are attending the party or not, you are asking for a response. Regrets or regrets only means you want to hear only from those guests who will not be attending.

Chips and Tips

For milestone events such as bar/bat mitzvahs, weddings, or anniversaries, send a save-this-date postcard to out-of-town guests once you have settled on a date to give them sufficient time to make travel or vacation plans.

Ma Bell Invites

If the event is no more complicated than asking your best friend over for a Sunday barbecue, you can, of course, do it quickly with a phone call.

If you have a lot of phoning to do, you can even start a *phone chain* among several of your guests. Just ask each guest to call one or two other people, and make sure you supply all the names and numbers. It's a great time saver.

Do not rely on phone calls if you have to give detailed information such as directions, special instructions for a surprise party, where to park, or which entrance to use. Remember: When the information is important, write it out and distribute it.

Shindig Sayings

A **phone chain** invitation means that you call one guest and ask him or her to call one or two others whose names and numbers you supply.

Party Pitfall

Never leave a party invitation on an answering machine. You have no way of knowing if the message was ever received. If you must leave an invitation on a recorder, follow up if you have not heard from the guest within a day or two.

Hand Delivery

Are you having a theme party and the guests are all located in close proximity? Or do you want to create a real buzz? Hire costumed couriers (or put your car-driving teens into service) to make the rounds and deliver the invitations by hand. Their outfits should match the party. For instance, if it's a western theme, have the couriers dress as if they worked for the Pony Express.

You've Got Mail

There are now Internet Web sites on which you can quickly extend your invitations via e-mail—in cyber-style. Some even offer programs that will track responses in a guest-list format and provide your own party-plan Web page.

If you know all your guests' e-mail addresses, you can send invitations via e-mail for a high-tech effect. These look like actual cards and can be animated or artsy, formal or fun. All you do is fill in the blanks and in seconds your cyber-invitation will be in their electronic mailboxes.

Best of all, since replying only takes a couple of keystrokes, you generally receive responses much more quickly, which is a big help in your planning. The surprise is that these cyber-summons are FREE! Check out:

➤ Blue Mountain Arts (www.
  bluemountainarts.com)

➤ Evite.com (www.evite.com)

➤ RSVPme (www.rsvpme.com)

➤ ersvp (www.ersvp.com)

Printer Party Goods

Use your desktop publishing or clip-art programs to help you design and print an invitation, a matching reply card, program, envelopes, and place card that are one-of-a-kind and totally customized for your event.

Whichever invitation you choose, make sure it matches the theme of your event. And, most importantly, have fun doing it!

Party Pitfall

With hand–delivered invitations, discretely call ahead to see if they will be at home or at their place of work (if you can deliver it there). It would be a shame to waste the fun and festivity of such a surprise on an unanswered door.

The Least You Need to Know

➤ The invitation is your guests' first glimpse into your party; let it be crystal clear.

➤ Match your invitation to your party style: casual for casual, formal for formal.

➤ All invitations must answer the five *W*s: who, what, when, where, why—sometimes how.

➤ There are limited occasions when word of mouth or telephone invitations are sufficient.

➤ You can design and send a variety of invitations.

Chapter 9

Tiny Bubbles: Stocking Your Bar

In This Chapter

➤ Learning the basics of serving alcoholic beverages

➤ Stocking your bar

➤ Essential garnishes to have on hand

➤ Buying just the right glassware

When your palate (and the occasion) calls for something a little more sophisticated than a six pack of beer or wine that comes in the gallon bottle with the screw-off cap, it's time to start setting up your own home bar.

A walk around a liquor store will reveal everything from wines to whiskey, from liquors to liqueurs, from apple jack to apple cider. Here's everything you need to know to set up a serviceable bar that should be able to handle most basic drinks.

Top Shelf

If you've ever bought a drink in a bar, you probably know that bar-brand liquors are one price and top shelf is a higher price. *Top-shelf* liquors are called that because they are literally kept on the top shelf—right in the eyeshot of the customer.

Top shelf, or *call brands,* are those brand names people ask for: "Give me a Chivas on the rocks."

The bar brands are usually used if you don't specify a certain brand, for drink specials, and as happy-hour promotions. These brands are less expensive and lower in quality than top-shelf brands.

While it's possible to find generic brands that might be the same quality as a top-shelf liquor, you would do better to invest the extra dollar or two in a premium bottle for your home bar. Just as a chef uses only the best ingredients, a good bartender looks for the highest-quality liquors.

Booze Basics

Chances are you have a liquor of choice, but to set up a bar that will appeal to all your guests, here is some information you'll need to be the best barkeeper in town.

Give Me a Whiskey ... Straight

Whiskey actually comes in three basic varieties. There's blended, bourbon, and Scotch.

Blended whiskey is made with a combination of grain and 20–40 malt whiskeys mixed together. It's also the main component in classic cocktails like a Seven and Seven (Seagrams 7 Crown and 7-Up), a manhattan, or an old-fashioned. Want a good whiskey for mixing with colas or clear soda? Choose Seagrams. For drinking straight up or on the rocks, try Dewars.

Bourbon combines at least 51 percent corn with rye, barley, and/or wheat. Bourbon is thought of as the quintessential American whiskey and the classic whiskey chaser in a *boilermaker*.

Festive Facts

When people ask for a bourbon drink made with Jim or Jack, they are referring to Jim Beam or Jack Daniels. Although Jack Daniels is a Tennessee sour mash, most folks drink it as they would a classic Kentucky bourbon.

Scotch, thought by many people to be the Cadillac of the whiskeys, is usually served straight or on the rocks (over ice). It's occasionally mixed with water or club soda, but for the most part people who favor it like the taste of the Scotch itself. If you really want to make people blanch, ask for a Scotch and 7-Up. Chivas Regal is the premiere brand, and Dewars also makes a very good Scotch.

If you are looking for a good Scotch, look for a single-malt made by one brewery and imported from Scotland.

In addition to the more common whiskies, there is also Canadian whisky (spelled without the e), Irish whiskey, and rye whiskey.

The Lighter Drinks

For folks who like to drink light, most choose a clear gin or vodka. A gin and tonic is still the classic summer drink—kind of like tart lemonade with a kick. Some folks also use gin to make martinis, although over the years vodka has become more synonymous with that drink. Gin mixes well with a variety of fruit juices, and Tanqueray or Beefeaters are good brands to buy.

Vodka is the main ingredient in martinis and is made from grain. Although there are flavored vodkas, keep a plain bottle of Stolichnaya (known more commonly as Stoli) or Absolut chilled in your fridge or freezer to be drunk straight. Vodka also mixes well with a variety of juices.

Rums come in both dark and light. The lighter varieties are used as the base for a number of tropical drinks including rum runners, piña coladas, or Long Island iced teas. The darker varieties, while used in some mixed drinks, are often drunk like a whiskey.

Tequila is an essential in most bars and is usually used as a *shooter*—a shot glass of liquor, served straight and swallowed in one gulp—or mixed into a margarita. Be sure you have coarse salt and lime juice on hand to make a classic margarita. Cuervo Gold is an excellent choice of tequila.

Dry vermouth is needed for gibsons and martinis, while sweet vermouth is needed for Manhattans.

Chips and Tips

Many bartenders recommend that if you want to buy only one bottle of alcohol, it should be vodka since it is so versatile.

Shindig Sayings

A **shooter** is usually made in a shot glass. The recipient drinks the liquor in one gulp, sometimes followed by sucking on a wedge of lime or lemon.

The Wine Cellar

It is also a good idea to have several bottles of wine on hand in your liquor cabinet. You should buy a bottle or two of a merlot or a cabernet for red-wine drinkers. Chardonnay and Chablis should satisfy your white-wine drinkers. If you are not sure which to buy or have a limited budget, split the difference and buy a rosé or white zinfandel.

These days, you can usually buy good inexpensive wines at any wine store. Just ask the clerk if you need help choosing a good wine.

Shindig Sayings

Liqueurs are a variety of sweet alcoholic beverages usually made from fruits, nuts, spices, flowers, or essential oils. Although they were traditionally served after dinner to aid digestion, today they are also used in the preparation of a variety of cocktails and cooking recipes.

A bottle or two of champagne or sparkling wine kept chilled for special occasions is always nice to have on hand.

After-Dinner Drinks

Liqueurs are generally served after dinner or with dessert. Made from fruits, nuts, spices, and flowers, liqueurs traditionally have been served to aid in digestion and cleanse the palate after a large meal. While these are nice to have on hand, they are not essential to a basic bar.

Aperitifs are often used synonymously with liqueurs, but are actually different. They are usually sipped before a meal to help whet the appetite. Again, these can be stocked in a more advanced bar.

For the more sophisticated palates, there are a variety of brandies, cognacs, schnapps, ports, and cordials. These, too, can be added to your bar over time.

Nonalcoholic Essentials

Having a wide selection of drink mixers available to your guests will not only help you stretch your liquor further, it also will offer your friends an alternative to alcohol.

In addition to mixes, a well-stocked bar also would have garnishes such as large green olives (without the pimento); orange, lemon, and lime wedges and peels; maraschino cherries; coarse salt; sugar; and pearl onions.

By having all these basics in your bar, you can pretty much guarantee that no one is going to go thirsty at your party.

Taking Stock of Your Liquor Cabinet

No one expects you to have every drink available at his or her favorite cocktail lounge, but there are some basic types that you'll want to buy and then add to your stock over time.

Booze Essentials

You don't have to bust the bank to set up a basic bar. You can buy a bottle at a time until you build up your stock. Ultimately, you should shoot for the basics listed here.

You will always need the following liquors on hand: blended whiskey, bourbon, gin, rye, Scotch, tequila, and vodka.

Since you can't always stock your bar with a collection of wines, unless you happen to be Donald Trump, try this to get yourself started: Rosé or white zinfandel, light white wine like chablis or chardonnay, and a red wine such as a merlot or burgundy.

Beer is one of the most popular party beverages and can be found in hundreds of styles and alcoholic and nonalcoholic varieties.

Every good party host has a collection of mixers, or beverages commonly mixed with liquor. With the mixers mentioned here you will be able to make almost any drink your guests request. They include club soda, colas, fruit juices, ginger ale, milk or cream, tonic water, and coffee.

And, of course, never forget the ice. Running out of ice can be a party breaker, so make sure that when you buy your liquor you stock up on bags of ice.

Chips and Tips

To salt or sugar a glass, rub the rim first with a wedge of citrus fruit (orange juice for sugar, lemon or lime for salt). Pour some coarse salt or sugar into a small saucer. Invert the glass into the dish and twist. The glass's rim will be coated.

Supplementing Your Stock

If you find that you have more money and can afford more expensive liquors, you might want to consider adding liqueurs, brandies, aperitifs, rum, and vermouth to your liquor cabinet. They will expand on the variety of drinks you'll be able to offer your guests. Keep track of your friends' favorite drinks to lead you to buy the best choices.

Chips and Tips

Juices mixed with sparkling water make a great nonalcoholic beverage for any guest who doesn't want to imbibe.

Again, mixers are essential to every party, and the more variety you have the happier your guests will be. As you increase your stock, consider purchasing Bloody Mary mix, daiquiri mix, grenadine, simple syrup, Tabasco sauce, and Worcestershire sauce.

Garnishes are the treats often served with a mixed drink. It is good to have at least some of the following on hand. Put in a stock of celery sticks, lemons, limes, maraschino cherries, unstuffed green olives, pearl onions, oranges, course salt, and granulated sugar.

As your bartending mastery grows, these drink-enhancing garnishes are sure to please and astonish your guests: angostura bitters, cinnamon sticks, cloves, nutmeg, powdered chocolate, paper umbrellas, and whipped cream. Check your drink recipes before your party to lay in a stock of what you'll need.

Winning Ways with Wine

For a cocktail party, it's good to have one or more bottles of a red, white, and rosé or white zinfandel wine on hand. For a dinner party, choose the wine that best goes with your meal and buy a sufficient quantity to pour two glasses per guest in the first hour, one glass per guest for each subsequent hour.

Red wine is generally served with heavy dishes such as beef or pasta. White wines help accent fish, pork, poultry, and salads. Rosé and white zinfandels are gaining in popularity as all-purpose wines but should not be used if there are wine connoisseurs present.

For those occasions in life that call for corks to pop, keep a bottle of champagne or a sparkling wine in your refrigerator at all times. You can't always predict those celebratory moments.

Beer Barrel Polka

While it's always nice to stock the favorite beer brand of your guests, a party is a good time to experiment with new flavors and brands. Purchase a six-pack or two of an imported beer or a local microbrew. If it is a sports-related event or for a big gang, you will probably want to tap a small keg and keep the beer free-flowing.

For the beer baron, you might want to consider stocking different varieties of beer. There are ales, stouts, lagers, pilsners, and more. The list is endless. Be sure to stock nonalcoholic varieties as well.

Party Pitfall

Beer should be poured and served in glasses. The bottle or can should never leave the bar area. There is nothing more likely to ruin photographs at a formal event than pictures of your guests holding bottles or cans of beer.

Tool Time

Just as a chef needs the right tools to cook, a bartender needs the right equipment to be a good mix master.

A corkscrew is essential for opening wine bottles. If you are not used to working with one, you would be wise to buy a wing corkscrew. They are easy to operate and make extracting the cork simpler for beginning wine stewards.

If you want to make the perfect martini, you will need a shaker. It's a container, usually made of stainless steel or glass, that looks like an oversized tumbler. A shaker often comes with a stirrer and a strainer. The strainer is essential for keeping ice cubes or fruit slices from falling into the serving glass.

To measure the right amount of alcohol in drink recipes, you will need a jigger. In a pinch, you also can use a shot glass.

Don't be fooled by your bar guide. When a recipe calls for a teaspoon, it is not referring to the spoon you use to stir your tea. Head to your nearest kitchen gadget store to pick up a real set of measuring spoons.

A "church key" can and bottle opener are still useful items, even with today's flip-top cans and screw-cap bottles. Many microbrews or imports don't use screw caps and you'll have to rely on old-fashioned bottle openers.

Swizzle sticks or straws (short and tall) are good to put into mixed drinks for stirring and sipping.

A pitcher with a long-handled spoon to mix and serve drinks is good to have for iced tea, lemonade, or a large batch of a frozen drink.

A wine bucket is nice to have to properly chill the champagne, but a good-looking ice bucket and tongs are essential.

Every good mixologist has several bar towels by his side for cleanups and wiping water spots off glasses.

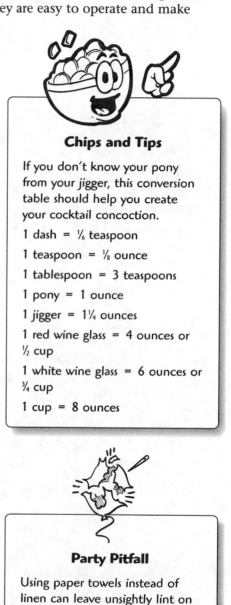

Chips and Tips

If you don't know your pony from your jigger, this conversion table should help you create your cocktail concoction.

1 dash = $\frac{1}{6}$ teaspoon

1 teaspoon = $\frac{1}{8}$ ounce

1 tablespoon = 3 teaspoons

1 pony = 1 ounce

1 jigger = $1\frac{1}{4}$ ounces

1 red wine glass = 4 ounces or $\frac{1}{2}$ cup

1 white wine glass = 6 ounces or $\frac{3}{4}$ cup

1 cup = 8 ounces

Party Pitfall

Using paper towels instead of linen can leave unsightly lint on your glasses or bar.

Toothpicks are helpful for skewering the cocktail garnish.

A small, sharp paring knife is necessary to cut garnishes and fruit peels.

Bar knife

Bottle opener

Ice tongs

Jigger

Ice bucket

Measuring spoons

Muddler

Pitcher

Shaker

Stirrer

Strainer

Winged corkscrew

Bar tools essential for every mixologist.

Make certain you have a supply of cocktail napkins on hand to give out with each drink. In addition to keeping the condensation from making the glasses slippery, it also will help to keep water marks off your furniture. Coasters are essential for fine wood surfaces.

Ice Is Nice

Red wine and straight-up drinks are about the only beverages served at room temperature at a cocktail party. Everything else you serve should be chilled.

Beer glasses should be kept chilled to avoid excess foam when the beer is poured. If you don't have room for the glasses in the freezer, swish ice cubes around the inside of the glass and dump the cubes out before pouring the beer. Make sure, however, that you have some glasses that are not chilled for those who feel it takes away from the taste of the beer.

On average, guests go through 2½ pounds of ice per person during a standard four-hour party, and more so in hot weather. Remember, you can never have too much ice. If you can't make enough, buy it. Keep it in coolers and use it to replenish your ice buckets. The bags of ice are not meant to be seen by your guests. Be discreet when you restock. For sanitary purposes, ice should be picked up with tongs, not your fingers.

Remember that you'll need more ice for frozen drinks.

Class with Glass

We know you loved collecting them, but when you're hosting a cocktail party, you probably should serve your guests' drinks in something other than your Flintstone jelly glasses or the matching Sesame Street cups from McDonald's. Relax, you can still use them at a theme party.

Besides your theme glasses, there are a few essential glasses you should have, or at least know about, when throwing a party.

Chips and Tips

When a twist of lemon peel is called for in a drink recipe, with a sharp knife, cut a strip of lemon peel from the fruit and rub around the rim of the glass. Twist the peel over the drink to release the skin's oil and drop the oil and peel into the drink.

Party Pitfall

Standard-sized ice cubes can damage blender motors and dull or break blades, so make sure to use an ice crusher before dropping ice into the blender when mixing your frozen drink.

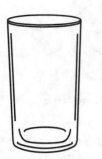
Highball glass

On-the-Rocks glass

Red Wine glass

Shot glass

Beer mug

Pilsner Beer glass

Brandy snifter

Champagne flute

Cordial glass

Irish Coffee mug

Martini glass

Sour glass

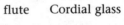
White Wine glass

Basic bar glassware.

A highball glass is a good, versatile glass. It will hold between 8 and 12 ounces of fluid. It can be used for a Tom Collins, iced tea, Bloody Mary, or a similar tall drink.

An old-fashioned or on-the-rocks glass is short and fat and will hold approximately 6–8 ounces. As its name implies, you can serve an old-fashioned or shots of liquor poured on the rocks. In daily use, it serves as a generous juice glass.

If you can only afford to buy just one type of wine glass, go with a larger stemmed red wine glass. The bowl shape will hold 8–10 ounces. This will also work well as a water glass. When your budget allows, purchase smaller matching white wine glasses that will hold 6–8 ounces.

In a pinch, you can use a wine glass to serve champagne. However, to help trap the champagne's bubbles and retain its sparkling flavor, you should invest in 6-ounce flute glasses.

To help make mixed drinks, find a 2-ounce shot glass. It's preferable to find one that's already marked for a 1-ounce shot.

As your bartending skills grow, there are some other glass styles you might want to add to your collection.

For the ultimate in savoir-faire, wrap your hands around a 12- to 20-ounce snifter and let the warmth of your hands heat your favorite after-dinner brandy.

Nothing looks quite the same as a classic 8-ounce martini glass. Here's lookin' at you, kid.

And for the ladies who lunch or for the trendy folks who prefer flavored vodka, there's the chic style of a 2-ounce cordial glass.

Another staple of sophisticated society is the 5- to 7-ounce sherry glass used to serve aperitifs or liqueurs.

Want to add some kick to your coffee? Pour your best brew into an 8- to 10-ounce Irish coffee mug along with a shot of Irish whiskey. Top with whipped cream and you'll have a drink that ballads have been written about. These mugs also can be used for layered drinks.

Chips and Tips

Always handle a glass by its stem when preparing a drink. You don't want your fingerprints to dirty the glass or the heat of your hand to warm the chilled surface.

Chips and Tips

To avoid wasting beverages, and glasses, personalize plastic beverage glasses with guests' names. If you prefer glass, buy labels to put on the glasses and then add your guest's name with waterproof ink.

Festive Facts

Greta Garbo, the legendary film actress, spoke her first American film words in the 1930 MGM version of *Anna Christie*. "Give me a whiskey, ginger ale on the side—and don't be stingy, baby." Dubbed the "Swedish Sphinx," she retired from films in 1941 and remained almost a recluse until her death in 1990.

Be Responsible

Finally, remember that if you're the one pouring the drinks or hosting the party, you are responsible for your guests. Even if you were not legally at risk, you are morally accountable to stop friends from driving while intoxicated or even marginally under the influence.

Set up a designated driver, take their car keys away from them, call a cab, or put them up for the night. The bottom line is, don't let friends drive drunk. If you do, you're not a good friend.

The Least You Need to Know

➤ Buy the best brand of liquor you can afford.

➤ You can stock a basic bar and build on it over time.

➤ Invest in the right mixing equipment.

➤ When you're starting out, buy glasses that can be used for a variety of beverages.

➤ Be responsible—don't let your guests drink and drive.

Chapter 10

Setting Up
Your Space

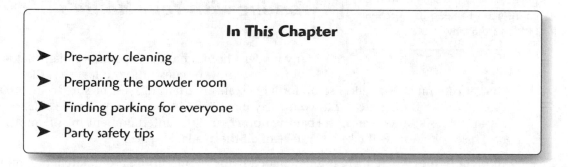

In This Chapter

➤ Pre-party cleaning

➤ Preparing the powder room

➤ Finding parking for everyone

➤ Party safety tips

The home you so carefully decorated and made into a snug sanctuary might not be a haven to the hoards of guests you've invited to your party. You undoubtedly designed it to suit your own day-to-day life—but that isn't necessarily conducive to company.

In fact, throwing a party at home might mean that you need to spend some time rear-ranging furniture, removing pictures, and even putting things in storage. In this chap-ter, you'll learn about just some of the things you can do to make your home into more of a party space.

The Party Is Here

Once you've decided on the type of party and the amount of guests, look around your home and decide where you want the group to gather.

If you've informally entertained before, where did your company congregate? Often during casual events, people tend to naturally assemble in one area of your home

more than others. If that's the case, will this room be suitable for a planned celebration? What is it about that room that makes it attractive for guests to gather? Can you duplicate that feeling in another room if you need to hold the party there?

Don't look at a room and assume it has only one purpose. While dining rooms might seem the most logical setting for a dinner party, a kitchen, den, or living room might work if they can accommodate more guests. In fact, many hosts say that whenever people are invited to their home, no matter where the party is planned to take place, everyone ends up in the kitchen.

Working with Your House's Layout

Many modern homes have an open floor plan that allows for a free flow of guests. If your layout is like that, it often makes an ideal setup for large-scale entertaining. Just be sure to incorporate all the adjoining areas into your party plan. For instance, you might be able to set up the food in one area, the bar in another, and the entertainment in still another. This way guests will take advantage of all the available space.

In older homes where there is a designated living room, dining room, kitchen, family room, basement, or den, choose the space that will best accommodate the number of guests and the activities planned, and has easy access.

Don't rule out any room or space for a party without careful consideration, even if the area doesn't initially seem primed to hold party-goers.

Additional Party Spaces

For some folks, the garage or unfinished basement is a great place to gather—especially when crafts or kids are involved. It's often an area that can take friends dropping food or paint being splattered. Just remove the car, do some quick cleanups, add some decorations, and these areas become Party Central.

Will the weather conditions cooperate? Then don't forget the great outdoors. Backyards, patios, terraces, and decks can be the site of a variety of celebrations, not just barbecues.

Once you've settled on a space, evaluate if you can make it more user-friendly.

Sit on It

Is your living room or den set up with the chairs facing the television set as the focal point? Unless part of the entertainment involves sitting and watching a program or video, change your seating. Arrange your chairs together in conversation groupings so guests can talk easily, even if it puts their backs to the television.

However, don't put the furniture so close together that people can't easily walk around. Most folks only need about 18 inches to comfortably move between pieces of furniture. Also, make sure that a table or flat surface is within easy reach of a seated guest for placing a cup or plate.

Unless it's a small group or sit-down dinner party, or you want your guests to stay fixed in their chairs like potted plants, provide seating for no more than one quarter to one half of your guests, depending on the age group.

If people seem glued to their seats when you want them to mingle, the amount of seating might not be the problem. It's possible that it's the wrong type of seating. Big, cushy couches aren't necessarily convenient when you need to get up and down at a cocktail party. You might do better to put in three dining room chairs and take out a loveseat. That not only gives you an extra seat, it also makes the arrangement more portable.

Party Pitfall

Don't plan to hold your event outdoors unless you know for certain the weather will be pleasant or you have arranged for a tent or other shelter should the conditions turn from fair to foul.

Party Pitfall

If your party list is filled with the elderly or infirm, do reserve adequate seating for all your guests.

It Looks Better Over There

If there is too much furniture in the room you plan to have your party in, move some of the pieces out. You might be able to use them in another area or store them elsewhere like a bedroom, basement or garage. You also might consider moving the pieces outside in good weather or taking them over to the house of a neighbor or friend.

When you have a lot of furniture to remove and not enough places to store it, consider renting a moving truck for the day to hold some of your belongings.

Too Massive to Move

You will find you have pieces of furniture that are simply too big to budge. If that's the case and it just looks out of place with your party decor, there are a few things you can do.

One way is through camouflage—covering a hutch with fish nets for a nautical party, for instance.

Chips and Tips

If you need to hire laborers to help with moving furniture, call a local college job board or look in your Yellow Pages under "Employment, Temporary." There are a number of agencies that specialize in manual laborers that can be hired for four hours or more.

You can also turn the seating away from those specific home furnishings. Move guests' focus to another object or objects.

Hiding the Heirlooms

If you have a favorite vase or a priceless painting put those precious pieces away for safekeeping. Of course you can show them off, but do it in either smaller groups or set up barriers around the piece.

Cleaning and Clutter

If your home could be described as having a lived-in look, you might want to do some basic housekeeping before your party.

Cleaning Away Clutter

It's difficult to clean around a stack of magazines, a pile of shoes, a week's worth of mail, arts and crafts projects, and general jumble. For the best results, before a cleaning product touches your hand, you must first clear the clutter.

Use Suitable Supplies

Chips and Tips

If you can, plan your parties to take place shortly after you've done your major spring or fall cleaning. This way your home looks its best, and your party preparations will involve little more than dusting, vacuuming, and washing the floors.

Once the clutter has been dealt with, it's time to start cleaning. To save time, purchase or make a cleaning belt similar to one a carpenter uses to keep nails, screws, and tools. A pair of cargo pants with multiple pockets also will work, as will a bucket or tray with a handle that is filled with cleaning equipment. Try to limit your cleaning products to a few choices. Use multipurpose products for greater speed and efficiency.

Clean Smarter, Not Harder

When you begin to clean, use the clock system. When you enter a room, clean it as if you were going around a clock and you have started at 12 o'clock. Move from there to 1, then 2, and so on, until you've worked your way around the clock and are back at 12. Don't backtrack. Dirt follows gravity and floats down, so dust the ceiling fans and light fixtures before you vacuum the floors.

Get all suitable members of the household involved in the cleaning. If they worked hard to make it spotless, they're less likely to want to see it get dirty again.

Remember, you're going for the "illusion" of clean. It's a party, not a military inspection of your barracks.

Off Limits

As much as you'd like to have guests feel complete-ly comfortable in your home, chances are there will be some areas that you will like to keep off limits. You have every right to keep guests out of certain areas, and there are a couple of things you can do short of posting a guard.

The simplest way to suggest that a room is off-limits is to close the room's door. That will gen-erally keep most mature guests at bay.

However, if you're having a party with lots of chil-dren in attendance and you truly want to keep the kids out of certain rooms, you might want to replace your doorknobs with ones that have simple locks or install a simple hook-and-eye lock near the top of the door out of a child's reach.

Preparing the Powder Room

The one room in the house you will want to make sure is spotless is your powder room. Provide a box of tissues on the counter and store an extra roll of toilet tissue under the sink or in a special reserve container.

Surveys say that most guests will snoop in a friend's medicine cabinet. Remove all medicines that could potentially cause problems if taken incorrectly and move them to a locked area.

If there are not going to be small children at your event, you might want to put to-gether a toiletries basket for your powder room with likely items your guests will need.

Chips and Tips

Black-and-white newspapers make excellent, lint-free cleaning cloths for windows and mirrors.

Party Pitfall

A computer can be very tempt-ing to nosy guests. To keep them off, install a password or a key lock so no one can turn on your computer without your permis-sion. It also might be advisable to simply unplug it and cover it with plastic.

Festive Facts

Even when you are not entertaining, a bathroom's medicine chest is not the ideal storage area for drugs. The warm, moist atmosphere can break down or change the chemical composition of some prescriptions. All drugs—prescription or over the counter—should routinely be kept in a cool, dry place.

Chips and Tips

Place an attractive can of air freshener within sight so that guests can use it at their own discretion.

Chips and Tips

Place a "Do Not Touch" sign over the thermostat to ward off a well-meaning guest who wants to change the room's climate.

The Comforts of Home

With a little effort, your guests can enjoy all the comforts of their home—in your home.

When the weather is raining or cold and guests will be wearing outer garments, try to arrange for closet space or another area where these coats and jackets can be hung. While many people routinely place coats on a bed, it makes it very inconvenient if your coat is on the bottom of the pile and you want to leave early. A sturdy clothesline, hung in your garage or spare room, will serve as a rack for coats on heavy-duty hangers.

In addition to providing coat racks, you should also be aware of temperature. Your guests' comfort might depend on your heat and air-conditioning system. Adjust your thermostat accordingly.

The Thoughtful Host

If you know that a friend has difficulty walking, place his or her chair at the end of a table and near the exit (and bathroom) to make moving about easier. Also, reserve a parking spot close to your house or in your driveway.

Speak with guests who may need special attention in advance to see if there are small changes you can easily accomplish in your home to make him or her feel as welcome and comfortable as any other guest.

Besides taking your guests into consideration, it is also important to consider how a party might affect those who live near you. If your neighbors live close by and it's possible your party will inconvenience them in some way, alert them to your plans. Better still, if it's a large party, invite them. Even if they choose not to attend, they are less likely to complain or feel put out if they know you have been considerate.

Park It There

Often one of the major challenges in home entertaining is providing enough parking spaces. If this will be a problem at your party, try these solutions:

➤ Move your own car out of your driveway or parking slot and tell a guest or two they can have your spot.

➤ Check with neighbors to see about using their parking spots or driveways.

➤ Suggest that friends park in a nearby parking lot and arrange for at least two cars to shuttle your guests back and forth.

When parking is truly inconvenient or extremely limited, you might consider hiring a valet service. This is especially true if your guests are older, would have difficulty walking a great distance, or during bad weather.

Better Safe Than Sorry

The majority of accidents happen around the home. Try to ensure they don't happen at your home during your party. Even if you don't have children of your own, you should try to make your space as safe as possible for your young guests. Use common sense and don't expect that parents will be responsible for their child's actions. In the excitement of a party, too often parents become distracted.

Take a walk through your home at the same time of day that your party will take place and check for safety points like proper lighting, steps in good repair, floor coverings are fastened, and doorways clear of "traffic-jam" items. Also be sure all pets are secure or boarded elsewhere to prevent mishaps. This little exercise can save you a lot of concern and will prevent any party problems.

Keep in mind that if you have something in your home that will make you say "Watch out" or "Don't touch" whenever anyone goes near it, it is best to remove it or secure it before your guests arrive.

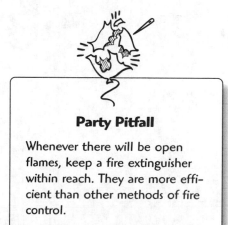

Party Pitfall

Whenever there will be open flames, keep a fire extinguisher within reach. They are more efficient than other methods of fire control.

The Least You Need to Know

➤ Rearrange, move, or camouflage your furniture as needed to make your home party perfect.

➤ Clear out the clutter before you clean up.

➤ Prep a pretty powder room.

➤ Notify the neighbors of your party.

➤ Make parking plans to accommodate all guests.

Chapter 11

Ambience: Beyond Balloons and Crepe Paper

In This Chapter

➤ Using your senses to create a party atmosphere

➤ Finding the perfect music for your theme

➤ Creating party ambience

➤ Making your buffet table a sensory success

Ambience is that indefinable something—the mood or feeling you get when you walk into a room. It's what makes you feel excited, scared, happy, relaxed, nervous, nostalgic, or sad without even necessarily knowing why.

In this chapter, you'll learn how to produce the right ambience by utilizing four of your five senses: sound, smell, touch, and sight. It is in weaving these elements so skillfully together that you are not totally aware of them separately that you create ambience. They just come together to create an atmosphere that affects you on an almost subconscious level. It's knowing how to utilize sound, songs, fabrics, flowers, props, and lighting.

Now Hear This

How often have you heard a song or a sound and been reminded of a different time and place? Sound is a very strong stimulus. Close your eyes and think about the beach. In addition to the water, sun, and sand, you're probably also thinking about the calls of gulls flying overhead, music playing from a radio, children laughing, and waves crashing onto the shore. Sound goes a long way to creating ambience.

At your party, sounds could be anything from piano music to creaking doors and crying ghouls as part of a haunted house theme. Specially created sound-effect tapes and CDs, along with music, are effective ways to add an aural dimension to all your parties.

Keep in mind when planning your party that it is important to select sounds and music that are appropriate to the event or location. For instance, it's unlikely a Sweet 16 party would feature the music of Mozart. On the other hand, rock and roll wouldn't be fitting for a high tea. Music, like other sounds, should be appropriate to the site, the occasion, and the crowd.

Choose the right sounds at a theme party and you have created another dimension that will make your parties stand out from any party your guests have ever been to.

Party Pitfall

Be sure to give your DJ a clear picture of your guests, theme, and occasion. You'd hate for a disc jockey to show up stocked with popular dance and disco music if your guests are all in their late 60s and 70s.

Festive Facts

Draped with trees and vines from floor to ceiling, the Rainforest Cafe, a national chain of jungle-themed restaurants, recreates all the visual elements of a rainforest. However, the designers went a step farther and included the aural atmospheric elements of animatronic animals, waterfalls, squawking parrots and macaws, and the sounds of a thunderstorm. The entire experience of dining is enhanced tremendously by the sounds you hear.

Sweet Smell of Success

Smell is one of the most effective senses to help remind you of a time or place in your past. While it's fun to use fragrances to enhance a party's theme, use scents sparingly and carefully. It is far better to have your guests tempted by the smell of steak sizzling on your grill than it is to have the heady fragrance of the stargazer lily in your centerpiece or scented candles. Strong scents can distort the taste of your dinner.

How Touching

If you think about why you love a favorite outfit, you'll probably realize that part of what you like is how the clothes feel next to your skin, their softness, and maybe their coziness. The elements of touch you select to create ambience for your party should also feel good next to your guests' skin.

Fabrics are a terrific way to stimulate the sense of touch. When decorating, you can use rich patterned tapestry wall hangings, downy-soft seat cushions, satin throws, the rustic texture of burlap tablecloths, the luxurious feel of velvet pillows, or the absorbency of cotton napkins. All of these fabrics can be a great way to capture guests' attention as well as sustaining the party's theme.

If you want to give your home the illusion of being a medieval castle, drape your chairs in tapestry. However, if you want to give guests the feel of being in the home of a peasant in the same time period, remove any soft cushions. Instead, give guests wooden seats or cover your chairs in burlap to make them scratchy.

A Soft Seat

The sense of touch has just as much to do with your guests' comfort level as anything else.

When providing seating for your guests, it is very important to consider what kind of party you are having. At a cocktail or networking party remove cushy couches and put out chairs that are more along the lines of a church pew—in other words, not exactly a place you would plant yourself for the entire evening.

However, if you have arranged for stage entertainment or a floor show, make the seating fairly comfortable.

A Touchy Theme

Just like music, what your guests touch at your party should vary from theme to theme. If the party has a Japanese theme, you expect to sit on pillows on the floor and cool yourself with paper fans. At a garden party, you might find a hammock or porch swing more appropriate.

Chips and Tips

Be sure the scents you surround your guests with don't interfere with the fragrance of your feast. The wrong or too strong fragrance can ruin their appetites.

Party Pitfall

During a lecture event or anything that could be considered slightly dull, make sure the temperature is a little colder than normal and the chairs comfortable, but not overly so. You don't want your guests to be lulled to sleep by a comfy chair and a warm room.

When you choose the items you'll need to convey your theme, consider not only what the materials or props will look like, but what they will feel like. For instance, do you want your guests to feel as if they have stepped into a sensuous Arabian nights fantasy with silk and satin cushions and table coverings? Or are they to feel as if they are experiencing the rustic retreat of the Wild West with wicker baskets, rough-hewn cedar tables, and well-oiled leather chairs?

Luminous Lighting

The bright light you use to cook and clean in your kitchen is probably a little harsher than the light you have in your bedroom and living room. In most other rooms of the house, your lighting is softer because you don't need that same bright intensity as you do when you are chopping vegetables.

To create the best lighting scheme, illuminate from above, below, and from the sides of the room, all at the same time. Use low wattage, soft white, pink, or frosted bulbs. Install dimmers for the greatest range of lighting effects.

There's a saying: "If all the world's a stage, then I want better lighting." Be sure your parties and your guests are seen in their best light.

Candlelight

For an overall flattering effect, you can't beat candle-light or a fireplace. If you want to create an instantly romantic or dramatic effect, eliminate every other light source and fill your room with candles. The flickering glow is an extremely effective way to illuminate a room and create a warm ambience.

Twinkle, Twinkle

The one Christmas tree decoration you should never pack away are the white twinkle lights. These strands of mini-lights are a powerful light resource. It's not that they illuminate so well—it's just that the effect they give is so dramatic.

String them in trees, line a walkway, outline a piece of furniture or a doorway, tuck them into bushes, weave them into a centerpiece, drape them on a curtain rod, wrap around poles, or let them shine through sheer fabric. Place these twinkle lights in almost any area

Chips and Tips

Check out your room at the same time of day as your party is scheduled to be held. Turn lights on and off, change bulb wattage, move lamps, light candles—experiment. Have someone sit in different parts of the room so you can see how the lighting makes your guests look.

Chips and Tips

To help candles stay drip-free, store them in your refrigerator until a half an hour before you use them. When it's time to light them, keep the candles out of any drafts.

you can think of, for almost every occasion. Twinkle lights are a great resource for creating interesting lighting effects.

Illuminating Luminarias

Often at Christmas you will see streets decorated with paper bags filled with glowing tea lights or votive candles. It's an impressive sight when you see them lining walkways, driveways, and the curbs in front of homes.

While you can buy premade luminarias, you can make them yourself for pennies. All you need is small plain paper bags, a hole punch, kitty litter or sand, and tea lights or votives.

In the top half of a paper bag, use a stencil or freeform a design. Cut out the design with a handheld punch. Fill a bag halfway with sand or kitty litter. Nestle a votive candle or tea light in the sand, light, and enjoy.

You Light Up My Life

One of the most interesting lighting effects you can use in your home, whether you are planning a party or not, is to set an *uplight* on the floor, underneath a tree or plant.

As the light shines up through the leaves, it will cast beautiful shadows and designs on your ceiling and upper walls.

Center of Attention

If you're short on money or time, the place to spend your decorating dollars would be on your centerpiece and buffet design. Since your buffet table is one of the focal points at any party, get more flash for your cash by focusing on your centerpiece and creative food containers.

With exciting and theme-related centerpieces, you can often forgo some of the more extravagant decorating ideas.

Chips and Tips

Tuck the strands of twinkle lights in your trees and plants in your home year-round, whether you are preparing for a party or not. They add an unexpected touch of whimsy like fireflies when flashing or elegance when in a nonflashing mode.

Party Pitfall

Don't emboss the pattern all the way through the luminaria bag's length, or the sand or kitty litter will seep out.

Shindig Sayings

Uplights resemble a wide tube or a can with the light bulb inserted at the bottom so that it can shine up.

103

Clothing the Table

Of course, paper and plastic tablecloths and napkins are less expensive than cloth, and they come in a wide variety of colors and patterns, but whenever possible splurge on lavish linens or clever coverings.

You don't need to own a warehouse full of linens to top your tables with style or imagination, nor do you have to break the bank to achieve the look you want. That's one of the advantages to renting. You can choose the size and style that suits your party and purse and you don't even have to press it! If your local store doesn't carry the design you want, have your chosen linens shipped. Panache Party Rentals (www. linenswithpanache.com), for instance, has a huge selection of high-quality rental cloths to choose from that are affordably priced.

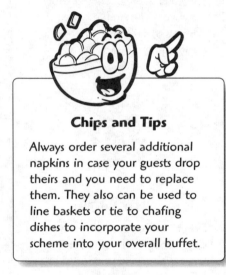

Chips and Tips

Always order several additional napkins in case your guests drop theirs and you need to replace them. They also can be used to line baskets or tie to chafing dishes to incorporate your scheme into your overall buffet.

Party Pitfall

Although you can put a square overlay on a round table, on an oblong table, a round overlay doesn't work as well.

Sometimes a tablecloth isn't your only option for topping the table. Perhaps there is a bedsheet in your linen closet that suits your needs, or you can buy fabric on sale often for less than the cost of a tablecloth.

Get creative! Here are some ideas for materials you can use to cover the table for a variety of themes: drop-cloths, blueprints, beach towels, flags, or baby blankets. This list is limitless. Look around your home for items that will inspire you to build a better buffet.

Unusual Place Mats

Place mats may be perfect when you have an odd-sized table or you want a layered look on top of your linen. On the other hand, runners are regal or rustic, depending upon the design and fabric.

You have a choice of items that can be used as place mats at theme parties. Here are a few ideas to get you started: diapers, kitchen towels, bandannas, or a large silk leaf.

Looking at Layers

Layering cloths is a lovely way to add multiple colors, patterns, and texture to your table. You can drape the top fabric (called an overlay) loosely, put it on the diagonal if it's a square cloth topping a round one, puddle it on the ground, or gather the top cloth and pin to form a scallop design.

On the Level

Have you ever wondered why buffets in magazines and restaurants look so much more artistic than yours? Levels. Most of us take the time to artfully arrange our food on platters, but then ruin the effect by placing the trays flat on the table. Take overturned pots, boxes, paint cans, books, bricks—anything with height—and loosely cover your arrangement with a tablecloth or coordinating fabric. Bunch the material decoratively and display your dishes at different heights for an eye-catching appeal. Or use cake stands, books or other decorative items that will give your buffet height.

Sensational Centerpieces

Centerpieces are the center of attention on your buffet or dining table. While flowers are the most common centerpiece material, they are not the only choice. Bring out your collectibles, trophies, book collection, toys, hats, candle assortments, fruits, vegetables or even a goldfish bowl. Almost anything, attractively grouped together, will make an inventive centerpiece.

Anything that makes you think of your theme will probably work as the perfect centerpiece. Take a moment to look around your house and see what catches your eye.

Clever Containers

Bowls, while generally used as food containers, are not your only serving choice. Depending on your event, there are a variety of selections that will keep your theme and the party's ambience alive. Some are more suitable for dry food, while others would work for a wet or dry dish. Keep in mind you often can nestle a bowl into a variety of these vessels to camouflage them and make them more suitable for display. Here are some items to spark your own brainstorms. Try hollowed-out fruits or vegetables, hats, baskets, coffee or tea pots, or flower pots for starters. What do you have that would work?

Whether purchased at Tiffany's or the thrift store, the components of your party atmosphere or ambience are a statement of your personality, creativity, and flair for fun. Take the time to explore your surroundings and delve into the depths of treasured or stored possessions.

Chips and Tips

You can group your collection together to make the centerpiece, or you can intersperse it with other items. For instance, you might sprinkle coins from your collection around like confetti on the banquet table that has a piggy bank for a centerpiece.

Chips and Tips

A child's wading pool is a great place to store iced drinks for a beach-themed party.

The Least You Need to Know

➤ Use your senses to create an ambience.

➤ Match the music and other sounds to the party and guests.

➤ Choose textures which will allow guests to get a feel for the effect you are trying to achieve.

➤ Twinkle lights make a great lighting effect for almost all situations.

➤ If you're short on money or time, invest in your table decor.

Part 3

The Hostess with the Mostess ...

To throw a really fantastic party you need to do more than just drop a six-pack of beer and a pizza on the table. You need ambience, the right guests, and that certain something that every good host has—that flare for keeping guests happy and things running smoothly.

Everyone dreams of hosting a party where all the guests get along, all the food tastes great, and everything is perfect. Unfortunately, that is rarely the case. Lucky for you, you have this book and us. We've put together this part for the hostess who wants to be the mostess. You'll learn how to greet guests in style, make them comfortable, and make sure that you have all the right food and drinks to keep the party a party.

Chapter 12

The Hospitable Host

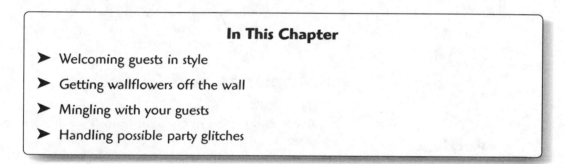

In This Chapter

➤ Welcoming guests in style

➤ Getting wallflowers off the wall

➤ Mingling with your guests

➤ Handling possible party glitches

The most important—we repeat, *most important*—thing for every host to consider is the comfort and enjoyment of their guests. Nothing short of the red-carpet treatment is acceptable. Each step of the way, in every aspect of the plan, the conscientious host puts herself in the shoes of the guest. In fact, one of your final planning steps is to walk from driveway to doorstep then through the whole event to departure. You will then experience, step by step, the flow of the party through your guests' eyes.

In this chapter, you'll learn how to become the host with the most and give your guests the party of their dreams. From the minute they walk through your door, you're going to want your guests to feel like royalty, and by following these simple tips you'll be able to do just that.

Roll Out the Red Carpet

One of the first steps to creating the ultimate comfort is to send a very clear and concise invitation. Ideally, it will provide every bit of information necessary for your guest to prepare for and attend the event, without a moment's stress or confusion.

In Chapter 8, "The Honour of Your Company …," you found detailed instructions for creating the perfect party invitation. Those instructions are dedicated to ruling out confusion for guests before arriving. This next section will take you through what a good host should do once guests arrive.

With this, the red carpet leading to your party has rolled out to your guest and he has planted his foot firmly upon it.

Continue the red-carpet treatment by leading your guests to your front door with markers such as balloons, signs, ribbons, or reflective tape. These helpful and welcoming symbols shout out, "We can't wait for you to get here!" Your thoughtfulness and thoroughness will bring guests to the party in a cheerful mood.

> **Chips and Tips**
>
> Even with a map and directions, guests can become lost while in an apartment complex or hallways. The height of hospitality is to place people at strategic points to direct guests. Dress your "living signs" in costumes to match your theme for added appeal.

One hospitable act leads to another, and with each gesture, your guests feel more and more pampered. They will move along the red carpet to your party portal ready for fun and festivity.

Meetings and Greetings

Have you ever arrived at a party and for the first several minutes stood in discomfort not knowing where to go or what to do? You tried to look confident as you looked around for some clue as to your next move. How special did you feel? Well, your party host made a big boo-boo. When each guest is met cordially and given the impression that the party could not possibly start without him or her, the host has done her job, and very well. Be sure there is always a greeter present for guest arrivals.

> **Party Pitfall**
>
> Bad weather will put even the cheeriest guest in a grumpy mood. Provide valet parking or at least umbrella escorts to offer the ultimate accommodation.

Coats, Hats, and Gifts

It is ideal to have a helper take coats, gifts, or potluck items from each guest or direct them on where to place items.

Something to Drink?

The most appreciated welcome is an offer of food and beverage. For crowds in a small area, trays of food and drink being passed is the easiest and fastest way to get refreshments into the hands (and mouths) of guests. Otherwise, place bowls or trays of snacks in several easy-to-reach places.

Placing Names and Naming Places

One of the best ways to make guests at a sizable party feel at ease is to give them an attractive name tag and remove the "What was your name, again?" anxiety. When using name tags, these basic rules apply:

➤ Prepare the tags ahead if possible.

➤ Never have guests print their own names.

➤ Type or print names in large block letters.

➤ Decorate blank tags with small trinkets to match your theme.

➤ Some fabrics like silk, velvet, and angora are too delicate for glue. Consider using a clip-on or pin-on tag instead.

Grab a Seat

A great way to make a guest comfortable at a dinner party is to assign each guest a "reserved" seat or table to sit at. Wandering through a room and feeling clumsy about finding an available seat is one situation most people can do without.

When you have more than one table, use tent cards and jazz them up with ribbons, stickers, trinkets, or fancy lettering. Budget-wise hosts will let their party favors double as seating assignments. Some other innovative party "placers" are …

➤ shiny red apples for a teacher's luncheon.

➤ boxes of Cracker Jacks™ for a baseball banquet.

➤ neon sunglasses for a beach bash.

Now that you have a place for everyone and everyone in his place, labeled and tabled, you can relax and enjoy your meal, the same as your contented and contained celebrants.

Chips and Tips

At large events without a check-in table, welcome guests with name tags alphabetically posted on the front door. Affix name tags to a decorative poster covered in plastic wrap to make it easier to remove them.

Give a newcomer a bit of time to become acclimated to the party, hang her coat up, set down gifts or food, and freshen up, before plunging into the festive fray.

Chips and Tips

For a mixed crowd of friends, family, and business associates, arrange seating by putting compatible guests together. In contrast, let guests seat themselves when they're familiar with each other.

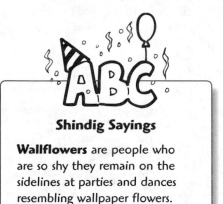

Festive Facts

Name tags should be placed on the right shoulder, so that when shaking hands, it is natural for one's eye to fall on that exact spot, making it easy to casually glance at the guest's name.

Getting the Wallflowers off the Wall

Not every guest at your party will want to plop a lampshade on his head and lead the conga line. Some *wallflowers* won't even want to get into the conga line, so as a gracious host, you must accept that. The ideal party plan includes entertainment and activities that guests can take or leave, as they please.

Shindig Sayings

Wallflowers are people who are so shy they remain on the sidelines at parties and dances resembling wallpaper flowers.

If you want to have any organized activities, keep them short and varied and allow your guests to participate at their own comfort level.

Making introductions and encouraging mingling is high on the host's to-do list. At a large party, it will be necessary to appoint official host's helpers to do party tasks, and leave the hosts free to introduce guests to each other. Make it a special point to know something about your guests so that you might find a common interest and say, "John, Bob is the regional vice president of a software design company. Bob, John is the guy I was telling you about who put together my Web site." Any opening that will make a guest comfortable talking to a stranger is welcomed.

The Most the Host Can Do

There are several do's and don'ts for party hosts. Some might seem obvious, but it is those evident details that often get overlooked. If you take these tips to heart, you will stay at the top of the best-host list:

➤ Act calm even though you may feel harried and hassled.

➤ Have fun yourself! Remember, it's a party.

➤ Set a realistic time for the party to end. You should always leave them wanting more.

➤ Set up a two-sided buffet line, or spread the buffet around so there are no long lines at large parties.

➤ Offer to serve elderly guests.

➤ Keep the thermostat and music at acceptable levels.

➤ Set your menu to consider the tastes and diets of your guests.

➤ Provide shady places at an outdoor event and spray your yard to keep insects at bay.

Sticky Situations

As perfect as the plan may be, there are always times when a host needs to use her fast fix-it skills. Unexpected and uninvited doesn't just pertain to guests, it also describes party situations. Handle these predicaments quickly and with calm, humor, and grace. It will go a long way to diffuse any uncomfortable dilemmas.

Party Pitfall

An enthusiastic hostess planned a birthday dinner for her husband. Unfortunately, she had so many events planned that dinner was delayed for two hours. The elaborate dinner was interspersed with video shows, toasts, songs, and more toasts. The guest of honor then opened 30 gifts. All this time the guests were pretty much expected to remain seated. When finally set free, the guests took with them a memory of not the delicious meal or the beautiful table decor, but the unbearable length of the party.

The Least You Need to Know

➤ The perfect host's first thought is the guests' comfort.

➤ A gracious welcome is a perfect start to any party.

➤ Name tags and place cards give guests confidence.

➤ Getting guests to mingle is easy with some help from the host.

Chapter 13

Smooth Moves

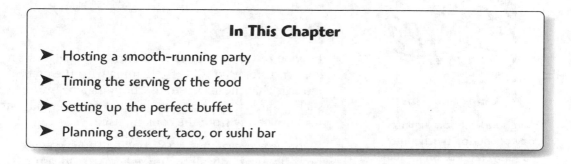

In This Chapter

➤ Hosting a smooth-running party

➤ Timing the serving of the food

➤ Setting up the perfect buffet

➤ Planning a dessert, taco, or sushi bar

The secret to hosting a successful party is to be an "enjoyee" rather than an employee. It is vital for you to organize your party with this goal in mind. If not, you won't be the only one not enjoying yourself. Your guests will have a tough time relaxing when you, the genial host, are dashing around, fussing over details, and not really landing in one place long enough to visit with guests. Having adequate help is not always the solution to this party panic. You need to know the art of smooth moves.

This chapter will help you because it's a collection of tried, true, and new tips to make sure your party runs like a Swiss watch.

Perfect Planning

How smoothly your party moves along depends greatly on how well you prepared before the first guests arrive. If you have been preparing properly, you should have a notebook full of checklists as well as a written schedule. Make sure all the supplies are in place and all your plans are on schedule. Keep your notebook in a convenient spot so you can check it off lists quickly as the evening progresses.

Don't try to be a superhero. You can't do everything yourself. If you live alone, assign a good friend or relative to serve as honorary cohost, or bring in professionals. By spreading out the hosting duties, no one is ever away from the fun for too long.

Party Pitfall

While cohosts are usually wonderful people, be careful not to bog them down too much with duties. They still expect to be guests and have fun.

Chips and Tips

Make sure you post a master copy of your party schedule on the refrigerator or on a cabinet. That way there are no excuses that someone couldn't find his or her list.

In addition to your master list to avoid forgetting something, put together a list of everything that you are serving and the order in which it's being served. Start with the appetizer and move through dessert. Proper preparation will reduce stress so you can have fun too.

Lay out your plan in time order so that you know if and when you need to take something out to thaw 30 minutes before serving. Not only mark the cooking times, but mark down every detail you have to handle along the way.

If you have several people working with you, be sure everyone has a copy of the master schedule and their duties are marked with their initials and their copy is highlighted in a distinct color in case they misplace their list.

Prep Chef

In good restaurants there is not just one chef, but several who are responsible for helping with the preparations. That means washing, chopping, measuring, slicing—any of the preparations that are essential, but take time away from the cooking itself.

If you've ever watched a TV cooking show, you've probably seen how all the ingredients are measured and kept in cups. Then, as needed, the dish or cup is emptied into the other ingredients. This will speed your preparation time. Use disposable bags and plates for your prep work to cut down on dirty dishes.

Keeping It Clean

To keep things in the kitchen running neatly and smoothly, get in the habit of washing and putting away your dishes as you cook. This will keep the disorder down to a minimum. Keep out a dishpan or pot filled with hot soapy water so utensils and plates can soak. This will speed cleanup.

Meals in Minutes

Whatever needs to be done that can be taken care of before the last minute is a time saver. For instance, put salad dressings in a carafe or place butter in a serving dish. Then all that's left is that they be placed on the table.

If possible, store foods in the container they will be cooked or served in so the only last-minute step is to put it on the stove or on the table as it reads on the schedule.

Avoiding Decorating Dilemmas

You should have all your supplies handy. Make sure you have everything assembled and the scissors, hammers, nails, or tape you'll need so you don't waste time looking for a thumbtack. If possible, pre-set your table the day before.

Picking Up

Keeping the kitchen and party area bussed—that is, clean—goes a long way in having your party run smoothly.

Provide a clean trash can in an area that's in sight of the food, but not too close to it. Keep extra bags in the trash can so as you remove one, you can immediately replace it.

Like a restaurant, keep a tray on hand to help you quickly remove dishes to bring to your kitchen.

They're Here and Hungry

Every single aspect of your event has a start, middle, and end, especially food and beverage service. Thirst and Hunger are the most unwelcome party guests. You'll find that people will usually show up at a dinner party famished, so you will want to feed them shortly after they arrive.

Munching Hors d'oeuvres

The first hour of a party, the cocktail and socializing time, is as easy or as complicated as you would like it. Blend elaborate appetizers with some pre-pare-ahead selections. It will result in less stress during the party.

Keep the Drinks Moving

Chips and Tips

Assemble all your serving dishes in an easy-to-access area. Label each piece with a small piece of paper naming the particular food that is going into that dish. Also, place the proper serving fork, knife, and/or spoon in the plate to save any last-minute frantic searches.

Party Pitfall

A trash can that is more than half full becomes an unappetizing eyesore. Empty the trash often.

Whether you have hired a bartender or guests are helping themselves, waiting lines are a moving violation. If you have a large group, set up a satellite bar for soft drinks, beer, and wine, making mixed drinks from the main bar only.

The key to timing the cocktail hour is to watch the clock before guests drink or eat too much. Call them to dinner in a graceful way; you can ring a bell, walk and talk while you shepherd guests to the table, or if you have an entertainer with a microphone, have him make the announcement. While you cannot drag them to the table by the scruff of the neck, a gentle nudge will work.

Plated to Perfection

One of the challenges of serving a big dinner is getting all of the food on the table at the same time and at the perfect temperature. Whatever the temperature your food requires, piping hot soup, chilled and crispy salad, hot main course, or frozen dessert, it needs to be served on time.

Self-Serve Situations

Buffet-style service is a boon to events from kickback casual to elegantly formal. There is a basic (and very flexible) set of rules for setting up a socially correct and smoothly operating buffet table.

Chips and Tips

Provide light snacks for guests to enjoy while they wait for their table to be called. A tray with raw vegetables or a basket of bread will work nicely.

Party Pitfall

To avoid running out of popular food items before all guests have passed through the buffet line, have a server mete them out. When everyone has been served once, guests are welcome to visit the buffet for seconds. Or you can serve seconds yourself so no one is embarrassed about looking like they're eating too much.

A basic buffet arrangement should begin at one end of the table picking up plates, then the main dish, vegetables, salads, breads, condiments, and finally flatware and napkins. For greater ease, wrap napkins around flatware.

If seating is available to all guests, then utensils, beverage containers, and napkins are set on the dining table at each place.

For 50 or more guests, your buffet should be available from two sides with identical access to food from either side. Or use a "traffic cop" approach to direct guests to start at both ends and work toward the middle. Set up identical service on both halves.

To accommodate a large number of guests, seat them and call them in turn by table numbers. Try to make sure the waiting line is only slightly longer than the buffet table itself.

Instead of one long table, separate two round tables to be used—one for salads, relishes, and breads, and the second for entrées and vegetables. This encourages guests to make one trip for salads and another for the main course.

If your guests will not be sitting at a table, serve only bite-sized finger/fork/toothpick foods. There should be no need for a knife in these situations.

Grazing

Another trendy form of serving buffet-style is called grazing, since it sends guests roaming from table to table, helping themselves to a variety of foods.

The grazing system requires guests to queue up in several mini lines. This is on-the-move mealtime at its optimum.

A fix-it-yourself grazing station usually features just one meal course such as beverages, salads, bread, sandwiches, soups, entrées, or desserts.

Festive Facts

In 1924 Caesar Cardini invented the Caesar salad at his restaurant in Tijuana, Mexico. He was deluged by a large crowd of Americans on July 4 and it caused him to run out of ingredients. Not one to give up, he hauled what he had out to the dining room and improvised the salad. Cardini's is the label he established in 1948 for the bottled version of his dressing.

Not Just a Salad Bar ...

One of the best innovations that developed from the buffet table was the salad bar. The idea of being able to heap a bed of lettuce, different salad fixings, and your favorite salad dressing onto your plate took the country by storm. There's no limit to what you can put on your salad bar.

There are a variety of theme food bars that will please your guests. These include breakfast bars, appetizer bars, potato bars, *crépe* bars, pasta bars, taco bars, sushi bars, and dessert bars. Almost anything can be put on a grazing bar.

Food bars are a solution to the dilemma of too little space, time, and help. What kind of bar do you want to build?

Here a Snack, There a Snack

When your space is small and your guests are many, make it simple for them to get food without having to fight their way to the buffet table. Place snack foods within convenient reach and you will be giving your guests a gracious gift ... food on demand.

Shindig Sayings

Crépe is the French word for "pancake." Not to be confused with the thick buttermilk variety Americans eat, these are super-thin and with a variety of fillings that make them suitable for appetizer, entrée, or dessert.

Place containers of snacks everywhere. With bites and bits just an arm's length away, your guests will be fed throughout the party.

Another way to make food accessible is by passing food on trays. Tidbits on toothpicks and other bite-sized selections work best for this process. Be sure to hand out napkins with each serving. This tactic will reduce the steady stream to the buffet table and the jams it creates, and can be delegated to a helper or volunteer cohost.

Party Pitfall

Avoid getting ambushed by hungry hordes when passing around appetizers. If you find yourself being "attacked" by a throng of people and you can't venture further into the room, place a clean napkin across one tray and take two trays out at once. While one tray is being devoured, the other tray can be passed to the other side of the room.

Throwing a party without a hitch from start to finish is an art form. The list of steps to follow is long and, for some, intimidating. No worry, though, because with the aid of your notebook planner, determination, and thoroughness, you will glide through your event gracefully and graciously—all thanks to your smooth moves.

The Least You Need to Know

➤ Have someone act as cohost to alleviate any party problems.

➤ Clean as you cook to save time.

➤ Buffet serving solves space, time, and flow problems.

➤ Specialty food bars score well with guests.

➤ Set containers of snack foods all over the party place.

Part 4
Classic Occasions

There are a number of reasons why you might decide to throw a party. You might be looking to impress your new neighbors, the boss, or even your future in-laws. Whatever it might be, we've put together a part that will make it easy and painless for you.

There are just some classic occasions in life that every person must face, whether it's a cocktail party, a black-tie dinner, or a business dinner; you'll learn how to entertain these crowds with the greatest of ease. Not only will you impress them, but you'll impress yourself with what a fantastic host you really are.

Chapter 14

The Cocktail Hour

> ### In This Chapter
>
> ➤ Serving food at your cocktail party
>
> ➤ Choosing wine for a wine-and-cheese party
>
> ➤ Planning a cocktail party for a large group
>
> ➤ Hiring a wine expert to help host your party

One of the most popular parties is the cocktail party. It usually starts between 4 and 7 P.M. and is relatively short—usually an hour or two—with a somewhat limited food selection. If you have never been to a cocktail party, think of it as happy hour at your favorite pub: a little food, a couple of drinks, a few laughs, and then back to your life.

It also can be a party that's held before another event. For instance, if you and friends are going out to dinner and a movie, you might get together for a couple of drinks first. It also might be the wrap-up after a get-together that's been too much fun to put an immediate end to. Whatever the reason, cocktail parties should be short and sweet.

If you are new to giving parties, hosting a cocktail event is a great way to put your big toe into the waters. And with the tips found in this chapter, you'll soon be a cocktail expert.

Party Pitfall

You will undoubtedly use more liquor and supplies if you make it a self-service bar. You may want to offset that by serving as bartender yourself or bringing in a professional.

Shindig Sayings

In years past, a **sommelier** was the steward or servant in charge of wines on large estates. These people were responsible for stocking, storing, and selecting wines for their employers.

Chips and Tips

Be prepared to have a clean glass for each guest for each wine. Paper or plastic are not good options as they affect the taste of the wine.

Belly Up to the Bar

Obviously, at a cocktail party you will want to serve drinks. It's not necessary that they be alcoholic, but those are the more traditional kind available to guests.

If you don't have an actual bar, you'll need to set up an area to serve as one. You will need two tables. The back bar is basically a work station. The front table is where the glass is placed for the guest to be served.

The best place to set up, if possible, is in the kitchen. It's easier to access ice, chilled glasses, and running water to wash glasses, pitchers, and shakers.

Best Cellars

Wine-and-cheese parties are probably the best known and most popular forms of cocktail parties.

If you're not familiar with wines, you can get a book on the subject, do some on-line research (www. epicurious.com is a great site), or check with the *sommelier* either at a liquor store that specializes in wine or your favorite fine restaurant. Be sure to let him know the price range of the wine you are interested in.

There are a lot of options in hosting a wine party. You can select a certain vineyard or producer (Perrier-Jouét, Berringer, Swanson Winery), type (Chablis, merlot, chardonnay), vintage (year), region (Bordeaux, Tuscany, Napa Valley), or a certain country. Some countries, like Australia, for one, are gaining a lot of popularity for its wines. Of course, France, Italy, Germany, and the United States are the most common.

You also will want to have a variety of cheeses to serve your guests. Remember, however, that you want the cheese to enhance, not detract from, the wine. Therefore, if you have chosen a variety of light wines, choose a light cheese.

The cheese is served with breads and crackers. Fruit—apples, pears, strawberries, peaches, and grapes are also delicious choices.

When planning your party, you will want at least four to six different wines and three to six different cheeses to accompany the wine.

Martini Madness

Another party that's taken on renewed popularity is a martini event. You will need to have a variety of vodkas (and possibly gins) to make a selection of these potent potables.

Proper glasses are a must for the martini mavens. Unless you are very up on what's popular, you might want to hire a bartender from a nearby martini bar or buy a book of martini recipes.

Festive Facts

W. C. Fields' propensity for drinking is legendary. Near the end of his life, he had severe liver trouble and bright red discoloration on his face due to excessive drinking. The studio makeup artists always had to apply heavy coats of cosmetics to hide his symptoms. Despite all that, the alcoholic funnyman was often seen drinking as much as 2 quarts of martinis a day.

Champagne and Caviar

For a truly special event, trot out the bubbly to wash down your caviar. Champagne is still the symbol of the ultimate celebration. So when it's time to wish the bridal couple well, celebrate an anniversary, praise a promotion, or just toast a milestone birthday, champagne is still the drink of choice.

Chips and Tips

When you are celebrating special occasions with champagne toasts, be sure to stock sparkling cider or other nonalcoholic bubbling beverages for those guests who prefer them.

In general, if you are going to serve champagne, it's best to go with a quality brand. Quality is easily discerned in champagne, even for someone who is not very experienced.

If you are serving champagne, the quality of your food should be appropriate to the occasion. That means that you wouldn't want to spend a fortune on a bottle of wine to wash down a hamburger— unless that's your guest of honor's favorite food.

Try jazzing up your party with a little caviar. Caviar is traditionally served ice cold and on plain toast points. However, you might want to have these toppings available: finely chopped hard-boiled egg, minced onions, and sour cream.

Cutting the Cheese

Since you are not trying to feed people a meal at a cocktail party, the food served might be a variety of cheeses with crackers or a more elaborate spread of substantial appetizers. Remember, you always should serve food to help offset the liquor's effects.

Chips and Tips

For a novel way to present bite-size appetizers, stick plastic forks or fancy toothpicks, holding the snack, into a melon half with the flat side down of the fruit on the dish. The picks will give a porcupine look to the melon.

For ease of serving, keep the food to one or two hot choices and one or two cold choices. Be sure these are small, bite-sized selections that require nothing more complicated than a fork to eat, and preferably just your hands or a toothpick.

Depending upon when you're hosting the party, the guidelines for appetizer quantities are as follows:

One-hour cocktail party before dinner:

3–4 light hors d'oeuvres per person

5–6 heavy hors d'oeuvres per person

One- to two-hour cocktail party without dinner:

5–8 light hors d'oeuvres per person

3–6 heavy hors d'oeuvres per person

5–8 combination of hot and cold per person

Great food, exceptional drinks, and pleasurable socializing are the makings of an event that is guaranteed to put you in the Hosts' Hall of Fame.

Beating the Balancing Act

Even though the typical cocktail party atmosphere is one of mixing and mingling, some seating is necessary.

Chips and Tips

Be sure to cover easily damaged surfaces like wood, marble, and glass with felt-back plastic tablecloths. You can cover these with lovely fabric to preserve your decor and party theme.

You can make eating-while-standing more manageable for your guests if you clear off the tops of furniture to make room for guests to park their drinks, or rent bar-height tables. Provide napkins or coasters, to absorb the moisture on glasses.

Since the cocktail party is quite uncomplicated and takes less time to plan than a full-blown party, it can be produced on short notice to acknowledge or celebrate any occasion in a spontaneous way. Just by keeping a bare minimum of party essentials on hand, you can throw together frequent and fast festivities that may rival those that have been planned for weeks.

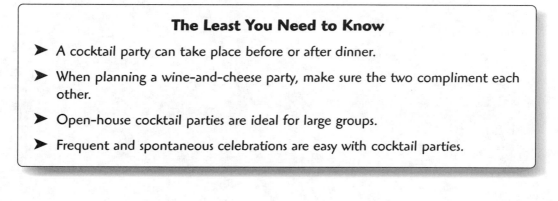

The Least You Need to Know

➤ A cocktail party can take place before or after dinner.

➤ When planning a wine-and-cheese party, make sure the two compliment each other.

➤ Open-house cocktail parties are ideal for large groups.

➤ Frequent and spontaneous celebrations are easy with cocktail parties.

Chapter 15

Black-Tie Affair

In This Chapter

➤ Setting a formal table

➤ Knowing which fork to use and when to use it

➤ Planning a multicourse meal

➤ Serving your guests

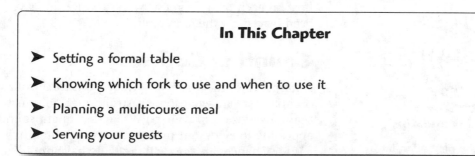

While most parties you play host to will be more along the lines of simple, one- or two-course meals, buffets, chips and dip, or pizza-and-beer gatherings, there will be times when you will need to entertain a little more formally.

Since most of us haven't been to finishing school and don't practice strict dining etiquette in our day-to-day lives, this chapter will teach you (or refresh) some skills you will need to be the perfect host no matter the situation. This way, when it comes time for you to pop the question, impress your boss, or meet your future in-laws, you will have the tools to entertain with confidence and panache.

Turning the Table

If you plan to entertain formally, it's important that you understand that this meal cannot be served on snack trays or on the kitchen counter. Ideally, a formal meal is served in a formal dining room. However, if you don't have a traditional dining set, you still can make accommodations for an elegant event. Dining tables and chairs can easily be rented for under $15.

It's not a good idea to cramp your guests. When you are seated at a dining table for the bulk of the evening, tight seating isn't cozy, it's annoying. Either rethink your guest list, or put together two dining tables.

Limiting the Guest List

Wherever you decide to hold the dinner party, try to invite no more guests than you have seats at one table. However, when a large guest list can't be avoided, you need to set up a second table. Do this only if you can keep the tables close to each other so guests sitting at the second table don't feel as if they have been invited to a different party.

If you are forced to have two separate tables, make certain that each table is decorated comparably. Also, be sure to place one host (if necessary, appoint a cohost) at each table so guests won't think they have been placed at "the kid's table."

Counting Courses

A formal meal may have anywhere from three courses on up. There are even some gastronomical journeys that have dozens of courses. While that might sound appealing to a guest, it probably seems frightening to a host. Chances are you will probably have only five courses to your meal. Trust us, this isn't as bad as it sounds. You will likely start the meal with an appetizer (possibly even served during a cocktail hour), then move on to a fish dish (oysters, clams, mussels, or shrimp cocktail), then a soup and/or salad. Then you will proceed into the entreé, and follow that with dessert.

There is remarkable flexibility in designing the menu for your formal dinner. However, take into consideration your guests' tastes and ease of preparation. Don't prepare a menu that will keep you in the kitchen longer than you will be in the dining room.

Creating the Cuisine

What you choose to serve is even more varied than the amount and types of courses acceptable.

Etiquette dictates it is important you have the proper dining service to present each course properly. In other words, if you don't have a special fish fork, you shouldn't serve a fish course to start your meal.

Now, let's get practical. Most people don't know what a fish fork looks like, much less own one; it seems silly that you would reject your best fish recipe just because you don't own the right fork. However, if at all possible, at least provide a clean knife, fork, and/or spoon with each course as needed.

When Money's No Object

If you can afford to choose whatever meal you wish to serve, feel free to create a menu with multiple courses and an extensive wine list. While this type of meal is generally reserved for a gourmet cook and friends who appreciate fine dining, it is fun to do on occasion.

Chef's Choice

Create menus with any dishes you feel comfortable cooking. Don't forget there are many excellent package mixes to help you as well. There is no rule that says you must cook everything from scratch. Consommé, for instance, can be made by heating canned beef broth and adding a splash of sherry. You don't have to create the dish by making beef stock from bones.

Tempting Takeout

Let's assume you've inherited a full set of china, crystal, and silverware, but unfortunately you didn't inherit any cooking skills. Can you still serve a formal meal? Of course. Remember that presentation is the key, so grab your takeout menus or head to your favorite gourmet delicatessen.

When hosting a dinner party, it is usually not your cooking skills that are being judged but your ability as a host. Don't let your lack of cooking skills prevent you from hosting an elegant event.

Chips and Tips

Do keep in mind that if you choose to offer multiple courses, keep the portions small so guests won't fill up before they reach the main course.

Chips and Tips

No matter how much or how little you will be spending on your meal, ask your guests if they have any dietary restrictions. Or simply make certain you have extra vegetables available should someone arrive and announce they are allergic to fish, don't eat meat, or are on some particular diet.

Festive Facts

A society woman was a great cook, loved to entertain, and enjoyed giving formal dinner parties. One day she inadvertently ruined a batch of chicken piccata just before her guests were scheduled to arrive. She placed a call to a local Italian restaurant, which surreptitiously delivered enough to serve her guests, and kept it warm in her oven. When it came time to serve the entreé, she replated the meal onto her china dinner plates.

As dinner proceeded, one of her guests remarked that the meat tasted remarkably like that served at the restaurant. The hostess simply said, "Yes, it's the same recipe. I hope you're enjoying it." That's grace under pressure!

Eliminate Experiments

One of the most common mistakes beginning hosts make is trying a recipe for the first time on their guests. Even experienced chefs can only guess what a recipe might taste like from studying the ingredients.

Chips and Tips

When you serve multiple courses with multiple selections of wine, you start with a mild course and mild wine, working your way up to heavier tastes in both food and wine as the courses progress.

If a recipe sounds appealing, try it out first on your family or a close friend or two. Don't let it be the possible ruination of your dinner party.

Perfect Place Settings

You may have purchased or been given a standard set of china. This generally consists of eight to twelve place settings, each with a dinner plate, bread/salad/dessert plate, soup bowl, cup, and saucer.

A typical flatware place setting consists of a dinner fork, salad/dessert fork, teaspoon, table/soup spoon, and a butter knife with a serrated edge. Add other pieces as your budget or needs dictate.

Formal glasses do not generally come in sets and are purchased by the piece or type. However, you should have a stemmed water glass and a wine glass at the minimum for each guest. (A complete list of bar glasses is included in Chapter 9, "Tiny Bubbles: Stocking Your Bar").

Topping the Tablescape

As host, it is up to you (or your waitstaff) to set the table. It is therefore important that you understand how place settings are laid out.

Since you know the menu, make sure there are a sufficient number of dishes, glasses, and flatware for each course. At the beginning of the meal, it is not necessary to have any more plates on the table than is required for the first course and bread plates.

Setting Up

The dinner or first-course plate is centered to each chair and placed one inch from the edge of the table. The bread-and-butter plate is placed at 11 o'clock to the dinner plate. The knife is placed horizontally and at the top of the bread plate with the handle pointing to the right.

Keep in mind, no round bowl should be presented without a flat plate under it. This means if you were to offer salad or soup in a bowl, you would not put it on the table without a flat plate underneath it.

You may preset the dinner plate under the first-course plate, but it is not necessary. However, if you do, you might wish to place a doily on top of the dinner plate so it will remain clean should something accidentally get spilled from the first course. The doily would be removed when the first-course dishes are taken away.

Use Your Utensils

Forks (except fish forks) are always placed to the left of the plate; knives and spoons go to the right.

Depending upon what would be needed for your meal, the forks would be laid out to the left of the plate. The largest piece is centered on the dish, and all the other pieces are lined up so the bottoms of the pieces form a straight line. Lay them out according to the menu items served and going from left to right: cocktail fork, salad fork, and dinner fork. On the other side of the plate, you would line up the knives and spoon. Starting from the inside and moving right there are: steak knife, dinner knife, fish knife or fish fork, and soup spoon.

Chips and Tips

If you own service for eight and you have ten or twelve guests, rent or borrow half as many place settings as you will need in total plus one. This will enable you to alternate the dishes at every seat and have one left over just in case.

Chips and Tips

To help you remember whether a piece of flatware goes to the left or right of a plate, remember the word *left* has four letters, and so does *fork*. *Knife* and *spoon* each contain five letters and so does the word *right*.

Chips and Tips

If you have a proper fish fork with a heavy left tine, that can be used to replace the fish knife.

Generally the soup spoon is the only spoon preset. However, you might place a dessert spoon above the dinner plate and horizontal to it with the bowl facing left.

If you were to also preset the dessert fork, it would be placed below the dessert spoon and facing the opposite direction.

A teaspoon, if needed, is placed on the saucer with the cup when dessert is served.

Properly set flatware.

Fish fork   Salad/   Dinner fork   Teaspoon/   Soup spoon
         Dessert fork   Dessert spoon

Place spoon   Butter knife   Steak knife   Dinner knife

Wash It Down

The glasses start with the water glass set at the 1 o'clock position to your plate and one to two inches away. The red-wine glass goes below and to the right, the white-wine glass goes below and to the right of that, and the champagne flute just below and to the right of the white-wine glass.

Wiping Up

The napkin can be placed to the left of the first fork, folded and placed inside an empty glass, or placed on top of your dishes if you are not presetting any of the courses. If you are serving a formal dinner you might want to consider renting, borrowing, or even buying cloth napkins.

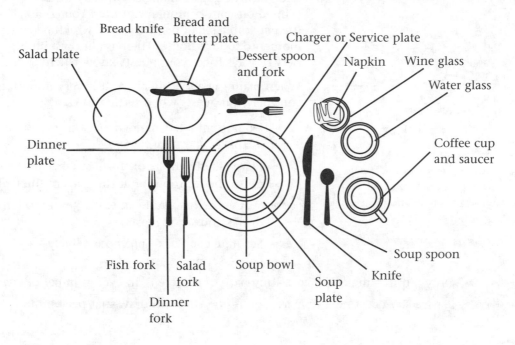

A formal place setting.

Charge It

For a very elegant presentation, you should use a *charger* or *service plate*. These are large, round platters that are put at each place setting under the dinner plate. Food is never served on the charger. It may be removed when the first course is served or the first course's plate may be placed on the charger.

Shindig Sayings

A **charger** or **service plate** is a large round platter that is put under or instead of a dinner plate as decoration only.

Chips and Tips

Take an instant photo of your guests upon arrival, or use a picture from past occasions and frame the picture as the place setting and memento.

Finishing Touches

As you would expect, there is more to a formal table than plates, flatware, and glasses. Here are a few things you should consider when putting together your tablescape.

Where Do I Sit?

While you can leave open seating at your dining table, it is far better to assign places.

These can be made from heavy paper stock folded in half with the guest's name beautifully inscribed or printed on your computer's printer. You could also put the paper in a small picture frame, which becomes a momento to take home. There is almost a limitless variety of ways to let your guests know where to sit.

When planning a seating chart, it is very important to consider your guests when setting the seats:

➤ Do not put a left-handed guest in the middle of a table of right-handers

➤ Place elderly guests or those in wheelchairs closest to the restroom or at the ends of the table

➤ Seat yourself so you can easily get up to refresh drinks and serve guests

➤ Separate couples to promote a lively conversation

➤ Only put in a male/female seating pattern if there is an even number of guests

➤ Place a shy guest next to a gregarious one who will draw that person out

Center of Attention

A centerpiece is usually used to bring color and style to your dining table. It is often made of flowers, but you can use a variety of items to suit a particular theme if you are having one.

The most important thing to remember about a centerpiece is that it should be below eye level or raised on a transparent platform above eye level to avoid interfering with your guests' line of vision and conversation.

Serving with Style

While you may preset your first course, you will need to determine how you are going to serve the rest of the meal. You must choose whether you are going to give your guests plated portions or have the guests served by you or a waitstaff member. Do not place the food in serving dishes and leave it on the table for guests to help themselves at a formal dinner.

Plated Portions

This is the most practical serving solution. It allows you to portion out the servings in your kitchen uniformly. This is important if you plan to serve multiple courses and want to serve small allotments of each dish. It also allows you to arrange the food on the dish attractively. Sprinkle herbs or colorful spices around the edge of the plate to give it color and to make the plate seem more full.

Serve from the Left

Whether you choose to bring each dish around for the guests to serve themselves, or the food will be served by you or a waitstaff member, serve from the left.

The logic behind this custom is that the majority of people are right-handed. This would allow them to use their right hand if they are serving themselves.

Chips and Tips

If you are unsure whether a centerpiece is too high, place your elbow next to the arrangement and raise your arm straight up. If the centerpiece is above your middle finger, it is too high.

Chips and Tips

If there is only one portion, it should be centered on the plate. When there are several foods, each should be given a distinct section of the plate.

Likewise, when the diners have finished their course, you should remove the plate from the right.

Keep in mind that there should always be a plate in front of your guest and that glasses are not removed until dessert is served.

Hiring Help

Should you decide you would like to hire someone to help serve the meal, there are a number of places to check.

If there is a culinary institute or hospitality management program at your local college, these students are usually trained in the art of presentation. However, be sure it is a student who has almost completed the program, not a beginner.

You also might check at your favorite fine restaurant (not the pizza parlor) for a lead. If your regular waiter is not available, he might be able to suggest someone else.

Do make sure you tell the waitstaff member how you would prefer he or she dresses. All of them are capable of supplying their own uniform to a degree (slacks, white shirt, and tie). However, fancy vests, dinner jackets, or evening coats might have to be provided if you require these. Many waitresses will own the equivalent costuming, but might not have a formal maid's uniform.

Whether you are serving the meal yourself or hiring someone to do it for you, the most important thing to remember is to relax, enjoy yourself, and sit back and wait for the compliments on what an excellent hostess you are.

The Least You Need to Know

➤ Formal dining refers primarily to the presentation.

➤ Place flatware from out to in, in the order it will be used.

➤ Forks go to the left, spoons and knives to the right.

➤ If hiring a waitstaff person, make sure they have appropriate experience or training.

Chapter 16

A Day of Dining

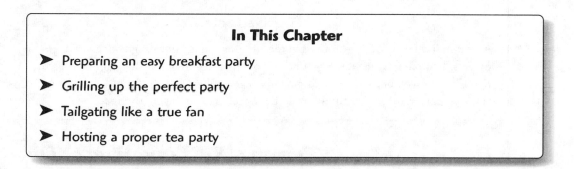

In This Chapter

➤ Preparing an easy breakfast party

➤ Grilling up the perfect party

➤ Tailgating like a true fan

➤ Hosting a proper tea party

One of the easiest ways to pick an occasion for a party is by picking a food. Have you discovered a great lasagna recipe that you want to share with friends, or has the weather turned warm and you want to try out your new gas grill? Whatever the reason, the party doesn't have to be fancy, just some good food and an excuse to celebrate.

In this chapter, you'll learn that there's no law that says you can't have a birthday party breakfast or celebrate a wedding anniversary with a backyard barbecue. We'll show you how to throw a fabulous fete at any time of the day.

Breakfast or Brunch for the Bunch

Mornings are a great time to gather together for almost everyone. Many busy business men and women are finding that breakfast meetings allow them to extend their work-days by starting out early. The same strategy works well for active families on weekends.

For just that reason, breakfast, brunch, and even lunch events can be an excellent option. These parties can start early, last only an hour or two, and not interfere with other plans for the day.

Bagels or Beluga

You have almost as many choices of what to serve at breakfast as you would at dinner; however, most of these events work best as simple breakfast buffets.

Bagels or biscuits, Danish or donuts, bran muffins or bran flakes, coffee cakes or croissants—these continental breakfast staples are great for serving the gang. Pick a few, or pick them all. Just put out fresh juice, tons of toppings (anything from butter to *beluga caviar*), hot coffee, and tea, and you have yourself a breakfast bonanza.

Festive Facts

An extended family of 20—brothers, sisters, spouses, aunts, uncles, grandchildren, grandparents, and parents—meet every Sunday morning after church for bagels and coffee. The timing works well because most commitments generally don't start until after noon on Sundays. Each family takes turns buying the bagels and supplying the space.

Shindig Sayings

Caviar is sieved and lightly salted fish eggs (roe). The best and generally most expensive type is **beluga caviar,** taken from beluga sturgeon that swim in the Caspian Sea. The sturgeon has large eggs about the size of pearls that come in shades from gray to black.

Two on a Raft and Wreck 'Em

For some guests, it's not breakfast unless there are eggs. Poached, boiled, fried, baked, over easy, steamed, scrambled, or in a casserole, quiche, or omelet, these versatile protein packets are big at breakfast. If the group's not too large, take individual orders.

However, if you are feeding a flood of folks, scrambled eggs are your best choice. They will hold their heat for a while in a chafing dish and you won't have to stand over the stove all morning. *"Two on a raft and wreck 'em!"*

A Balanced Brunch

If the hour that everyone can get together is later in the morning or early afternoon, you will undoubtedly want to add a few more substantial items to the continental menu.

You might wish to offer pancakes, French toast, omelets, quiche, or egg casseroles. Depending on the group and your wishes, perhaps bacon, sausage, ham, or another meat is needed before your guests declare it a meal.

For really late brunches, you may want to skip the breakfast selections altogether and put out an array of cold cuts and salads to feed your guests. Offer a variety of toppings, sliced bread, fresh rolls, baguettes, flour tortillas (for wraps), or bagels all set out for guests to build their own *Dagwood* sandwiches.

Shindig Sayings

In diner talk, **two on a raft and wreck 'em** means scrambled eggs on toast.

Festive Facts

Dagwood sandwiches are named after the husband, Dagwood Bumstead, in the "Blondie" comic strip. He is famous for his sandwiches made from a collection of cold cuts and toppings piled sky high between two slices of bread.

You even can offer standard dinner fare or casseroles at lunch. This often happens with holiday meals such as Thanksgiving or Christmas.

Parties on the Move

Progressive parties are another entertaining alternative. They work especially well when the participating hosts live nearby.

At a progressive party, each course is served in another person's home. As the meal progresses, so do the guests, moving from house to house, course to course.

There are a variety of ways these events are hosted. Money may be pooled and allotted for each segment of the meal. Or, the host absorbs the cost of what is being served at her house. If that's the case, these parties are routinely held so that one person doesn't get stuck paying for the most expensive item, while another only pays for ice cream.

Memorable Meals

If you opt for having a dinner party, there is no reason you can't make it a theme meal. You can choose foreign foods, meals based on one dish or ingredient, or food preparation technique (such as grilled, fried, or baked foods).

Feasts with a Foreign Flair

When you and your friends get together to go out to dinner, how often do you hear, "What do you want to eat? Italian? Chinese? Thai? Mexican?"

You may choose to do all the dishes based on the cooking of one country, or you may put together a selection of different dishes from a number of lands.

Festive Facts

Within many ethnic groups there are subcultures. For instance, in Chinese cooking many restaurants base their cuisine on a particular style or region. Cantonese (from the south-eastern region of Canton) is the most common. However, you also may find dishes or menus based on other areas such as Fukien (east coast), Peking-Shantung (northeastern), Honan (central) or Szechuan-Hunan (western).

One Taste Sensation

Another tasty theme is to base the entire menu around one key ingredient or one type of food.

For instance, if you were to choose garlic as the key ingredient, each dish would center around the use of this one spice. Choose a canapé, appetizer, soup, salad, meat, side dish, bread, dessert, and beverage all containing garlic as an ingredient.

Be aware that if you choose a spice like garlic, you'll probably want to confine this particular party to very close friends!

Just like choosing a spice, you can make one food the focal point of your party.

Tomatoes, for instance, are a wonderful choice because not only are they plentiful and there are so many varieties, you also can find endless recipes to choose from that use this fabulous fruit.

Festive Facts

There are literally dozens of garlic festivals throughout the United States and Canada each year that bring in hundreds of thousands of patrons to eat and drink all things garlic including ice cream and sweet garlic jelly.

To host a one-taste sensation party, you need to determine what you have a lot of, what you like, or what's on sale. Then look through your recipe files for meals with a common ingredient or browse through searchable data bases for a common thread (epicurious.com has an excellent one) to select a complete menu.

Chips and Tips

Selecting a menu based on one type of food is a particularly good idea if you have a home garden. Often the entire crop of a vegetable will be ready to harvest at the same time.

Bring on the Barbecue

Grilling is great in summer months because it gets everyone outdoors and it doesn't heat up the kitchen. Foods cooked on a grill take on a flavor that you have trouble duplicating on a conventional stove.

Inside or out, there are so many alternatives to the types of grilling you can do. You can try a built-in, brick, charcoal, or wood-chip barbecue, gas grill, smoker, or hibachi. One of the hottest trends is to install a grill inside the kitchen so you can enjoy barbecues year-round, no matter the weather. There are even inexpensive attachments you can put on your standard stove burner to make it act like an outdoor grill. Or buy a portable and affordable electric grill.

Grilling is great to gather the gang in a casual atmosphere.

Dining Alfresco

After a long winter stuck indoors, there is little that is more enjoyable than being able to dine *alfresco,* or outside. This is especially true when the days are warm and the cool evening breeze brings blessed relief from the heat of day.

So sit back and drink in the heady fragrance of the night-blooming jasmine. These parties are a delight.

Shindig Sayings

Alfresco is an Italian word that means taking place in the open air. It usually refers to dining outside.

Party Pitfall

Be careful when spraying insect foggers or bug spray. While they might work well at keeping the bugs away, they shouldn't be sprayed near food or guests.

Chips and Tips

For a refreshing taste, take sliced peaches and put them in the bottom of your wine glass. Then eat the wine-infused peach at the end of your meal.

Backyard Banquets

Where is it written that you can only enjoy fine dining indoors? When you want to entertain in style, there is an elegance to eating outdoors under the glow of moonlight that no room can duplicate.

Take out your best linen tablecloth and napkins, your crystal vase, your sterling silver flatware, candlesticks, and your crystal goblets. For complete enjoyment, set your dining table up under the canopy of a spreading tree, or on your terrace.

A meal under the stars is a special occasion, no matter what you serve your guests. As far as the beauty of the surroundings, well, the sky is the limit.

Picnics with Panache

In the middle of the eighteenth century, the aristocracy of England and France had extremely elaborate picnics. Their servants would load carriages full with tables, chairs, fine china, crystal, and huge banquets to take a meal out in the country.

Over time, picnics have become less and less refined. For many people, cold fried chicken, thick slices of ham, or sandwiches make the perfect picnic. However, putting together something more elaborate doesn't have to be too difficult.

The next time it's your turn to pack the picnic, put together a Mediterranean feast with cold marinated shrimp, grilled vegetables, smoky sharp provolone, Greek olives, a crisp rosé and ripe peaches. Or create another meal that's a little more interesting than salads and sandwiches.

Don't forget a corkscrew, salt and pepper shakers, trash bags, insect repellent, moist towelettes and sunblock. In fact, if you picnic often, you might want to keep these items in your car.

Tailgating for the Team

Years ago, tailgate parties were limited to fall football games. These days, folks are tailgating year-round for a variety of sports. It's a great way to get together with your friends and to interact with a group of fans for camaraderie or friendly rivalry.

With the rising prices at professional sporting events, tailgating also helps to defray costs of feeding your family at the stadium.

You can make your tailgating gathering as simple or complicated as you like. If you want, you can prepare your meal entirely at home, store it in coolers or insulated thermoses, and eat when you get to the event.

Tea and Crumpets

These days, the simple pleasure of sitting down in the afternoon (traditionally tea is served at 4 P.M.) to enjoy a soothing cup of tea, light refreshments, and good company has made tea parties appealing to men and women from all walks of life.

For a high tea party, you will need to use your best china or tea service and good linens. While white linen or lace is traditional, pastels and soft floral prints also work well.

Proper tea is made from loose tea (although today bags can be used) measured out 1 teaspoon per cup (and 1 for the pot). Tea can either be brewed in the cup or in a heated teapot (swish hot water in the pot and pour it out to warm it) and then strained into the cup—never drink tea from a mug.

Tea sandwiches are essential and must be made on whisper-thin bread with the crusts cut off. They are then shaped into a square, triangle, or round using a knife or cookie cutter.

Scones, crumpets, shortbread cookies, and *Madelaines* are essential to a proper tea party and can be topped with sweet butter, clotted cream, lemon curds, and/or jams.

To learn more, read *A Guide to Tea Parties for Ladies of Any Age* by Dawn Hogan (www.partyexperts. homepage.com).

Rarely lasting longer than an hour, teas are a great way to entertain when you are tightly budgeting time and money.

Chips and Tips

If you love sporting events but hate sitting in traffic after the game, bring extra food to cook up before you go home. This way you can relax, have something to eat, and discuss the game.

Chips and Tips

While you should cut the bread yourself into thin slices, you can cheat by using presliced bread and rolling it thin with a water tumbler or rolling pin.

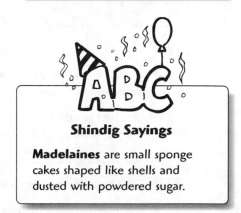

Shindig Sayings

Madelaines are small sponge cakes shaped like shells and dusted with powdered sugar.

145

Festive Facts

Queen Victoria started the 4 P.M. tea-time tradition that is still popular in England today as an early workingman's supper. In addition to tea, small sandwiches filled with watercress, wafer-thin cucumber slices, shaved turkey breast, chicken salad, or tuna salad, along with dainty cakes, English biscuits and toppings are usually served.

Shindig Sayings

Flan is a Spanish baked custard coated in caramel. It is also known as *créme caramel* in France and *crema caramella* in Italy.

Decadent Desserts

Perfect for after a play or movie, dessert parties are a sweet indulgence.

Putting together a party like this is like being a kid in a candy store … because you really are. You can choose cakes and candies, pastries and pies, tortes and tarts, parfaits and puddings, *flan* and fruit. It's a celebration for your sweet tooth.

Pair these sweet treats with a selection of flavored coffees, teas, and dessert liqueurs for a party that may not be good for the waistline, but certainly is food for the soul.

Breakfast, brunch, lunch, tea, dinner, or dessert—most anytime of the day or night is the right time to party.

The Least You Need to Know

➤ Continental breakfast buffets are a great way to feed a group of people at an early morning event.

➤ Add more substantial foods to a continental breakfast, including hot meat dishes, and you have created a menu suitable for brunch, lunch, or dinner.

➤ Backyard dining can be as elegant as in the dining room.

➤ Picnics can have more panache by serving foods other than cold cuts.

➤ High tea or dessert parties are excellent ways to entertain when time is short.

Chapter 17

Strictly Business

> ### In This Chapter
>
> ➤ Planning your business party
>
> ➤ Timing a successful open house
>
> ➤ Producing a business party with a theme
>
> ➤ Inviting the bigwigs home for dinner

Special events and parties are a big part of doing business in any sector of the commercial world. To "party," regardless if used in relationship to workmates, employees, clients, or prospective clients, is a common method of interaction in the business community.

The main thrust of this book is for home parties, but since business functions are so important in our lives, you will find here information that can be applied to a variety of parties that may be planned for companies at home or elsewhere.

Plot the Party Plan

When it's your turn to produce a celebration for employees, clients, customers, or associates, it is essential to keep your plans uncomplicated, personalized, and within your budget. With close-knit companies, you can host a casual gathering or one that is very detailed and customized. For entertaining clients and customers, however, you will want to plan something creative and original but which somehow relates to your business.

Party Pitfall

Make sure all members of the committee are actively involved and that you aren't ignoring their ideas just to do things your way.

Chips and Tips

Set up fewer chairs than the amount of people you expect at your volunteer recruitment party. The subliminal effect of having to bring in more chairs is that this event must be extra special if there is such a huge interest to help. Just be sure the extra chairs are easily accessible so that the momentum of the meeting isn't slowed.

The most important tool that you have for planning events for your company is the consensus opinion of your fellow employees. It is therefore best to put together a committee. Even if you do the bulk of the work, the advisory committee allows everyone to feel they have had the necessary input into the occasion.

If you're trying to build excitement and get the committee to "buy into" your concept and pass along enthusiasm, you need to make your planning sessions a party, too. For instance, if you were planning a golf outing, you might put green tablecloths down on the conference table or hold the meetings at the planned golf course. For refreshments you might serve juice and coffee with pieces of cake with chocolate icing and sprinkled with coconut flakes dyed green. On top of that would be a donut hole covered in powdered sugar sitting on a tee.

Give each member a notebook with a golf theme or a pen shaped like a golf club, or one of those short pencils used to mark a score card.

It's the attention to fun and the details that will generate excitement and make your committee members goodwill ambassadors who will promote the event throughout the company. This is very important with morale-building events.

Open Your House or ...

Generally, an open house, whether it's in your home, office, or retail store, is the best way to entertain large groups. Guests can come and go and spend as much time as they care to. This relaxed plan of celebrating is very popular with business people because it fits easily into most schedules.

In most cases there will be a specific purpose for having your open house. It might be to kick off a new business, introduce a new product or service, or to show off a new facility. The bottom line is that you are trying to drum up additional business with your clients and enthusiasm with your employees.

Perfect Timing

Open-house festivities scheduled from 5 to 8 P.M. on weekdays are best for business contacts, potential clients, or customers. It is more convenient for "9-to-5'ers" to take time at the end of their workday.

A Business Theme

With your motive or goal in mind, you can set a theme by playing on any words or phrases that fit as illustrated below:

➤ "Have We Got News for You!" Use newspaper effects all the way through, including a tabloid-style invitation; newspapers fashioned into flowers; and favors, prizes, or gifts wrapped in newsprint.

➤ "We're Truckin' to Our New Address!" Invitations are fashioned after official forwarding address cards from the post office. The hosts don jumpsuit coveralls, company logo hats, and T-shirts. Easy decorations are made from packing boxes, barrels, and a variety of packing materials. Serve food from takeout containers. This is a great theme for a transportation company.

Party Pitfall

A business function planned on the weekend will likely be poorly attended. Most people do not want to interrupt their time off for a work-related outing. The exception is when it's a family affair; then Sunday afternoon events are better attended than Saturday events.

Festive Facts

When one of the offices of an international shipping company moved to a new facility in Miami, invitations to an open house were printed on paper that resembled packing material. The cocktail tables were clothed in the company's colors and the centerpieces were small wooden shipping crates filled with items representing all 43 countries where they had offices. A robot greeted guests to represent their state-of-the-art facility and a band played music. The highly successful event received write-ups in industry publications.

RSVP Calls

For open-house events, request a "yes or no" answer, then e-mail or phone one week ahead to gather late responses. This short, enthusiastic phone call will determine that all invitations were received and also generate pre-event excitement.

Bring the Whole Family

When organizing committees for family events, encourage involvement of members' families. It will not only provide a larger pool of talent, it will give your associates a chance to spend hard-to-find quality time with their loved ones.

Bill of Fare with Flair

For curb service, there are catering companies that specialize in picnics and open houses for families. They will load your buffet tables with staples like hot dogs, hamburgers, ham, and chicken. There also are chuck wagons, hot dog carts, and salad bars that can be brought in. Many off-site caterers can serve your guests a full gourmet meal when they set up their kitchens on the property or on specially equipped trucks. Your only restriction is your budget.

Fun for Children of All Ages

For family parties you must give special consideration to providing enjoyable activities and entertainment for all ages. Party entertainment may include bands or variety performers such as clowns, face painters, jugglers, magicians, or kiddy rides, pony rides, games of chance, booths, and concessions will add to your event fun.

Children love nothing more than seeing their parents acting silly. Organize games and activities that pit teams of grownups and kids against each other.

Chips and Tips

Send a separate invitation to each child with instructions to bring a parent(s) along. This will result in almost 100 percent kid turnout—and, of course, mom and dad, too.

Festive Facts

A college wanted to bring families onto their campus. They began by hosting a carnival and cookout. In addition to the fun, tours were given of some of the classrooms and programs offered. That way, in later years, when college choices are being made, the families would have a "relationship" with the hometown college.

Happy Holidays

These days, holiday parties are anticipated, like a reward, by employees. Of course, a holiday bonus is very much appreciated, but a festive and entertaining party also does a lot for morale and company spirit. Here are just two ways to boost morale with a different type of holiday celebration.

➤ "Tour of the Lights": Load your guests onto a bus, serve traveling treats and toddies out of thermos bottles, and feast your eyes on your town's extravaganza of holiday lights.

➤ Hold a party to salute the holiday traditions of other countries. Encourage employees to come dressed in clothing from their ancestral heritage and explain the holiday customs of their forebearers. Guests also should be encouraged to bring food specialties to share.

> **Chips and Tips**
>
> Since employees often feel a little awkward when they are in a social situation with coworkers, employers, and their own families, invest in a few well-placed entertainers to help break the ice until everyone feels comfortable in their surroundings.

> **Festive Facts**
>
> One company routinely collected food and toys from employees at the annual holiday party to be distributed to local charities. After finding out that some of the company's own employees were struggling financially, the company changed its policy. It still collected from the employees, but instead of going to strangers, huge baskets were assembled for needy employees and anonymously given to them. Once employees knew their donations were going to co-workers in need, the amount of contributions increased dramatically in both quantity and quality.

Dressed to the Nines

A perennial party favorite is the adults-only dinner dance. It is the chance to get out of work clothes and show up at the party looking like you stepped off the pages of *Glamour* or *GQ*. These dress-up occasions are appreciated by employees and customers alike.

For small numbers, this party can be comfortably given in your home, as elegantly and formally as you like. If your group is sizeable though, you may want to take it out to a more suitable site or adapt your home by adding on a tent.

Festive Facts

One company wanted their super sales staff to have no concerns about enjoying themselves at a black tie party held at a local hotel. They not only provided overnight accommodations, but they also set up a huge pajama party for the employees' children that included babysitters, food, and entertainment.

Company and Community Pride

Many companies are getting involved in community activities. This not only helps the community, but also helps increase employee morale. Companies work on projects like adopting a portion of a road and keeping it clean, helping to build a house for Habitat for Humanity, or working with their local United Way to raise money. These "workdays" are often followed with a social gathering of the employees.

Chips and Tips

Set up a variety of community-boosting activities so that employees can choose something that best suits their personality or skills.

Inviting the Bigwigs

It happens. There are just some occasions that make it important or essential to invite your boss or clients to your home to entertain. Don't panic. Here are some suggestions to help you get through the event relatively unscathed:

➤ Put out the "good" dinner service.

➤ If you're hiring someone to help for the night, don't act as if you have maid service all the time. Also, think twice about bringing in help if it's a small dinner party. It takes away from the intimate feeling you are trying to convey.

➤ Choose a meal (or buy takeout) that doesn't require a lot of last-minute preparation. Check with your client or boss's assistant to find out about favorite foods or, more importantly, food allergies.

➤ Don't choose a meal that's messy or difficult to eat. Stay away from whole lobsters, for example.

➤ Don't drink alcohol, or drink only in moderation.

➤ If you have young children, introduce them to your guests, but have them eat their meal with a babysitter.

➤ If spouses are in attendance, draw them into the conversation.

➤ Don't talk business if you've invited your guests under the guise of a social occasion.

➤ Relax and try to enjoy yourself.

Awards and Rewards

Giving kudos and congratulations for quality of performance or length of service are standard reasons to call your fellow employees together. Another purpose for a party is to thank customers for patronage or entertain them to generate future business.

Sometimes these occasions are manageable in a private home, plant, or office location. However, when the amount of guests spills out of your living or work space, a venue should be the chosen party place.

Getting the Gold Watch

Retirement parties can be given for family members or co-workers. They can be casual or formal. They can be roast or boast events depending on the person honored and the situation.

You can choose to review their past work life or theme it around their retirement plans. The main responsibility of the host is to make the honoree feel that they are special and will be missed at the workplace.

You Did a Great Job

"Salesperson of the Year" or "Project Completed" are just two attainments that merit festive celebration and commemoration. Awards, bonuses, prizes, and incentives of all kinds are presented at big and small parties, both formally or in a casual mode.

Everyone deserves to be recognized for a career coup or a work win. It doesn't have to be life-changing or newsworthy, either. Just take the time to publicly celebrate those who deserve a special pat on the back for a job well done. Champagne or chili. The choice is yours.

Chips and Tips

Be sure to give awards—elegant or token—suitable for showing in the recipient's office so the guest(s) of honor will have a lasting reminder of your tribute and can show it off.

Pat-on-the-back parties, whether planned elaborately or simply, will keep company morale at its highest. Efforts that bring great results should not go unrewarded or un-awarded. Make them fun. The light side of a workmate or associate is usually unem-ployed during the workday, so it is appealing to bring it out in these social settings.

If achievement awards are presented regularly, invest in an "Employee of the Month" plaque showing a photo of the honoree and host a mini celebration at lunch or a cof-fee break.

Thanks, Mr. and Ms. Client

"Thank-You" parties for clients and customers are a fantastic way to tell them, in per-son and in all sincerity, that you appreciate them and their patronage. Inviting these important people to your home or office is the best way to introduce them to em-ployees that are a voice or an e-mail address.

An appreciation open house is a sure way to solidify a business relationship. Remem-ber, it's difficult to pull your business when you know these colleagues as human beings with families and lives.

Don't forget to acknowledge your support staff as well. It's surprising how often an account is kept because of the way your receptionist responds to phone calls, or how your shipping department maintains a friendly relationship with the letter carrier who stays around to pick-up last minute shipments.

Business entertaining, whether done as a marketing tool or employee recognition, is an important part of our hosting lives. And since we spend so much time involved with work, it's nice to be able to find ways to incorporate those times with our fami-lies so we can combine business with pleasure.

The Least You Need to Know

➤ Special events are good for business.

➤ Let employees have a say in work-related parties.

➤ Open houses are effective business entertaining options.

➤ Rewards, awards, and honors all fulfillment to work and help increase produc-tivity and morale.

Part 5

Seasonal Celebrations

With every season there comes a new reason to celebrate. And why not? There's no reason that you should be sitting around and waiting for the next birthday or major holiday—like Thanksgiving or New Year's—before you allow yourself time to party.

We've matched over 10 different holidays with a party plan. As the host, you'll hardly have to think when planning one of these festive gigs. Just copy the invitation ideas, plan the food accordingly, and buy the suggested souvenirs. The only thing you'll have to prepare on your own is the guest list.

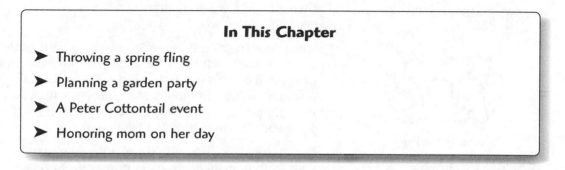

Chapter 18

Spring Flings

In This Chapter

➤ Throwing a spring fling

➤ Planning a garden party

➤ A Peter Cottontail event

➤ Honoring mom on her day

The long gray winter is over. The crocus, tulips, and daffodils have peeked out of the ground. Children are giggling in the street. Neighbors are emerging from the cocoons of their homes to remove their storm windows, sit on porches, and air out their houses. A better time to gather family and friends you probably haven't seen since the holiday hoopla.

Whether you are honoring mom on her special day, planning for the arrival of the Easter Bunny, or just joyful about planting your garden, spring can make anyone, old and young, feel like a party. In this chapter, you'll get tips on planning the perfect garden soiree, special ways to celebrate Mother's Day, and ideas for Easter above and beyond an egg hunt.

Great Gardening

It's time to spring into action and cultivate your relationship with family and friends. What better way to plant the seeds to social success than by throwing a great garden party for the gang? Once you start to plan, this party will take root and grow into something beautiful!

Dig out your address book, and send your guests wildflower or vegetable seeds with the invitation printed on a label and attached to the packet.

Shindig Sayings

A **cornucopia** is a goat's horn depicted as overflowing with fruit, flowers, and corn, signifying prosperity and abundance. Today, woven, ceramic, or clay cornucopias are used in table decor.

Shindig Sayings

Crudités are raw vegetable pieces that are used as an appetizer and often served with a dip.

Garden-Fresh Food

Serving a *cornucopia* of farm-fresh fruits and vegetables is an appetizing approach to the menu for such an event. Pick up a vegetarian cookbook or do a search on the Internet (www.FoodTV.com). There are hundreds of recipes so tasty, even your steak-and-potatoes friends won't miss the meat.

Start your dinner by cultivating the taste buds of your guests with an appetizing array of fresh vegetables on a *crudité* platter. Prepare several different dips or simply buy salad dressings. Be sure to include a low-fat or fat-free option in your selection for guests with dietary restrictions. Buy or make a vegetable pizza and have it cut into bite-sized pieces to use as an appetizer. From there, if you are serving dinner, proceed with a vegetable-based soup.

Since your guests will be working hard in your garden, you'll probably want to whet their whistles with fruit- or vegetable-based drinks like a strawberry daiquiris, orange blossoms, or Bloody Marys. Beers, wines, and most liquors are plant-based, so almost any drink you serve will fit into this theme scheme.

For your main course, guests can enjoy the snap of your fresh ingredients in pasta primavera, vegetable lasagna, grilled portobello mushrooms (which have a delicious beefy taste and texture), vegetable kabobs, fried rice, couscous, or any other garden-fresh dishes of your choosing.

And for the final hurrah, just-picked and washed fresh fruit is always a favorite dessert. You also can serve it in pies, on top of ice cream or cake, or in a fruit salad.

Serve your garden buffet in style by using lead-free flowerpots and garden tools as your serving utensils. Just make sure the drainage holes are covered.

You might find these vegetarian meals so memorable, you will want to use them for many of your themes.

Frolic and Fun

Garden parties are a great source for a variety of entertainment options. Obviously, your first choice would be to gather your guests to germinate your garden. Whether you have an acre or just a window box, digging into the dark dirt is an activity even the most staunch city slicker will love once you get him or her to try.

Looking for other ways to make merry? Host a sing-along of spring or garden songs: "The Lusty Month of May," "April Showers," "Paper Roses," "You Don't Bring Me Flowers," or "Garden Party" are popular songs that have grown on us.

Landscaping the Layout

Garden parties are ideal when held outdoors. However, even Mother Nature can use a little help now and then, so whether your party is indoors or outdoors, try these design details to jazz it up:

➤ Use cloths with pastel, floral, or vegetable motifs to bring out the gardening scheme.

➤ Pile fresh fruits and vegetables on a plate or in a basket. Tuck in greens and edible flowers, and you will have created a double-duty display that can be enjoyed both with the eyes and the palate.

➤ When your garden party is going to last until the evening, set lighted candles on the tables. Cover these with hurricane globes to keep them protected from the wind.

Seasonal Souvenir

To say thanks to your group of gardeners, reward them with remembrances of their day in the dirt. Treat them to potted plants, watering cans, or gardening books.

Party Pitfall

Be sure that your pots are lead-free. If you have any doubts, insert a pot liner or bowl in the pot first.

Chips and Tips

For great music to accompany the merriment, check out Vivaldi's "The Four Seasons." It's classical music that sounds as if it were meant to be played in a garden setting.

Bunnies and Baskets Brunch

Bunnies, baby chicks, baskets, and bouquets of flowers all say Easter. Luckily, it is very easy to put them all together for a fabulous spring brunch buffet.

Write your invitation on paper that can be rolled or folded to fit into a large plastic colored egg, seal, label, and mail at your post office.

Bountiful Baskets Buffet

Whether you are serving an Easter brunch, lunch, or light dinner buffet, this menu is hearty enough for almost everyone.

Bunnies & Baskets Brunch invitation.

Begin your Easter brunch with a toast using a mimosa, Bloody Mary, or Virgin Mary. For the children, serve straight orange juice or mix it with ginger ale and pour into a plastic champagne glass.

Once the toast has been made, present your guests with the perfect spring appetizer, a cold fresh-fruit *compote* or salad featuring some of the season's freshest produce.

Shindig Sayings

A **compote** is fruit that has been cooked or stewed in syrup.

For tradition and ease of preparation, pick a prepared ham as your entrée. Since they come fully cooked, you can easily serve it cold—just unwrap and slice. It can be accompanied by different flavored mustards, mayonnaise, sauces, or relish.

When you want to make a hot dish, unwrap the ham and place it into a roasting pan. Baste it with your favorite glaze or coating. Heat according to package directions for the type and size of ham you have purchased until the internal temperature of the meat is 140°F. Slice and serve. Garnish the serving tray with greens, colored eggs, and fruit.

If you are serving ham, you will probably want a salad on the side. Potato salad and ham go hand in hand, so offer a variety of spud salads with a typical mayonnaise or a German potato salad base.

A just-picked-from-the-garden green salad or a steamed vegetable medley will add color and crunch to the meal.

And in case a bunny comes hopping along, don't forget to have plenty of cooked or raw carrots on hand.

An Easter-licious Brunch

For an Easter brunch, you can really impress the crowd by making individual omelets to order. Fill a pitcher with beaten eggs (you might want to offer an egg substitute or whipped egg whites as well), and put out small fry pans along with butter, margarine, or cooking spray. Offer a variety of whatever fillings, such as cheese, diced peppers, mushrooms, onions, and tomatoes.

French toast will hold its heat for a while in a chafing dish, making it ideal for a buffet. Offer it with cold or heated syrup and fruit toppings.

You will want to put out baskets filled with muffins, sweet bread, buns, biscuits, and bagels with a variety of toppings to spread on the breads.

Gelatin molds or fruit toppings with cake and chocolate complete this bountiful buffet.

Hopping-Good Fun

It is almost impossible to have an Easter celebration without an egg hunt. Here are some egg-hunt ideas that will appeal to kids of all ages:

Chips and Tips

Orange marmalade thinned slightly with orange juice makes a delicious and easy ham glaze. Take whatever mixture you have left-over after you have coated the ham and thin further with more orange juice, then heat to make a sauce that can be used to pour over the ham.

Party Pitfall

Do not use real eggs. If one is not found, it will begin to rot and give off a very foul stench. If you must use real eggs, especially in an indoor location, be sure to keep track of the location of all the eggs. After the hunt, double-check that all the eggs have been found.

Jump in the fun and fill plastic eggs with chocolate candy or jelly beans. If you prefer not to give the children too many sweets, include small novelties such as trinkets, erasers, stickers, buttons, pennies, or small toys. Should there be a teens-only or adult party, fill the eggs with items that would appeal to someone more mature. If your budget allows, fill the eggs with costume jewelry, movie tickets, key chains, makeup, golf balls, money, lottery tickets, and other token gifts that would appeal to your adult guests.

When there are children of a wide variety of ages, put some eggs out in easy-to-see spots. Send the youngest children out first to gather up those eggs. Once those have been collected (and make sure each child finds at least one egg), you may send the older children out. For an egg-ceptional solution, team up an older child with a younger child.

Chips and Tips

Don't be fooled into thinking that older "kids" don't enjoy finding candy and toys in their eggs, too. Be sure to include some of these when you are stuffing them for teens or adults to make everyone "hoppy."

Chips and Tips

While any florals would work, for a true spring ambience, try to select tulips, hyacinths, lilies, hydrangeas, roses, daffodils, or other pastel-colored flower varieties.

Once the egg hunt is over, the fun has just begun. Here are some terrific ideas to keep your party hopping. Do the bunny hop, bring in a baby animal petting zoo, show *Bugs Bunny* cartoons, or have everyone decorate a hat and then host an Easter Parade of their designs and give prizes for the best entries.

Decorating the Den

Holding this party outdoors will go a long way toward creating the perfect atmosphere. However, if the weather or your home doesn't allow for this, create spring in your own home with these sensational springtime suggestions. Display spring flower arrangements, put all your bowls in decorated baskets for your buffet, sprinkle jellybeans on your table like confetti, hang fake butterflies, and make each guest's placecard by writing their name on a colored egg.

Spring-Has-Sprung Souvenirs

This hopping holiday will be remembered for years to come when you give your guests these springtime souvenirs: carrot-top plants, toy bunnies, chocolate eggs, or a copy of the Velveteen Rabbit.

Have a hoppy Easter!

Queen for a Day

Hear ye, hear ye, lords and ladies of the realm, we gather to honor the woman who gave us life and love. We celebrate and rejoice our Queen Mom.

This event works best when children, grandchildren, and spouse (or significant other) all get involved. There is nothing a mom likes better than seeing her entire family working together.

It's possible, of course, that you could simply walk into the next room or pick up the phone to invite your mother to this party; however, don't. Make her feel special by giving her a formal invitation.

You can put it in a card, write it on pretty decorative paper, or create something using a clip-art software program. You can use a fancy font on your computer or neat hand-writing, or hire someone who does calligraphy to write it out.

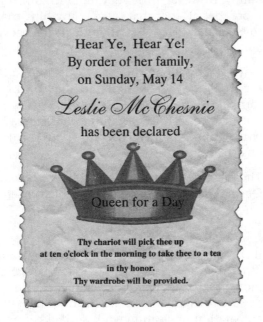

Honor Mom with this special invite.

Hear Ye, Hear Ye!
By order of her family,
on Sunday, May 14

Leslie McChesnie

has been declared

Queen for a Day

Thy chariot will pick thee up
at ten o'clock in the morning to take thee to a tea
in thy honor.
Thy wardrobe will be provided.

If you can afford to, attach the invitation to a dozen pink roses or her favorite blossoms and have them delivered. If not, have one of the grandchildren deliver it, or send it through the mail. The point is to give her an invitation she can save forever as a keepsake.

A Spot of Tea

This may be one of the few times in your life that you will get to use your grandmother's silver tea service. Drag it out and polish it. If you don't own one, rent a complete tea service or go to your thrift shop to mix and match a pretty teapot and cups.

And if some guests require something a little stronger than tea, offer small glasses of sherry or champagne.

Most importantly, serve the meal with style and elegance and make sure the Queen Mom is waited on hand and foot.

Party Pitfall

Admittedly, trying to sell this menu to men might take a bit of doing. However, once they realize that it's delicious and that it will earn them points with mom, they really enjoy it.

Chips and Tips

Buy inexpensive but elegant and colorful gladioli and place in a tall vase. If the gladioli are tightly closed, you can force them to open within hours. Cut 1 inch off the ends and crush the stems' bottom so they will absorb more water. Remove excess leaves and two or three buds at the top of the stalk. Place into a tall vase filled with warm water. You will have beautiful blossoms to enjoy for days.

Command Performance

The perfect entertainment for a Mother's Day tea is the family. However, treat your mom to something a little more special—not that there is anything more special to a mother. Play classical music in the background to add a genteel atmosphere to your tea setting.

Since you are honoring your "Queen for a Day," nothing would be more appropriate than command performances for her royal highness' benefit. Put together skits, create a photo exhibit of her life, read poetry written about mothers (or write your own), or sing her favorite songs.

The main point of the entertainment is that the Queen Mom was offered the gift of yourself.

Preparing the Palace

If this party can be held in the home of someone other than mom, that will help to make the event more special for her. However, if that's not possible, be sure the party-givers are the ones who do any preparation or cleanup work needed before and after the event. Take the royal honoree out for a few hours to let the setup team do its majestic best. Set the banquet table with your best china, the "good" tablecloth, and fresh spring flowers.

Seat the Queen Mom in either a dining chair with arms, wingback, or easy chair placed at the head of the table in exalted comfort. Remove her shoes and place a velvet pillow at her feet.

Royal Indulgences

Perhaps your queen is very informal and might initially protest the attention. Do not be fooled. She will be touched to see her young princesses in skirts and young princes in shirts and ties. Her heart will be full when she sees the effort you made, knowing you did it to honor her.

Paying Tribute

To ensure she will have token reminders of her day in power, bestow the "crown jewels" and other examples of her subject's largess. Provide her with a toy crown, a family portrait, or a gift certificate for a day of pampering at a local spa or salon.

Spring is certainly the season to celebrate, and whether you are planting a garden, giving mom her due, or hiding Easter eggs, remember that pastels are the color and that flowers will brighten everyone's day.

The Least You Need to Know

➤ Make guests a part of your spring fling by asking them to help you plant your garden.

➤ Egg-based dishes make the perfect Easter brunch food.

➤ An Easter egg hunt is perfect fun for guests of all ages.

➤ A Mother's Day tea will make any mom feel like a queen.

Chapter 19

The Heat Is On

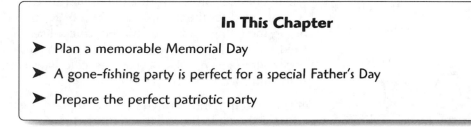

In This Chapter

➤ Plan a memorable Memorial Day

➤ A gone-fishing party is perfect for a special Father's Day

➤ Prepare the perfect patriotic party

There is nothing better in the heat of summer than a party outdoors. Whether you are honoring the fallen soldiers of the Civil War, celebrating our country's independence, or giving Dad his due, these are the barbecue picnic ideas you'll need for the perfect event.

In this chapter, you'll not only get ideas for throwing the perfect picnic, but find tips on decorating for Dad's special day and a variety of ways to celebrate our nation's greatest holidays.

Memorable Memorial Day

Memorial Day, formerly known as Decoration Day, was created in 1868 to honor fallen soldiers during the Civil War. It is now celebrated on the last Monday of May and is generally considered the unofficial beginning of summer.

After the parades and speeches, to honor its roots in Dixie, gather the gang together for a memorable Memorial Day backyard blowout in true southern style.

Since the temperature is likely to leave you parched, affix your invitation to an envelope of lemonade. A powdered drink packet will fit nicely into a standard-size envelope.

As God Is My Witness, They'll Never Go Hungry Again!

Park yourself at the picnic table, in the gazebo, or under a spreading oak tree and get ready to put a little South in your mouth for this Memorial Day spread.

Begin your meal by settling back to dunk fresh garden vegetables into a low-fat honey-mustard dip ladled into a hollowed-out red pepper. Don't pass up your favorite deviled eggs made crunchy by adding bacon bits as a topping.

As you sit sippin' your long, cool iced tea flavored with a sprig of mint, or a traditional mint julep, remember to save your appetite for the main course.

When your clan gathers with an "I'm famished" look on their faces, set them down to a feast of southern favorites, including cold fried chicken, thick slices of baked Virginia ham, a wedge of sweet-potato pie, tangy collard greens, black-eyed peas, cole slaw, corn bread, and fried green tomatoes.

Set the food in hand-painted bowls and platters garnished with edible flowers for a cultured presentation. And create shady places with parasols or umbrellas to protect food items.

After your kin comes back from playing in the afternoon sun or taking a dip in the swimmin' hole, refresh them with watermelon, Mississippi mud pie, and praline ice cream.

Mmmmm, that's good eatin'!

Minstrels and Mirth

While the young folk wear themselves out playing Johnny on the Pony, having a game of croquette on the back lawn, or hitting the badminton birdie, you can relax in a hammock and listen to the music of Tammy, Dolly, Tex, Shania, and other country stars.

After supper, gather the gang and put together a barbershop quartet or Sweet Adelines to sing classic songs of the Confederacy: "When Johnny Comes Marching Home Again," "Dixie," "Mammy," or "Swanee River." You also can put together a washboard, spoons, and banjo band to play alone or accompany the singing.

If you feel like kickin' up your heels, hire a square dance caller and get everyone up for the Virginia Reel. But don't forget to pencil in your best beau on your dance card for a Tennessee Waltz.

If the weather's not cooperating, enjoy some indoor activities. Rent *Gone with the Wind, Steel Magnolias, Driving Miss Daisy,* or *Fried Green Tomatoes* to keep you in a southern state of mind.

High steppin' or laid back, there's fun for all the folks at this festive feast.

Enhancing the Estate

White wicker and floral prints are the perfect accompaniment to a pretty picnic. Fill your chairs with overstuffed floral-print cushions. Adorn the tables with pastel prints and pitchers filled with flowers. Jonquils, magnolias, or jasmine would be exquisite in this antebellum setting.

Chips and Tips

Contact dance schools or square dance clubs to find a square dance caller. These schools and clubs are often listed in the Yellow Pages. If not, call your reference librarian or your local parks and recreation department to put you in touch with a caller.

If you prefer a more masculine design, use tapestries with fox-hunt patterns or velvet skirting with heavy fringe. Accent the tableau with French horns, confederate hats and flags, stuffed foxes, bronze horses, and riding crops.

When the sun starts to set and fireflies light the night, burn citronella candles to discourage mosquitoes. Oil lamps and twinkle lights add a combination of authenticity and whimsy to your personal Tara.

Souvenirs of the South

As a gracious way to say, "Thanks for showin' up. Y'all come back now, heah," grace your guests with these southern-style somethings including a bottle of Southern Comfort, a bag of biscuits, or a CD of country classics.

Life with Father

He's your biggest hero, first love, fiercest protector, and the smartest man on earth … he's your father. And each year we are given one day to show him how much we love him.

Here's how you can honor this very special man on Father's Day or any day. Although this party plan is geared to a dad who loves fishing, it will serve as an outline for whatever hobby suits your dad's fancy.

Unless he's the one who brings in the mail or checks it daily, locate the place that your dad is most likely to find your invitation.

Festive Facts

In 1966 Lyndon Johnson signed a presidential proclamation that the third Sunday in June was to be Father's Day, and Richard Nixon established it as a national observance in 1972. To you, however, one day a year isn't often enough to say "Thanks, Dad."

Draw a fish shape on cardboard, cut it out, and decorate it like his favorite fish. Write your invitation on it with wording like this: "No need to fish for compliments. We reel-y think you're the best, Dad. Hope you fall for the bait and join us …."

A "fishy" invitation.

Fisherman's Feast

If you and Father the Fisherman had a successful early outing at his favorite fishing hole, then the best part of the day is getting to eat the fresh catch. If not, purchase your fish fare at the market or a nearby seafood store.

Not only does fish taste best when it's grilled and eaten outdoors, it also leaves the odor outside of your house, so by all means plan on a barbecue.

Serve grilled fillets, skewered shrimp, or stuffed clams—whatever you caught or purchased.

If cooking is not possible, what else could you serve to dad? A *hero sandwich,* of course! Load it with seafood salad to follow the theme. It's a meal he can wrap his hands around. For a large crowd, order the "big sandwich," sometimes six feet long from your local deli or Subway sandwich shop.

No matter the menu, let dad enjoy it in his favorite easy chair, hammock, or at the dining room table set with the "good dishes and glasses" usually reserved for special company. Let him know there's no one more special than him, your admired angler.

Antics and Activities

Besides fishing, indulge dad in the recreation of his choice, or put together an afternoon of leisure activities you know he'll love.

Sit with him and watch the game of his choice or rent a classic "dad" movie such as *Life with Father, Father's Day, Parenthood, Mr. Mom,* or *Father of the Bride.* Otherwise, if he prefers, he can watch movies made by "other action heroes" like Bruce, Arnold, or Sylvester.

Decorating the Lion's Den

Since it's said a man's home is his castle, why not decorate it to look like one? Use some of these ideas to give dad the royal treatment. Perch a toy crown on the back of his favorite chair, tie napkins with fishing line and decorative flies or sinkers, serve food in lined, wicker fishing baskets or fill his minnow bucket with ice to cool his drink.

Make the room as comfortable and regal as you would to suit the king that he is.

Chips and Tips

To remove the smell of fish from your hands, rub them with lemon juice and wash as usual with warm, soapy water.

Shindig Sayings

In New York a sandwich made with French or Italian bread, cold cuts or salads, and toppings (lettuce, tomato, onions, peppers, olives, etc.) is called a **hero sandwich** or wedge. In New England it's a grinder, while in Philadelphia it's called a hoagie. The folks in New Orleans call it a muffaletta. Those on the West Coast call it a submarine, or sub, for short.

Festive Facts

Mark Twain wrote, "When I was a boy of 14, my father was so ignorant I could hardly stand to have the old man around. But when I got to be 21, I was astonished at how much the old man had learned in seven years."

Alms for a King

Give dad reminders of his very special day and to tell him that even though you may not show it, every day is Father's Day by writing or reading a poem about fathers, create a crown for him, make a coupon book for you to do his chores, or give him a magazine subscription of his favorite hobby.

Red, White, and Blue Barbecue Blowouts

Pick a patriotic summer holiday—Memorial Day, Independence Day, Labor Day—and bring the folks together for a red, white, and blue barbecue.

For these most festive of holidays, display your colors. This is a great way to show off that you're proud to be an American! From the red, white, and blue food to red- and white-hot blues music, this party will have them standing to salute.

Attach the invitation wording to a small flag, roll, and send in a mailing tube. If you want, this is a great project to recycle cardboard tubes from paper towels and wrapping paper. You can paint the cardboard or cover it with decorative paper. Glue small cloth or paper squares to seal the ends of the tube.

All-American Meal

No one will doubt the occasion when they spy this patriotic bounty of red, white, and blue food and drink choices.

Chips and Tips

Clear the area of any bills or anything that might serve as a reminder of chores that need to be done once this "King for a Day" celebration is over.

Chips and Tips

Although this event is planned for a USA celebration, the concept can be easily transformed to match the colors of other countries.

172

Welcome your guests with a Blue Hawaii cocktail. It's made from one part each rum, cream, Cointreau, and Blue Curacao. You also can offer white piña coladas or red Rum Runners. For the kids, serve pink lemonade dyed red, or white lemonade dyed blue. And before dinner, put out bowls of white and blue corn chips with red salsa.

Nothing beats a refreshingly spicy and chilly gazpacho or cold and creamy blue-potato soup on a hot day. If you prefer salad to soup, make fruit salad with white grapefruit sections, red grapefruit sections, Red Delicious apple slices, strawberries, pitted cherries, and blueberries.

For your main dish, what else would you do but fire up the grill and cook a batch of blue crabs, red snapper, lobsters, or shrimp? You can add a dollop of blue cheese and turn any rare beef or lamb dish into a red, white, and blue featured selection.

For side dishes, serve grilled red peppers; red- and white-bean salad; beets; red, white, and blue potato salad; blueberry muffins; tomato salad; red potatoes boiled in their skins and topped with blue cheese dressing; or red beans and rice.

For a flag-waving feast finale, fill a bowl with scoops of vanilla, strawberry, and blueberry ice cream.

Strike Up the Band

For entertainment while you eat, play a collection of music from George M. Cohan and John Philip Sousa. The music's lively, and they are great to sing along with or march to. If singing's not your thing, put together an all-kazoo band.

Other music that is also distinctly American is jazz and Dixieland. And don't forget red- and white-hot blues to heat things up after the sun goes down.

As a preamble to the festivities or as a rainy day alternative, have a video viewing of *Stars and Stripes Forever*, *1776*, or *Yankee Doodle Dandy*.

For less-musical entertainment you could try, ask your guests to tell the crowd why they're proud to be an American or to pick a person from history and tell why he or she is a hero to them, help the kids make and fly red, white and blue kites, or play a lively game of softball or volleyball.

Chips and Tips

Want to keep your mayonnaise-based salads or other picnic foods chilled and fresh longer? Nest a slightly smaller plastic bowl into a larger one. Put some heavy soup cans into the smaller bowl for weight. Fill the space between the two bowls with water. Freeze, then remove the cans and fill the interior bowl with your favorite prechilled salad. The ice will keep the dressing cold and help avoid spoilage.

Party Pitfall

For a holiday picnic, plan to see the fireworks at a municipal event. Don't play with firecrackers yourself. These seemingly small explosives are powerful enough to blow off a finger or two or cause blindness.

Don't lose sight of the purpose of these parties. Remember those who fought so that we could enjoy the freedom and celebration of these days.

Shindig Sayings

Even today, gents wear a flat straw hat or **skimmer** to keep the sun off their heads and faces. Mostly associated with Dixieland and Gay Nineties dappers (sharply dressed fellows), they are a theme-party staple.

Flying the Flag

No patriotic party decorations would be complete without flying our flag of freedom. Show off your colors proudly. You can even place an old flag on the table and cover it in clear plastic for a patriotic display.

Use these celebrations as opportunities to use the red napkins or tablecloth you purchased at the after-Christmas sales. Try some of these other ideas to spark a patriotic tone. Tie your red napkins with white and blue ribbon, turn plastic *skimmers* into bowls, float helium filled patriotic balloons, criss-cross blue and white ribbon on your red tablecloth, and sprinkle small star-shaped confetti on your table.

Be true to the red, white, and blue, and that's all you need to do for a perfect patriotic party.

Patriotic Party Favors

To be sure your guests remember this patriotic party, send them home with copies of the Declaration of Independence, a CD collection of patriotic music, or jars of red, white, and blue jellybeans.

The Least You Need to Know

➤ Send Memorial Day invitations with packets of lemonade.

➤ Make dad's day special by giving him time out with his favorite foods.

➤ Use leftover red Christmas napkins for the perfect patriotic party.

➤ Marching music by John Philip Sousa makes the perfect Independence Day accompaniment.

Chapter 20

Fall Festivities

> **In This Chapter**
>
> ➤ A harvest moon blowout you'll swoon over
>
> ➤ The spookiest haunted Halloween party
>
> ➤ Plans for a truly stuffed Turkey Day
>
> ➤ Projects to entertain young Thanksgiving guests

Fall is a beautiful time of year spanning the last warm days of Indian summer to the clear and wintry crisp days of autumn. Exploding in an array of exquisite colors, the countryside gives us one last show before the trees shed their leaves and begin their rest through the long winter. Autumn also is the beginning of the end-of-year array of holiday parties.

Use the ideas in this chapter to throw the perfect autumn fest. These parties are easy to follow, and easier (and less expensive) to host because they all start with a set of decorations that get added to or subtracted from for each type of party, but remain primarily intact throughout the season.

Autumn Leaves and Harvest Moon Ball

We "be-leaf" they'll want to come to your party when they get your autumn party invitations. Use a large real leaf to outline a design, print your wording, then splatter fall-colored watercolor paint on the design to resemble a fall leaf.

Bountiful Harvest

When the weather starts to chill, there's nothing so welcome as the stick-to-your-ribs warmth of a bowl of soup. Try warming up this crowd with pumpkin soup, of course!

An autumn leaf invitation.

We
be-leaf
you'll want to
come to our
party!

Saturday, September 29
1 p.m. to 6 p.m.
Joe & Ruth's
284 Belmont, East Madison
Apple & Leaf Gathering

R.S.V.P. by September 15
(888) 555-2704

Outdoor Casual   Luncheon

To begin your meal you'll want to try an appetizer of *crostini* topped with herb-roasted garlic and apple chutney.

Shindig Sayings

In Italian, **crostini** means "little toasts." These thin slices of Italian bread are brushed with olive oil and toasted. They're then covered with a variety of toppings.

While your guests are munching on crostini, they'll also be enjoying the smells wafting from the Crock-Pot, where you've cooked up a big batch of chili or hearty beef stew. Using the Crock-Pot will also free you to join your family and friends for a walk in the woods to see what Ma Nature has served up.

Serve corn bread with chili or crusty Italian bread with stew. Zucchini and pumpkin bread are also great choices with either main dish.

Garnish the chili or stew with corn chips and serve in individual bowls.

Serve heated apple cider in mugs with cinnamon-stick stirrers. If you want, you can add applejack or spiced rum to your cider for an added kick. And for the big ending, serve baked apples with vanilla ice cream.

Fall Frolicking

Since fall weather is still warm enough for outings, the perfect entertainment is the season itself. Gather everyone together to go check out the fall foliage. You might want to drive to an area where the colors are particularly spectacular. Then go for a hike and gather a variety of leaves, branches, cattails, Chinese lanterns, nuts, and berries to create enough decorations to last the season.

And while you're out, don't forget to pick out your pumpkin or fresh apples. Keeping fresh fruits and vegetables, including your pumpkins, in a cool, dry place will help them last through all your favorite fall holidays, even Thanksgiving. Or combine food and fun by making caramel or candy apples, or baked pumpkins. You could even get a press and make your own apple cider.

Revel in the last days of summer or the invigorating first days of fall, but most of all just enjoy good times with your guests!

Fall Festoons and Autumn Adornments

To jump-start your decorations with a fall focus, cover your table with a gold, burnt orange, red, brown, or bronze tablecloth, runner, or place mats.

On a tray or platter, put out a collection of autumn leaves. While you can use the ones you found on your hike, the preserved leaves you buy in craft shops or florists will last longer. On top of the leaves, artfully set a collection of small gourds and pumpkins, or place a large pumpkin in the center of the table with a number of smaller ones around it. Tuck in dried branches of wheat or Chinese lanterns, nuts, and berries into the arrangement. Periodically test to see that the pumpkin and gourds haven't begun to soften. Once they do, dispose of them and replace.

Here are a few other ideas to create a autumnal atmosphere. Top your curtains with grapevines, recover your pillows in a fall-themed fabric, heat orange peels with water for an inviting scent, or fill baskets with pine cones and leaves.

Reaping the Rewards

To give them warm reminders of these good times during the long, cold winter, present your guests with bags of apples, potted marigolds or packets of toasted pumpkin seeds.

Chips and Tips

Cut all the vegetables and meat for the stew into bite-sized pieces. This way, even if the meal is served as a stand-up buffet, it won't require anything other than a fork to eat.

Party Pitfall

Fall weather changes quickly. What seems like a warm fall day can suddenly turn bitterly cold. Make sure all the hikers are properly clothed with an extra sweater or sweatshirt on hand.

Chips and Tips

If you find yourself with more apples than you know what to do with, slice and dry them using a food dehydrator or oven method. It's much less expensive and healthier than the dry fruits you buy and eat as snacks.

Chips and Tips

If you have silk floral arrangements around your house, give them autumn appeal by adding a couple of dried sprigs of wheat, Chinese lanterns, or berries.

Party Pitfall

Touching dry ice directly with you hand will cause burns. When handling dry ice, make sure you use oven mitts or leather gloves.

Haunted Halloween

Out of the darkness spirits lurk to spin an evening of fright guaranteed to raise chills and goosebumps on all who enter your haunted mansion.

And to get those brave souls to enter your spooky home, you need to send an invitation that will spark interest in even the most cowardly. Create an obituary or newspaper story in the *Tombstone Gazette* describing the death of an unnamed guest to take place at the party. Ask your friends if they're brave enough to come find out who the victim might be.

Goblin Goodies

While you can serve whatever you would like to your Halloween guests, here are a couple of ideas that will turn them all into guests of horror.

Greet your friends with a cup of punch in a black plastic witch's cauldron made more deadly-looking by this frightening ice form. Begin by cleaning out latex gloves and filling them with green-colored water, then seal with a twist tie. Place the gloves on a cookie sheet and freeze. Once frozen, the gloves will easily slip off the ice. As the ice melts in the punch, the green dye will make it change to a more "toxic-looking" combination.

Add raisins (bugs) and peeled seedless grapes (eyes) and perch gummy worms on the sides of the punch bowl.

For an added kick, place dry ice in a tray under the cauldron. Camouflage the tray and tell your guests to drink at their own risk.

Offer up Bloody Brains as an appetizer (raw cauliflower broken into flowerettes and served with a red-colored dipping sauce).

For gourmet ghouls, cook up a batch of black linguine. Available in specialty stores, the pasta is made black by the ink of squid. Ladle on your favorite tomato sauce, stuffed Spanish olives, and pearl onions (eyes). If you prefer, toss the linguine with olive oil, roasted garlic, and capers (bugs).

For dessert serve orange sherbet or frozen pumpkin pudding inside hollowed-out minipumpkins.

Festive Facts

It is said that the history of Halloween dates back hundreds of years to the Celts, a group of people who worshipped nature and had many gods. The Celts celebrated their New Year on November 1. On the eve before their new year (October 31), it was believed that all the dead people were called together, the bad spirits taking the form of animals. The most evil spirits were said to take the form of cats.

The Tombstone Gazette.

Tombstone Gazette

Vol. 13   Dead Man Publications

Ghost Gala

Guests are wondering if they'll be in Death's notebook when he arrives at the Ghost Gala on Saturday, October 31.

The party is being touted as a who's who of the Renaissance festival society by event host, Bobby Rodriguez.

Will Death take a holiday when the party producer puts together the Happy Halloween party of the decade? Or will the celebration be short a guest or two at the end of the evening?

You are invited to find out for yourself -- if you dare.

It's a short broom flight from anywhere. Meet your host or meet your maker at Casa El Diablo on Cemetary Court. The Gala starts at 9 and continues past the witching hour.

A full selection of delectable will be served.

Rodriguez tells guests that the party will be a scream.

Hopefully the one screaming won't be you!

Death Is On Guest List for Party

Chips and Tips

When serving spaghetti, linguine, or other long pasta on a buffet, break it in half before cooking to make it easier to eat.

Chips and Tips

Instead of carving pumpkins, an easier option is to decorate them with markers, glitter pens, or tape pieces. You might just lay out a variety of craft supplies and let guests create their own creepy creatures.

Dead Man's Dance and Ghostly Gambol

Frighten your guests as they approach your haunted home by playing *Sounds Abound on All Hallows Eve* (www.doglake.com) for a masterful mix of monstrous music, scary sounds, and tales of terror.

Keep the aural environment going inside, too, as the revelers are greeted by the Grim Reaper, Frankenstein, or other horrible hosts.

If you want to have a scary activity for young kids, show them a bowl each of fish eyes, worms, and goldfish. Then blindfold them and tell them you want them to feel around and eat one of the things in the bowl. Substitute a bowl filled with peeled grapes, short pieces of fat pasta coated in oil, and canned peaches without syrup and floating in water. Then have them hold their nose (it diminishes the ability to taste), pick one item, and swallow.

For an older crowd, you can give everyone a pumpkin and a sharp knife and hold a contest for the best jack-o'-lantern.

Here's a fun activity for kids of all ages. Pair the guests up and give each team a roll of toilet paper. The object of the game is to wrap your partner completely with the entire roll of toilet paper like a mummy.

Festive Facts

Although Halloween traditions started in Europe, today it is celebrated much more widely on this side of the Atlantic. In England, every November 5, Guy Fawkes Day is celebrated. Instead of trick or treating, children light bonfires and burn Fawkes in effigy for his attempt to blow up the English Parliament in 1605.

Don't forget: No Halloween party is complete without a costume contest, dancing to "The Monster Mash," or a reading of a ghost stories such as *The Legend of Sleepy Hollow*. You can even try *Goosebumps* for the younger crowd.

Decked Out for Doom

No self-respecting haunted mansion would be complete without a cemetery. Create your own ghastly graveyard by making a collection of tombstones. You can use wood or insulating foam blocks found in home-improvement stores. Draw the styles you want and cut out with a jigsaw, sharp knife, or handsaw. Paint your headstones gray, write epitaphs, and season them with dirt, glue, moss, and other aging effects.

If you have a high ceiling and fan, tie a small ghost to one of the blades and set the fan on low. It will look as if the ghost is flying around the room.

Drape gray sheets or drop cloths over your furniture to give your place the look of an abandoned home. (Besides, it has the added bonus of keeping your furniture clean from spillage during the party.) If you don't want to cover everything, at least cover your buffet table. Make sure you have candelabras draped with spider webs and sprinkle the table with plastic bugs and spiders.

If you have uplights in your home, buy orange or red light bulbs. Position the lights under trees or plants so that they not only cast a shadow of the branches, the plants will be tinted in orange or blood red for a more eerie look.

Scary Souvenirs

When you send your guests home with their trick or treat bags, don't fill them only with candy. Try candy apples, Halloween-themed stickers or their own sound-effects tape.

Party Pitfall

Use only water-based paint on Styrofoam. Any other type of paint will cause the foam to melt. If you are not sure, test a small piece before using the product or ask at your craft store for the paint brand that would work best.

Chips and Tips

If you are having young children at your party and you don't want to have lit candles in your pumpkins, you can either use battery-operated lighted disks or strings of twinkle lights. You can also use battery-operated taper candles.

Chips and Tips

Picnic coolers work well to keep foods and beverages cold or hot. If you need extra space, wrap your meal well in leak-proof containers and keep on ice. If you live in cold country, your back porch or deck will serve as a roomy cooler. Or, if you have dishes you need to keep warm, cover well and wrap in towels for additional insulation and put into an empty cooler.

Chips and Tips

If there aren't a lot of children or they are widely differing ages, give them a chore to do in the kitchen: making the salad, washing the vegetables, folding the napkins—something to teach them a skill and keep them busy. Then make a fuss over their accomplishment during dinner.

Let's Talk Turkey

When the pilgrims landed in the New World, they began a celebration tradition to give thanks for their new home and good harvest. History has it that they shared their bounty with Native Americans. Today, Thanksgiving is a time we gather to give thanks for our good fortunes with our friends and family. Follow this plan and your guests will be truly thankful they were invited to your Thanksgiving celebration.

Create your invitation using pilgrim and autumn leaf clip art designs and write how thankful you'll be if they join you.

Bountiful Harvest

The best meals are those that share in your family's heritage—Mom's sausage stuffing, Aunt Rosie's breaded asparagus, Aunt Josie's potato salad, your mother-in-law's applesauce cake or gravy, or your cousin Dora's gelatin mold. A few phone calls will undoubtedly get you all the recipes you need to put on a Thanksgiving feast just like Mom's.

You may choose to start your own traditions, or you might want to prepare a totally meatless meal. Either way the bounty that you are grateful for will be the people who sit at your table or who can't be with you in any way except in your heart.

Keep an extra supply of disposable pie pans or plastic containers to send your guests home with leftovers.

Half-Time Show

In most homes, like it or not, it will be difficult to get any of the men (and some of the women) involved in something other than a football game. However, since the children need something to keep them busy, here are some ideas. Play touch football, have the children gather leaves for your table, make turkeys from pinecones and pipe cleaners or put together a kazoo band to play "Turkey in the Straw." At dinner, ask each guest to tell something they're grateful for.

Festooning in Fall Fashion

To recycle the fall decorations you made earlier in the season, you only need to discard the cobwebs and spiders from your base designs. Add pilgrims, Native Americans, or turkeys to the collection to give it a Thanksgiving look.

Rather than a large centerpiece, scatter beautiful leaves down the center of your table, add gourds, pumpkins, sprays of fall flowers, grapevines, and candles in various heights.

To dress up each place setting, tie each napkin and stemware with raffia. If you want to add uniformity to thrift shop or other nonmatching utensils, wrap a length of ribbon around the handles.

To help each guest find his or her seat, carve or write the guest's name on a minipumpkin or gourd to use as a place card.

Go beyond table decorations by tying the back of each chair with raffia and a sprig of autumn leaves, an ear of corn, or a cattail.

If you are serving a meal that is made up of recipes from family members or friends, or if someone brought a dish, put out a menu card listing their contributions.

Don't forget to put out the turkey, pilgrim, and Native American salt and pepper shakers and other Thanksgiving-related doodads you've collected over the years.

Chips and Tips

While it's often customary to have all food platters and bowls on the table, if space is a consideration, set up your ironing board nearby. Drape it in fabric and use as a temporary buffet so people can get their second helpings. Then once dinner is over, fold it up and reclaim your space!

Chips and Tips

After the holiday, put out the ears of Indian corn in your yard or a nearby park for the birds and squirrels to eat.

Turkey Tokens

In addition to the leftovers you'll invariably send home with your guests and the projects the kids have made, here are some other things you might want to give to say "I'm thankful for you." Choose a small pot of mums, a turkey- or pumpkin-shaped magnet, or baskets of dried fruits.

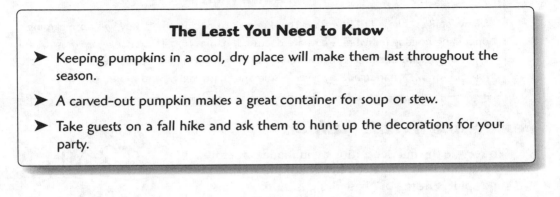

The Least You Need to Know

➤ Keeping pumpkins in a cool, dry place will make them last throughout the season.

➤ A carved-out pumpkin makes a great container for soup or stew.

➤ Take guests on a fall hike and ask them to hunt up the decorations for your party.

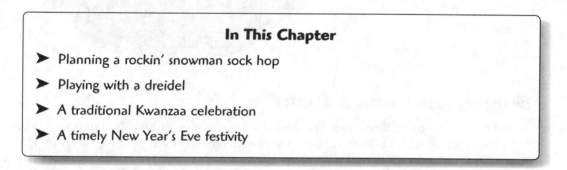

Chapter 21

Happy Holidays

In This Chapter

➤ Planning a rockin' snowman sock hop

➤ Playing with a dreidel

➤ A traditional Kwanzaa celebration

➤ A timely New Year's Eve festivity

The end of the year is almost a blur with the wide array of parties happening almost every night. To make sure all your celebrations stand out, we've created four totally terrific holiday parties to help you celebrate Christmas, Hanukkah, New Year's, and Kwanzaa in singularly spectacular and unforgettable fashion.

Read on and you'll find tips for decorations that stand out, terrific food, and entertainment that everyone will love. With party plans like this, you'll guarantee your holidays to be a smashing success.

Snowman Sock Hop

They'll be rockin' around the Christmas tree at this snowman's sock hop. You'll love this event because it takes the fun of a fabulous '50s party and puts a holiday spin on it. You and your guests will wish it was December all year long!

Put the stress on the hop rather than the sock, by affixing your invitation to a 45 record label. Decorate the envelope with holiday stickers.

A snowman sock hop invitation.

Friday
December 20
8 p.m. to Midnight
"SNOWMAN SOCK HOP"

Come in
'50s
Fashion

Dinner
&
Drinks

by
Michael and Carol
49 Bay Drive
RSVP 555-5982

Burger, Fries, and a Shake

The 1950s—now, those were the days, a time when most folks had never even heard the word *cholesterol*. To bring back that sweet naïveté, plan your menu around the '50s favorite foods: burgers, pizza, fries, chips and dip, popcorn, Cokes, and shakes.

To give your dishes a real '50s flip, find some old 45s, preferably from that era. Slip a disk into a red or green party plate so the colored rim shows through. Put a clear plastic plate on top of that and you'll have a leak-proof dish with a rock-and-roll holiday design.

Chips and Tips

Don't forget to place two straws in your drink—one for you and one for your honey.

Talk about eating off "The Platters"! You can even cover old 78s with plastic wrap and use these as serving platters or charger plates under your dishes. Likewise, cover '50s record album jackets and use them as serving trays on the buffet table. You can find scratched records for pennies at most thrift stores.

Dig through items at garage sales and flea markets to find old Coke glasses. Replicas also are available for sale at some specialty stores. In them, you can serve ice cream floats (softened vanilla ice cream in a glass slowly filled with Coke). Call your Coca-Cola distributor to arrange to buy the drink in individual-serving glass bottles.

Festive Facts

Although still an icon almost 50 years after his death, James Dean had major roles in only three movies—*East of Eden, Rebel Without a Cause,* and *Giant*. One of only five actors to ever receive an Academy Award nomination for his first movie, he died in a car accident on September 30, 1955 at age 24. It's prophetic that he once said, "Dream as if you'll live forever. Live as if you'll die today."

You absolutely have to have a pink party punch. What's in the punch doesn't matter, but it has to be a bright pink! If you have some "hoods" at the party (think James Dean in *Rebel Without a Cause* or Marlon Brando in *The Wild Ones*), you probably can have one of them sneak some rum into the drinks.

Rockin' Around the Christmas Tree

Roll into the opening activity and decorate the tree, or, weather permitting, build a snowman.

After the tree decorating, snowman building, and carol singing you need to spin some disks, so get yourself "Rockin' Around the Christmas Tree" by Brenda Lee or play "Blue Christmas" by Elvis Presley. There are lots of holiday albums from that time by artists of that era like Frank Sinatra, Burl Ives, Bing Crosby, Perry Como, and Johnny Mathis. Or, you can just play good "make-out" music.

Since most teenage parties turned into make-out sessions, you will have to make sure this party comes with something no self-respecting '50s party could have been without—a chaperone! That's right, you need to bring in a chaperone to make sure that the boys and girls don't dance too close. ("Leave enough room for the Holy Spirit" was a favorite reproach of Catholic nuns.) For fun, see if your parents are willing to take on the job of '50s chaperone. (This is particularly funny if you are adults.)

For those who don't enjoy the dancing, try sing-alongs, or have some of the guys compete in an *a capella* doo-wop contest or host a Marilyn Monroe, Elvis, James Dean, or Marlon Brando look-alike competition. And finally, twinkle-toes or not, everyone must get up to do "The Twist."

Shindig Sayings

To sing **a capella** means to sing without instrumental accompaniment.

187

Decking the Diner

Having a snowman or the beginnings of one on your front lawn is the perfect decoration, but if you can't have one you'll need to at least have a Christmas tree.

Shindig Sayings

Angel hair is spun white fiberglass that is draped on the tree like tinsel. It was used to give the tree a soft glow.

Christmas trees in the '50s had tons of tinsel (each strand carefully placed) or *angel hair* and plain red and green ornaments or fancy blown glass ones. The tree lights were large and brightly colored, not like the small twinkle lights used today. Tie red licorice in bows for another sweet memory.

There are lots of old and replica trays made for Coca-Cola bearing the famous St. Nick image. These would be particularly fun to have for this '50s Christmas sock hop.

Instead of large tables, it would be fun to have 36" round cocktail tables set like a soda shop. As a centerpiece or buffet-table arrangement, put a plain white canvas sneaker with red-and-green shoelaces, tied with jingle bells, on the table covered in a red or green cloth. Place a water glass inside a red or green sock and stuff it in the shoe. Tie or pin a bow with a jingle bell on the sock. Fill the glass with straws or candy canes. Adorn your room with lights and pictures of '50s movie stars.

Festive Facts

Artist Haddon H. Sundblom created his famous painting of Santa in 1931 showing him with rosy cheeks, red nose, bright blue eyes, and red-and-white costume for a Coca-Cola ad. The popular depiction of the "jolly old elf" was created to sell more soft drinks. The campaign was so popular that this commercial drawing created and sustains our contemporary Santa image.

Out of Santa's Sack

It wouldn't be a Christmas party without presents, so give your guests personalized Santa hats, jingle bells, and Christmas jewelry.

Remember, the best gift you can give during happy days is yourself.

Menorahs and Dreidels

Although a minor holiday on the Jewish calendar, Hanukkah has come to mean a time when Jews, like the Christians, can join with their family and friends to remember a miracle.

In the time when the ancient Greeks oppressed the Jews and banned the lighting of the temple candles, the Maccabees banned together and eventually defeated their tyrants and rededicated the Jerusalem Temple. In celebration they lit one of the temple lamps. Despite only having enough oil to keep the lamp lit for one night, it stayed lit for eight nights. Hanukkah, the Festival of Lights, is the holiday which remembers that miracle by lighting a menorah over an eight-day period, one candle for each night.

Shindig Sayings

Bubbe is Yiddish (a Jewish-German dialect) for grandmother.

To begin your Hanukkah celebration, ask family and friends to join you to light the menorah's candles. On a plain invitation, draw a menorah on the front cover. Hot-glue the Shamash—the middle candle which is lit first and lights the others—in place and ask your guests to pray with you as you light the Shamash and your first night's candle (or whatever night applies) on your menorah.

Mama's Kitchen

For a meal that tastes as if your mama or *bubbe* made it, you will love this traditional Hanukkah menu.

Chopped liver and gefilte fish serve as your appetizers for this special meal. You'll then enjoy chicken soup and matzo balls or beef and barley soup. The main course for this feast is a brisket of beef topped with homemade apple or horseradish sauce, or you can enjoy a roasted turkey with mushroom stuffing.

Shindig Sayings

Potato latkes are potato pancakes made with grated potatoes, eggs, onions, matzo meal, and spices. **Kasha varnishkes** are roasted buckwheat grouts with bow-tie noodles and chicken stock. **Challah** is a traditional Jewish bread, airy and rich with eggs.

On the side, you must have the traditional *potato latkes* (potato pancakes made with grated potatoes, eggs, onions, matzo meal, and spices), green beans and sautéed onions, *kasha varnishkes* (roasted buckwheat grouts with bow-tie noodles and chicken stock), beets, and *challah* (traditional Jewish bread, airy and rich with eggs).

For dessert, *kugel* (baked pudding served as a side dish with noodles, or as a dessert when raisins, nuts, and sweet spices are added), *blinis* (small buckwheat pancakes usually served with sour cream and smoked salmon or caviar), and *loukoumades* (fried honey puffs). A sweet wine often accompanies this meal.

Songs and Stories

The most important part of the Hanukkah celebration is lighting the menorah. This is the significant religious observance of the holiday. When possible, children who are going to temple school or who have learned the prayers are given the privilege of lighting the menorah and leading the group in prayer.

In addition to the gifts often exchanged, it would be great fun to have the children take parts and perform the story of the Syrians and the Maccabees. They could also read the story or the adults could take turns reading poems.

Another part of the evening is the game where children spin the dreidel. You can help the children form the top out of clay, or you can try the following method.

Get a small square box—a pint milk box would work—and fold down the top so it stays flat. You might have to cut or staple it, but try to get it flat. Paint the box and draw these symbols:

➤ *Nun*—the first letter of the word *nes*, which means "miracle."

➤ *Gimel*—the first letter of *gadol*, which means "great."

➤ *Hay*—the first letter of *haya*, which means "was."

➤ *Shin*—the first letter of *sham*, which means "there."

In Israel it would spell out "A Great Miracle Happened Here."

To get the top to spin, poke a sharpened pencil or chopstick through the box from the top through the bottom so the point sticks out the bottom. You can use the top end of the stick or pencil to spin the dreidel.

There are numerous games associated with the spinning of the dreidel. Here is one of the most popular.

All the players are given an equal number of pennies, raisins, or gelt(chocolate coins). Each player puts one token in the pot.

The youngest child spins the dreidel first. The letter that is facing up determines what the child is to do:

Shindig Sayings

Kugel is baked pudding with raisins, nuts, and sweet spices. **Blinis** are small buckwheat pancakes usually served with sour cream and smoked salmon or caviar. **Loukoumades** are fried honey puffs.

Nun: Player does nothing

Gimel: Player takes all the tokens in the pot

Hay: Player takes half the tokens in the pot

Shin: Player must put one token in the pot

Decorations and Dreidels

Let the children get involved in making your home ready for the holiday. They can cut and color the Star of David, dreidels, gelt, and menorahs and hang them strung together around your party site or on the back's of chairs.

Here's a recycling project for you or your children. Save six tubes from paper towels and spray paint them silver. With a hot-glue gun, connect three of the tubes into a triangle. Make a second triangle. Place one triangle on the center of your table. Set the other triangle on top with the point facing the opposite direction to form a Star of David. Run blue ribbons through the tubes, and cut them so they are draping at least six inches off the end of the table.

Let the children make a menorah using alphabet blocks, metal nuts sized to fit small Hanukkah candles, a box of small Hanukkah candles, and a hot-glue gun. Spell out C-H-A-N-U-K-A-H or H-A-N-U-K-K-A-H and glue the blocks together. Place a nut on each block with an extra one in the center for the Shamash and glue.

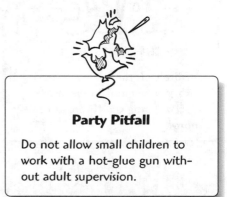

Party Pitfall

Do not allow small children to work with a hot-glue gun without adult supervision.

Letting the Tradition Live On

To create the warm memories of a lifetime of religious pride, family unity, and fun, give each guest a small menorah, a bag of gelt or a toy dreidel.

The light you will ignite in their hearts will last much longer than eight days.

Kwanzaa—The Symbol of Hope and Remembrance

Back in 1966, during a period of great civil unrest for the African-American community, Dr. Maulana Ron Karenga introduced a festival called Kwanzaa (Kishwahili for "first harvest"). She hoped the event would spark pride and create a sense of self-esteem and spiritual development among the nation's African-American population.

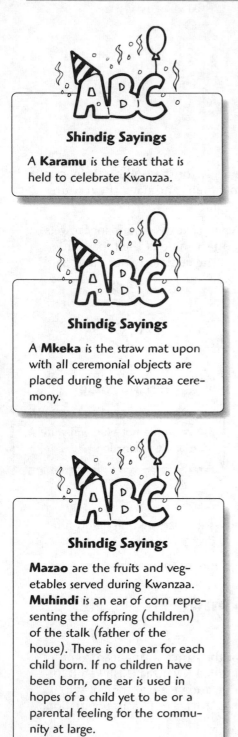

Shindig Sayings

A **Karamu** is the feast that is held to celebrate Kwanzaa.

Shindig Sayings

A **Mkeka** is the straw mat upon with all ceremonial objects are placed during the Kwanzaa ceremony.

Shindig Sayings

Mazao are the fruits and vegetables served during Kwanzaa. **Muhindi** is an ear of corn representing the offspring (children) of the stalk (father of the house). There is one ear for each child born. If no children have been born, one ear is used in hopes of a child yet to be or a parental feeling for the community at large.

The festival, which runs from December 26 through January 1, is based upon seven principles to coincide with the weeklong celebration. On December 31st, a *Karamu* (feast) is held to bring the community together to celebrate accomplishments and to give thanks to the Creator for his gifts.

Prepare the invitation for your own Kwanzaa celebration in traditional black, green, and red colors and roll it into a *Mkeka* (straw mat) upon which all the ceremonial objects would be placed in the ceremony.

Feast to Give Thanks

Much of this celebration is symbolic, and the food served is very much a part of tradition.

On a Mkeka serve a feast of *Mazao* (fruits and vegetables) and *Muhindi* (ears of corn). These are eaten to give hope to the future.

Also, on part of the Mkeka are dishes from all the nations of Africa such as leg of lamb, grilled shrimp, chicken, black-eyed peas, salad, and bread. Dessert might be southern-style pecan pie to remember the ancestors who lived as slaves.

Kikombe cha Umoja is the unity cup used to toast African-American ancestors. The libation placed in it is drunk by each member of the immediate and extended family. It also is used as a pledge to continue the struggles endured by their forefathers and a commitment to the future.

Designs of Our Past

In addition to African fabrics and artwork, there are very special symbols of the Kwanzaa celebration. In many ways, the *Kinara* (special candleholder) is reminiscent of a menorah. On the Kinara, there are seven candles—three red, three green, and one black, the colors of the African flag. One is lit for each night of the festival.

Starting on the day after Christmas, each day's candle (*Mshumaa*) symbolizes a different goal: *Umoja* (unity), *Kujichagulia* (self-determination), *Ujima* (collective work and responsibility), *Ujamaa* (cooperative economics), *Nia* (purpose), *Ukuumba* (creativity), and *Imani* (faith).

Celebrations of Our Heritage

At the Karamu, there is much singing and dancing in the way of the African ancestors. Tales are told of past accomplishments and praising the heroism of those that came before. The focus should be on traditional African entertainment rather than anything that would further represent the west.

Zwadi are the gifts that are given by the parents to reward their offspring. These should be educational or artistic in style. The giving and opening of the gifts is also a part of the celebration.

Symbols to Remember

To help remind all who participate in the Kwanzaa celebration, give them token Zwadi such as books of African history, red, green and black painted nuts or pieces of African art.

While Kwanzaa, this uniquely African-American holiday, is celebrated during the week between Christmas and New Year's Day, it is more than a festival. It is a way of life. It is a way to have African-Americans remember their past and to strive for a better future.

Shindig Sayings

Kikombe cha Umoja is the unity cup used during Kwanzaa to toast ancestors.

Shindig Sayings

Zwadi are the gifts that are given by the parents to reward their offspring.

Countdown to a New Year

Out with the old, in with the new—that's the idea behind a New Year's celebration. Father Time is clicking down toward midnight, but the fun starts well before then.

Here's a collection of old and new ideas that all spell a good time and guarantee excited guests.

To get the fun and excitement growing, send each guest a toy clock and put the invitation wording on it with the clock's hands pointing toward the hour your party will start or midnight.

Before It's Diet Time

Just about everyone resolves to start a diet on January first, so give them one last chance to indulge in some decadent delights.

To keep with the old and new theme, Father Time or Baby New Year, each of the menu items will feature timely or age-appropriate words in its name. Here are some ideas:

➤ OLD-fashioned roast turkey and giblet gravy

➤ MINUTE Rice

➤ BABY back ribs

➤ BABY carrots, corn and greens

➤ NEW potatoes

➤ MINUTE steak

➤ BABY Ruth candy bars

Label each dish on a card with a clock face design with the clock's hands pointing toward the dish.

They'll love every *minute* of this menu and will surely be asking for *seconds*.

Festive Facts

The concept of using a baby to signify a new year is not a recent one. As far back as 600 B.C.E in Greece, a baby was used in the new-year ceremonies. To celebrate Dionysus, the god of wine, a baby was paraded in a basket to symbolize the god's rebirth as the spirit of fertility. Records also show that Egyptians used a baby as a similar symbol for rebirth.

Rockin' Round the Clock

Have Father Time greet your guests upon arrival to remind them they have only a few more hours to party that year, so they better not waste a minute. Videotape guests giving their New Year's resolutions, to be viewed at a later date.

Play any game that has a time element in it. If you have to use an egg timer, stopwatch, or second hand, that game will fit into the overall theme.

Put together a music selection that has time in the title such as: "Time After Time," "Time is on My Side," "Rock Around the Clock," "My Grandfather's Clock," "Time in a Bottle," "For the Good Times," and "It Was a Very Good Year."

At midnight, be sure the New Year's baby makes an appearance to let everyone know what a good time they'll have that year.

Design Time

When it's *time* to decorate for the party, *watch* the fun begin as you *count down* the *minutes* and *clock* your guests' arrival for a good *time*.

Sundials and stopwatches, wall clocks and wristwatches, desk clocks and digital displays, analog and egg timers—if it tells time, show it off. Add wings to all the clocks to represent how time flies.

Synchronize all the clocks to the same time and set as many alarms as possible, so that when the New Year rings in, no one will be able to doubt it for a *second*.

Timely Gifts

So they'll be counting the *hours* until your next party, here are some gifts or prizes to remind them of their good *time: time*pieces, subscription to *Time* magazine, or egg *time*rs.

You need not worry about this party being a *time* bomb. Your guests will have the *time* of their lives.

The Least You Need to Know

➤ A snowman sock hop isn't complete without burgers, fries, and shakes.

➤ Include kids in helping to make Hanukkah decorations.

➤ Activities for Kwanzaa should be kept to traditional African-American entertainment.

➤ Clocks make the perfect decoration for a New Year's party.

Fighting the Winter Blues

You've barely recovered from the holiday festivities when it's time for another party! Just as surely as you'll be writing the wrong year for a couple of weeks, you are going to find yourself playing host to another spectacular celebration.

Whether it's a bowl game to keep the crowds cheering, the starry-eyed looks that tell you love is all around on Valentine's Day, or you have the luck of the Irish to throw a great St. Patrick's Day party, you know that this chapter will give you all the information you need to make your fete fabulous.

Bowl Game Gambol

Right behind Christmas and Thanksgiving, according to the National Football League, Super Bowl Sunday ranks as the third-largest occasion for Americans to consume food.

Americans will hold more parties in their homes on Super Bowl Sunday than any other day of the year, and you can be among them with these great ideas for inviting your guests. Or gather the gang for the Rose Bowl, Cotton Bowl, or Fiesta Bowl. Whatever it is, grab your jersey and cheer on your team!

Festive Facts

Super Bowl I, the first Super Bowl ever, was played January 15, 1967, at Memorial Coliseum in Los Angeles between the National Football League's Green Bay Packers and the just-founded American Football League's Kansas City Chiefs. The Packers won by a score of 35–10.

Box-Seat Tickets

As long as your television's working and the beer's on ice, don't worry, your guests will be waiting for an invitation to join the gang and root for the home team. However, that doesn't mean you can't have a little fun with the planning.

How else would you send out an invitation to a bowl game? That's right, you're learning … in a bowl! Buy a batch of inexpensive plastic bowls with lids, stuff them with the party info, label, seal, stamp, and send them from your local post office.

Feeding the Fans

The timing of the bowl game is going to greatly affect the specifics of what you are feeding your fans, but the basics will be the same.

No matter what meal you're serving, guys can't seem to watch football without having something to snack on. This is especially important if you are serving alcohol.

Chips and Tips

When the game is starting late, you might want to serve your meal beforehand instead of making everyone wait until halftime.

If you want to serve the main meal during halftime, that's fine, but put out light appetizers or chips and pretzels for games that run from early afternoon to evening.

Of course, you can theme your menu to the game. If it's the Fiesta Bowl, then Mexican cuisine is called for. Oranges would be a key ingredient in all the menu items for the Orange Bowl, a luau is perfect for the Hula Bowl or honor the regions the teams playing are from. For instance, if the New Orleans Saints are playing the Buffalo Bills, you might serve jambalaya and buffalo wings. Finally, of course, you may stick with the basics and offer hoagie sandwiches, pizza, chili, or barbecue ribs.

Scream for the Team

Obviously, your main function as host to a bowl game crowd is to keep the refreshments rolling and the TV set in working order. However, there are a couple of other things you can do to help the crowd really enjoy themselves.

To add to the festivity, mark everyone's name tag with the name of the team they're rooting for. Then as the game progresses, with each quarter, give a special prize to the fans whose team is leading. Prizes don't have to be anything expensive, just something to spur along the competition.

If you have a lot of spouses attending who are obviously not interested in the game, you might want to set up a TV in another room to play a movie or do something else to keep them amused while the game is on.

Show Your Team Colors

For many bowl games you won't be sure until a week or so before if your team will be playing. That sometimes makes it difficult to come up with decorations that are geared to those teams. To play it safe, you can go with a generic football decor and just add a couple of pieces to signify the two teams.

Turn your oblong buffet table into a football field. Cover it with a green tablecloth and use white tape to mark off the yard lines. Use mailing tubes or balloons to make the *goalposts* on the ends of the table. For fun, you might want to paint each goalpost to match the colors of the teams.

Make or buy team pennants, or if you are going to be hosting several of these events, keep them generic with writing that reads, "Go Team Go," "Score!", or any of a number of encouraging cheers. Team posters, footballs, shoulder pads, jerseys—any football-related item will add to the look.

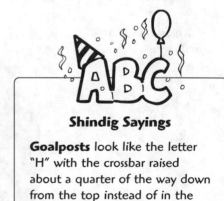

Shindig Sayings

Goalposts look like the letter "H" with the crossbar raised about a quarter of the way down from the top instead of in the middle.

To really get the crowd cheering, buy or make pom-poms in the team colors; it's a great activity for the kids that requires little more than crepe paper, scissors to cut the strips, and tape to attach them to a wooden dowel.

Stadium Souvenirs

Finally, send your guests home with trophies of their day such as team pennants, team t-shirts, or toy trophies for best fan.

The Celebration of Love

Valentine's Day is typically a day for sweethearts. However, this party could be a day of making love connections for friends who haven't quite found "the one." So dust off your wings and sharpen your arrows, because you're being cast in the role of Cupid.

Festive Facts

History says there may actually have been a real Valentine, a third-century priest who de-fied Emperor Claudius II's ban against wartime marriages. According to legend, Valentine performed secret marriages until he was discovered and put to death. However, there's another legend in which a persecuted Valentine had a secret correspondence to which he signed his name "your Valentine."

To begin your matchmaking plan, write your invitation, attach it to a red silk rose, and mail it in a long narrow box. Or make a paper Valentine for a heart-felt invitation.

A Valentine's Day invitation.

Give Cupid some help!
Valentine's Dinner
February 14
Cocktails at 7 Dinner at 8

Bring Your Own Bachelor or Bachelorette

Sharon and Glen
38 Maple Drive, Lawrence
RSVP - 555-8289

The best part of this party invitation is that it requires each person to bring along a member of the opposite sex, someone they are not romantically interested in. Your friends will all be playing matchmaker because even though Cupid's arrow missed them with this person, doesn't mean they won't be right for someone else. It's kind of a B.Y.O.B. event: Bring Your Own Bachelor(ette.)

The Way to Their Hearts

If the way to a person's heart is through his stomach, then this menu is one they'll love. In keeping with the Valentine's theme, the foods served are going to be red, pink, or white, or any food that is considered an *aphrodisiac*.

Something to keep in mind when planning your menu is that it's difficult to get to know someone when you're chewing heartily on a piece of fat-laden beef. Plan a meal that's light and tasty—filling, but without making you feel bloated.

Begin your matchmaking feast with a tray of oysters Rockefeller and watch the heat rise. Or tempt your young lovers with red caviar on toast points with a dollop of low-fat sour cream.

Fondue is a food of love, especially when someone else feeds it to you. In fact, if you prefer to have an evening of finger foods instead of dinner, a fondue is a great way to serve your guests something hot with very little effort on your part. It's also a food that is truly fun to eat.

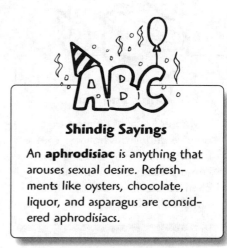

Shindig Sayings

An **aphrodisiac** is anything that arouses sexual desire. Refreshments like oysters, chocolate, liquor, and asparagus are considered aphrodisiacs.

But if you're going for the candlelit dinner on your best china, it begins with a hearts of palm appetizer splashed with balsamic vinaigrette. Your entrée is broiled salmon, fluffy white rice, and white asparagus. Serve white wine, white zinfandel, or a rosé with dinner, but be light-handed. A little wine may help a romantic mood, but too much will drown it.

After a leisurely meal, dessert should be moved to the living room in case dinner partners didn't work out. This will give your guests another chance to move about and find Mr. or Ms. Right.

Raspberries, strawberries, and white chocolate hearts should be spread on a silver tray or be overflowing out of a crystal bowl.

I'm in the Mood for Love

During the cocktail hour you'll want music that's upbeat without being too loud or bouncy, something that your guests will be able to talk over. When dinner begins, switch to a more romantic selection, possibly classical. The soundtrack from *Somewhere in Time* by John Williams is lovely. After dinner, move into blues and soul—Billie Holliday or The Temptations.

Designed for Romance

Here's another chance to bring out those red linens you bought for the Christmas holidays. Soften it by topping the cloth with a white lace overlay or tying the table-cloth's corners with white lace trim.

Chips and Tips

Red roses are at their most expensive during this holiday. You can save money by creating your centerpiece out of hearts and cherubs left from your Christmas holiday decorations.

If you only have a white tablecloth, let it look more festive by sprinkling red rose petals on the cloth (white on a red cloth), or sprinkle heart-shaped confetti or candy hearts.

Other ideas for table decorations include setting a love sonnet or poem at each place setting to be read, adorning napkins with a rosebud or ribbons, using lace doilies under dry foods, and tying lace ribbons to the backs of chairs.

If you picked up red or white unscented candles at the after-Christmas sales, be sure to adorn your table and room with a selection of them in all sizes and shapes.

And most importantly when setting the stage for love, adjust your lighting to be soft and flattering, but bright enough so guests can see each other and their meal.

Tokens of Love

Even if Cupid's arrow still didn't make a connection, send your guests home with love in their hearts with a book of poetry, box of candy, CD of love songs, or small cherub.

Everyone will fall in love with this party.

Wearing of the Green

St. Patrick's Day is one of those holidays that makes you feel glad to be alive. Italian, German, Greek, or French … everyone is Irish this one day a year. So don your tweed cap and raise your glass in a toast because this party is pure fun from the land of green hill and dale.

To ask lads and lasses to come to your event, write your invitation on a box of Lucky Charms cereal.

Festive Facts

The leprechaun is an Irish fairy who looks like a small, old man. According to legend, leprechauns are aloof and unfriendly, live alone, and pass the time making shoes. They also possess a hidden pot of gold. Treasure hunters can often track down a leprechaun by the sound of his shoemaker's hammer. If caught, he can be forced (with the threat of bodily violence) to reveal the whereabouts of his treasure, but the captor must keep their eyes on him every second. If the captor's eyes leave the leprechaun (and he often tricks them into looking away), he vanishes and all hopes of finding the treasure are lost.

Shamrock Spread

While some consider corned beef and cabbage a must at any Irish event, here are a couple of other dishes you should consider to warm the cockles of their hearts and stomachs. Serve split pea soup, lamb stew, *bangers and mash,* or steak and kidney pie. Wash it all down with a mug of Guinness, a popular Irish beer.

Shindig Sayings

Bangers and mash is sausage and mashed potatoes, delicious for breakfast, lunch, or dinner.

No meal would be complete without warm soda bread, potato cakes or Irish oatmeal biscuits (cookies) washed down with a piping pot of tea. For particularly cold days, fortify yourself with a mug of Irish coffee.

If you are going to say Irish toasts, you'll need a wee bit o' somethin' to toast with, so try some Irish whiskey. Or, if you prefer something sweeter, Bailey's Irish Creme is delicious.

Eat, drink, and be Irish, 'cause everyone's Irish on St. Patty's Day.

Songs and Sass for Lads or Lass

It's difficult to walk into an Irish pub and not find a dart game going, or a few of the town's gents revelin' everyone with some tall drinks of Guinness and taller tales. Find the tenor in the group and start him singing "Danny Boy." There won't be a dry eye in the house. "McNamara's Band," "When Irish Eyes are Smiling," "Four Leaf Clover," "Irish Lullaby (Tura Lura Lura)," and "Galway Bay" are all great sing-along tunes.

If you have a good sport with a bald head, proclaim it the official Blarney Stone. Not a soul can leave the party until they kiss the Blarney Stone for good luck.

Not Only Kathleen Gets Taken Home

Give your green-wearin' guests a small gift to carry home with them without spending a rainbow's-end fortune. Charm them with four-leaf clovers, Irish linen handkerchiefs, or, for fun, a bar of Irish Spring soap.

You'll be enjoyin' the luck of the Irish to get invited to this Gaelic gala.

Chips and Tips

Print out the words to the songs for your guests so everyone can sing along.

The Least You Need to Know

➤ Plan party activities other than just football watching for those who aren't fans.

➤ At a matchmaking party, move the dessert course to another room in case all your guests aren't hitting it off.

➤ Serve a traditional Irish meal for St. Patrick's Day.

Part 6
Life's Big Events

From the moment we are born it seems that there's always a reason to celebrate. Whether you're planning the birth of a newborn, celebrating 50 years of marriage, or just rejoicing in a graduation, you'll always find that a party is the way to go.

In this part we were only able to touch on a few of life's finer moments. But use them as a guide when celebrating any of life's milestones that your friends or family have good reason to enjoy.

Chapter 23

From Tots to Teens—Total Party Plans

In This Chapter

➤ A party of comic book proportions that any child will enjoy

➤ Throwing kids a sports–theme party

➤ Visions of music videos dancing in their heads

One of the most exciting things about being a kid is that you look forward to your birthdays. It's always a time of friends and family gathering to celebrate. There is the fun of playing games and being entertained as the center of attention. Even though that might feel a little awkward, it is still, in the long run, an enjoyable experience for most.

So the next time you want to plan a big birthday blowout for your best buddy, your child, or a sibling, here are some ideas that will help you to make them memorable.

Comic Book and Cartoon Capers

Like it or not, kids spend a lot of time reading about superheroes and watching cartoon characters. While you might wish they would spend more time with schoolbooks, this fascination does provide a great theme for your kid's next party.

Although we'll be focusing on classic superhero celebrations, these ideas can be adapted to Barney, Pokémon, Power Rangers, Snoopy, Rugrats, Blues Clues, or whatever characters interest your child. You can find a huge variety of themed party goods at www.1800partyconsultant.com/1625.

Chips and Tips

Encourage your guests to dress as superheroes or villains, in their character capes, masks, cloaks, and monogrammed bodysuits.

While you only need to flash the bat signal to get Batman's attention, chances are you're going to have to take a little more traditional approach to gathering your gang of party guests.

If you or a pal can draw, you might want to include a sketch of a comic strip with the invitation printed in the dialogue featuring the images of popular superheroes, or even create your own superhero. Another zowie invite idea is to insert the invitation into a Superman, Batman, or Wonder Woman comic book, seal with a superhero sticker, label and mail at the post office.

A Daily Planet invitation fit for Superman.

208

Fueling the Power Packs

Even the Caped Crusader needs to eat to build his strength to battle the forces of evil. And luckily for you, your guests will eat these super treats faster than a speeding bullet. Serve dishes like Batman Burgers, Superman Subs, Mr. Freeze Milkshakes, Lois Lane Lasagna, or Peter Parker Punch.

Festive Facts

The superhero we know so well as Batman was first introduced to the world in May 1939. Batman is unique from most other superheroes because he has no super powers, but instead relies upon superior training and intellect (as well as some of the greatest toys ever invented). He lives in Gotham City and is the alter-ego of millionaire playboy Bruce Wayne.

Here's a heroic idea. If you prepare any of the dishes on the previous list or create your own, place a name card next to it along with an action figure of the character it is named for.

Good vs. Evil Games

It seems that the best games for a superhero party all need a show of strength. Whether your guest list is made up of superheroes and arch enemies or Batman and Spiderman, here are some great games to answer the age-old question: Who is really stronger? Try tug-of-war or arm wrestling. Or test their speed with relay races.

Chips and Tips

Instead of having your tug-of-war teams dumped in a mud puddle or swimming pool, draw a line on the ground. The first team over the line loses.

For a couch-potato party, rent a series of movies and television episodes featuring your favorite superheroes or set up a comic book or trading card swap.

Heroic Hangings, Super Swags, and Dyno-Decor

If your party focuses on a particular superhero, use the colors associated with him or her for your party's decor. When including a variety of them, you might want to use primary colors. With the exception of Batman, most of the other characters wear bright colors.

You also could give your room different looks. For instance, make your buffet table Gotham City. Use boxes to create a landscape of the city. Spray everything gray and black. Cut out windows and either put yellow paper behind the openings or shine a yellow light underneath. This will cause yellow light to come spilling out of the windows and will show off the hometown of the *Dark Knight*. If the boxes are sturdy, you then can use them to support different food platters so they will sit on different levels.

Shindig Sayings

The **Dark Knight** is another name for Batman.

You also could create a crystal-like ice structure of Superman's Fortress of Solitude, *The Daily Planet*, Gateway City, or any of a number of environs of various superheroes instead.

Make paper chains of comic-page strips and hang from corner to corner, over doorways, or on stair rails. Or cut pages from comic books and piece them together to create a tablecloth. Protect it with clear plastic or glass overlay.

Super Souvenirs

Select one of these comic or cartoon carry-homes: comic books, superhero T-shirts, videos, or trading cards.

Speaking of Sports

Football, basketball, golf, horseback riding, gymnastics, soccer, baseball—whatever the interest of your guest of honor, he or she will have a ball at this party. You can focus on one sport, several, or all.

Invite guest athletes to try out for their spot on this all-star team. Suggest they come wearing team jerseys or T-shirts to support their favorite team. Whatever you do, here's an invitation idea to ensure that your guests have their ticket. Create a ticket for the big game that lists the party information to give your guests admission to the celebration using a desktop publishing program or clip art.

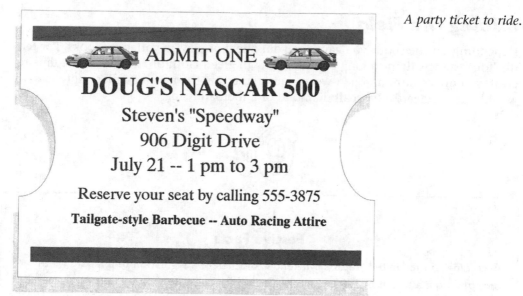

A party ticket to ride.

Concession Stand

No day at the ballpark or stadium would be complete without a trip to the concession stand or buying a hot dog from one of the stadium's barkers. "Get ya red-hot hot dogs right heah!!"

Put together a menu of Ballpark Franks, pretzels, popcorn, peanuts in the shell, minipizzas, cotton candy, or whatever food is a favorite.

Have your server (could be Dad) wear the hat and apron of the ballpark hawker and carry the food in a tray he wears around his neck.

Chips and Tips

Serve food in cardboard trays, bags, and boxes to duplicate game-style gourmet.

Are You Game?

If possible, organize everyone together in a short game of whatever sport you're focusing on. Many sports also have indoor or video versions.

If you have wide-open spaces and lots of folks, you might want to construct a field of play where guests go from game to game, or put together your own triathlon with running, jumping, and swimming (or whatever combination of activities you choose). Or watch filmed highlights or bloopers available at most video stores.

Chips and Tips

Check with your local toy store for safe versions of your favorite sport that can be played indoors.

Furnishing the Field

Depending on the sport, you can give your "field of play" a variety of looks. For tennis, for instance, drape a long banquet table in green cloth or felt. Use white tape to create a tennis court and open-weave fabric to create the net. A similar approach would let you create a baseball diamond or a football field.

Festive Facts

According to the United States Lawn Tennis Association, a regulation tennis ball, when dropped from a height of 100 inches on 4 inch thick concrete should bounce between 53 and 58 inches.

Whatever the theme, transform each table into something that suits the occasion. You can cover the table or just make a centerpiece to represent the sport. Party goods come in styles to represent almost every athletic pursuit.

Trophy Case

So that every guest goes home feeling like a winner, give blue ribbons, trophies, gym bags or sporting equipment.

Music Video Visions

Madonna or Michael Jackson, Brittany Spears or Ricky Martin—virtually everyone at one time or another has wanted to be a rock 'n' roller like these superstars. In order to give all those wannabes a shot at stardom, send out audition notices looking for the next rock 'n' roll star.

Be sure to tell all your guests they'll get a chance to strut their stuff on video so they should come prepared and in costume to perform their song of choice.

CASTING CALL

Do You Have What it Takes to be a Rock Star?

You sing the hits and we'll record your "audition" and you get to keep the tape.

You bring your own music or choose from one of our pre-recorded selection.

Stacy's Sweet Sixteen
September 6
8 PM to Midnight

473 Ises Road, Hartman
Please call to confirm your "audition."
(888) 555-1823

A music audition invitation.

Entertainers Eatery

To emulate a filming atmosphere, set up *craft services* to offer continuous refreshments to the cast and crew. The type of menu you choose, to be laid out on long banquet-style tables, can take several directions. You might want to do a "build a better burger" bar, serve favorite foods of pop stars or stick to the choices of your guest of honor.

Soft drinks and water in sports bottles are a must, but if you want to toast the guest of honor, put nonalcoholic sparkling cider on ice.

Decorate the birthday cake to look like a stack of CDs. Talk about "cutting a record!"

Shindig Sayings

The services provided by caterers on film sets are called **craft services**. The term is used for food-and-beverage providers for fashion shoots, film and video productions.

Festive Facts

Born December 2, 1981, Louisiana pop queen Britney Spears is always a hit with the teens. Serve her favorite foods—pizza, chocolate chip cookie dough ice cream, pasta, hot dogs, and Sprite—at your teen's next bash.

Quiet on the Set!

The entertainment at this party will be putting together video performances of the guest of honor and friends. They can choose to sing to backup music only, sing along with the recording star, or lip-synch completely. (Hey, it worked for Milli Vanilli!)

Shindig Sayings

Karaoke means "empty orchestra" and is a wildly popular entertainment concept originated in Asia. The guests sing to the recorded background music, reading the words scanning across a video screen.

A *karaoke* machine can usually be rented and is a big help in putting together this entertainment. You also can download songs on the Internet. Otherwise, contact a local DJ service—some of them will bring all the needed equipment with them.

If you can't afford to hire a company, you can achieve a similar filming effect yourself. While it will likely lack professional quality, you can more than make up by using your imagination. Use your camcorder to shoot a variety of backgrounds like a forest, ocean waves, or even just the kitchen, and project them on a large screen TV while your "star" is recording his or her tune.

Chips and Tips

Use a white board, chalkboard, poster board, or computer program to add titles and credit lines to the videos.

If the guests are old enough, let them make the videos themselves. In fact, if you can arrange to get several cameras, you could have a couple of "film crews" working at the same time. Then you can act as the executive producer for all the projects.

For fun that will last, set up a Web site where the videos can be uploaded. Since you never know who is checking the site, you might find one of your guests has been discovered. However, be sure to get permission from the participants and their parents before doing it.

Dressing the Set

Greet your rising stars with sound effects like screaming fans and sights of popping film flash bulbs. Get older or younger siblings and their friends to play these parts.

Hang inflatable musical instruments, a shimmer curtain, giant records, and miscellaneous electronic equipment and other props around the "studio" for effect.

It's a Wrap

Each guest should receive a copy of his or her own performance, of course. However, it would be nice if everyone could also receive a copy of the other guests' performances. This would likely have to be sent to them at a later date to allow time for duplication.

Chips and Tips

Great props for use in the videos can be found at garage sales, in attics, in thrift shops, and at swap meets.

The Least You Need to Know

➤ Show-of-strength and speed games are perfect entertainment at a superhero party.

➤ Organize a game of football, baseball, or even a triathlon where everyone wins at a sports party.

➤ Make sure everyone gets a copy of their own music video to take home.

215

Congratulations Goes To ...

Life's most important occasions are those that mark a milestone such as a 30th, 40th, 50th, or 60th birthday, or an anniversary celebration. Children grow from year to year celebrating not only birthdays, but receiving degrees starting at kindergarten and advancing as far as earning the title of doctor in their chosen field.

In this chapter you'll learn how to celebrate all of life's greatest milestones, from anniversaries to graduations. Remember, when it comes to parties, these are important and should be planned with the greatest care and love.

Love Is Still in Fashion

This anniversary party is a tribute to married love that, unlike fashion, has not faded through the years. This spoof on "ages ago" apparel and accoutrements such as the Nehru jacket, leisure suit, or slinky polyester flare-leg jumpsuit?

There will be giggles and guffaws when your guests receive an invitation explaining the gist of the celebration. Their mental wheels will start turning with illusions of how garish or gaudy their outfits will be.

It'll be a groovy invite baby!

A truly "un"-fashionable invitation.

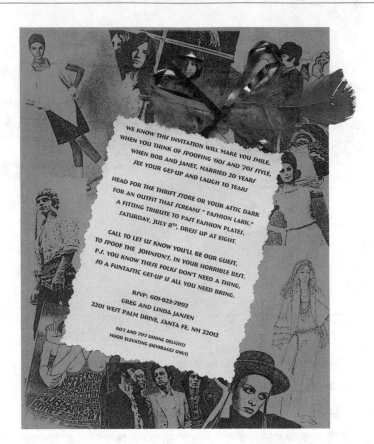

WE KNOW THIS INVITATION WILL MAKE YOU SMILE,
WHEN YOU THINK OF SPOOFING '60S AND 70S STYLE,
WHEN BOB AND JANET, MARRIED 20 YEARS
SEE YOUR GET-UP AND LAUGH TO TEARS

HEAD FOR THE THRIFT STORE OR YOUR ATTIC DARK
FOR AN OUTFIT THAT SCREAMS " FASHION LARK."
A FITTING TRIBUTE TO PAST FASHION PLATES,
SATURDAY, JULY 8TH, DRESS UP AT EIGHT.

CALL TO LET US KNOW YOU'LL BE OUR GUEST,
TO SPOOF THE JOHNSON'S, IN YOUR HORRIBLE BEST.
P.S. YOU KNOW THESE FOLKS DON'T NEED A THING,
SO A FUNTASTIC GET-UP IS ALL YOU NEED BRING.

RSVP: 601-823-7892
GREG AND LINDA JANSEN
2201 WEST PALM DRIVE, SANTA FE, NM 22012

60'S AND 70'S DINING DELIGHTS
MOOD ELEVATING (BEVERAGES ONLY)

Fad-tastic Food

Lay out a spread for your hungry "has-beens" including snacks reminiscent of the '50s, '60s, and '70s (or whatever was popular during the years you are highlighting): potato chips and onion dip, vegetables and dip, Hi Ho Crackers, Chex party mix, little pigs in the blanket, English muffin pizzas, Sloppy Joe's, and Swedish meatballs.

For decadent desserts dish out brownies, Toll House cookies, S'mores, Rice Krispies treats, root-beer floats, and hot fudge sundaes. Be sure your festive fuel station dispenses Boone's Farm apple wine, Yago sangria, Chianti (remember to save the bottles for candleholders), beer, and Coca-Cola in a bottle.

Chips and Tips

Add the addresses and phone numbers of thrift and resale shops on costume party invitations.

Far Out Funtime for Fashion Flops

While the sights alone should keep the gang occupied for a good long time, entertain them further by comparing stories about "when we wore this" and "did you really wear that?" or "I mean, what were we thinking?"

Show videos of that era and display photos of Twiggy's micro miniskirts, bell-bottoms, see-through shirts, fringy vests, disco duds, Jackie O. outfits, or Cher bare-belly chic.

Get hairy with Beatle bangs, Farrah flips, or *Mod Squad* Afros.

Let the guests of honor judge a funny and funky fashions show and award a "Best of the Worst" contest. Have one of your gregarious guests do the commentary and don't forget to get it on videotape!

Whether in platform shoes or go-go boots, your guests will want to get down and bop or boogaloo. Play the music of whoever rocked your world and have them dancing in the streets.

Decoration or Disaster

The fashion fads of the decades will dictate your party decorations and props. Forgotten fabrics and trims such as *tie-dye,* geometric, floral prints, neon colors, and florescents bring back the flourish of the '60s and '70s.

Hang both grungy and glamorous garments and accessories like hats, scarves, jewelry, and purses on the walls and stair rails. Drape them dramatically over furniture or from the ceiling. If you are going for a festive and fad-fashioned look, mix in tie-dyed balloons and streamers.

Light the site with a black light, lava lamps, and the ever-popular *pole lamp.* Deck the dance floor with a mirrored disco ball and don't forget to have a spotlight dance.

Chips and Tips

Try to dig up some pictures of the guests of honor in their far-out fashion flops.

Chips and Tips

Take a serious, sweet moment and honor the anniversary couple with a reverent anniversary waltz or the song they used for the first dance at their wedding.

Shindig Sayings

Tie-dye is a method of producing irregularly colored fabrics by tying the fabric with string before placing it in the dye.

Don't forget the velvet paintings of doe-eyed children or Emmett Kelly-like clowns. Plaster the walls with posters of concerts, movies, or sports events. Hang a few plants from macramé holders and decorate doorways with beaded curtains.

Fashion Favors and Stylish Souvenirs

These retro items are fab as favors and prizes for your groovy guests: tie-dye ties, love beads, or oldies tapes.

"G" Is for Graduation

One of the easiest ways to establish a theme is to build your entire party around the first letter of the key word. A graduation party is ideal for this initial concept, especially if student earned lettered degrees like BA, MA, or Ph.D. So now, when this great goal has been reached, it is time to spell "party" with a *G*.

Obviously, the first thing to do is explain the gist of your *G* gimmick and all of the guidelines for the gathering. The invitation you send will be clear as glass and with a grade A message. Whether you decide to be grand or generic, use gilded or gold lettering, on gift wrap or a garbage bag, be sure to go for the gusto.

Print the wording on a piece of 8½" × 11" goldenrod colored paper. Trim the edges with a fancy-edged scissors and run a metallic gold pen over the edges to create a gilded effect. Punch two holes 2 inches apart at the top center of the sheet, run an 8" length of gold ribbon through the holes and tie it into a bow. Mail in a 6" × 9" white envelope, addressed in gold ink, decorated with rubber stamp art or gold glitter. When you write "G is for Graduation" in big letters across the top side of the envelope, they will get the message.

Go for the Getups

Once the invitations have landed, your guests will be giving some thought to what they will bring as a G-rated gift. Some of the more gutsy guys and gals will even go all out and dress in *G* garb. Have a list of gifts and costume ideas handy. Guests can gussy up in gauzy gowns, groom's garments, gabardine, or gold lamé. Generous guests will give good or goofy gifts such as garters or galoshes. And won't the grad be grateful?

Graduation invitation.

> "G" is for graduation, and we're glad to say,
> John made the grade, it's a G-Letter day.
> We're going to gather, to salute the guy,
> Then he'll go to college, we'll say goodbye.
>
> Bring the whole gang over, in casual gear.
> We'll giggle and gab, and grab a beer.
> The gimmick is the letter "G."
> It's the gist of the whole party
>
> At the Johnson's, June 15th, 4-9 PM
> Please R.S.V.P. by June 10th 614-555-2823
> (Gag Gifts only-Goofy or Gaudy)
> Good Grub, too!

Goodies Galore

Go all out for this gastronomical gourmet; grilled or griddled food will be great. Along with a basic party menu of your choice, add the G-factor with a selection of snack items such as goose liver, Gorgonzola cheese, goat cheese, guacamole, Gruyère cheese, garlic bread, goldfish crackers, gefilte fish, Gouda cheese, gherkins, or grapes. Desserts including glazed donuts, gingerbread, gingersnap, guava, ganache, graham crackers, Granny Smith apples, gumdrops, and glorified rice will bring grins.

Let guests guzzle Gatorade, grape juice, ginger ale, and for the grown-ups, grasshoppers, gibsons, ginger beer, gin fizz, gimlets, gin, Galliano, Grand Marnier, or golden Cadillacs.

Chips and Tips

Guide your guests through the grub line with small signs labeling the G-rations.

Graduation Glorifications

From the gravel drive to your garage, through the house and out to the gazebo, glorify every *G* as you go. You could even make up signs that label each of these items with a big *G*. When decorating, use every shade of the color green, from green goblets to a gallon jug. Drape the walls with gossamer and gauze, or suspend grapevine from the ceilings.

Guessing Games and Go-Go Dancing

Plan a full gamut of games for the guests, including gin rummy, a game of touch football on the gridiron, or minigolf. They'll go gaga over scenes from *Grease* or *Gone with the Wind* flickering on the video screen, or the recorded sounds of George Gershwin, Glenn Gould, the Go-Gos, or Gale Garnet all gems of gold-record fame.

Toast the glittering grad with a gang of "great going"s, "go get 'em"s, and glad-handings in a glorifying gala toast.

Festive Facts

In the Middle Ages, a piece of spiced toast was often added to a drink for flavor. In the seventeenth century, legend has it that in Bath, England, a man took a glass of the public bath water his fair maiden was in, put a customary piece of toast in it and drank to her health. He then offered the glass to his friend, who declined the drink but said he would like the toast.

After the gaiety and giddyness subside and the graduate has said his good-byes to the guests, you can be guaranteed that your "*G*-whiz" get-together was great.

Go-Home Gifts and Gee Gaws

After Grandma and Grandpa have gloated over their grand-graduate's glory, it's time to send guests home with goldfish, gadgets or games.

House Sweet House

What a thrill it is to buy a new house, especially a first one. No matter if it is a bungalow for two or a condominium on the Cape, excitement and pride are abundant. It's an ideal time to plan a "come see the new house" party.

This theme is quite easy to produce and will be the ideal way to show a newly built house, a remodeled house, or a home with remodeling potential. Building and decorating materials like fabrics, wallpaper, carpet, and tile samples, fixtures, general construction equipment, and building materials will be the frame of the plan.

Here's a definite "key" to a successful housewarming/open house invitation. Send either new or used metal keys that have been sprayed gold and affixed to a sheet on which the party details have been printed. The invitation begins, "Our new home is always open to you."

A key to your home.

THE DOOR

TO OUR NEW HOME
IS ALWAYS OPEN TO YOU

Please come and take a
tour of our new home,
(now that's remodeled.)
We can't wait for you to see
what has kept us busy
every spare moment
for the last year.

Open House: June 15, 2001, 2-6 PM

2546 Ivy Lane, Brighton, CA 98002

RSVP: (Yes or No, Please) 201- 568-0431

Your presence is our gift of choice.

Casual Attire   **Light Refreshments**

Since this is the first time most guests will have been there, include clear directions or a map. Also be sure to festively decorate your home with balloons or a banner, so guests can be certain they have arrived at the right home.

Glad to Meet Ya!

Hang out the welcome sign, lay down the welcome mat, and put a light in the window. From the moment your guests step across your threshold, grace and hospitality are your hosting goals.

It's a particularly good idea to invite your neighbors to this open house. It's a great way to introduce yourself to them and you will surely win them over.

> **Party Pitfall**
>
> It is considered tacky to make mention of gifts, "registry" or preference information. If guests should ask about gifts, politely tell them that their presence is present enough.

> **Festive Facts**
>
> A younger couple moved into a quiet neighborhood comprised mostly of older retirees, and there was a little concern about if they would fit in with the quiet residents. The couple posted a notice on the communal mailbox inviting the neighbors to their open house. Seventy-five percent of them attended and many were thrilled to see their neighbors socially for the first time in years.

Decorative Dining

You may be hesitant to serve food in your new home. While understandable, it wouldn't be very hospitable. To increase the chances of your home coming out unscathed select menu choices made up of bite-sized pieces that don't require anything more than a toothpick and a napkin.

At open-house occasions, bar service might be too congested, and since guests may just pop in, serving light refreshments is the best option. A punch bowl, if spiked, should be kept in an area where youngsters won't be able to sample.

If you do have a bar, have it tended by someone who will keep it tidy and replenished when necessary.

Display and serve food in containers related to home improvement projects. Cover tables in dropcloths, blueprints or fabric swatches. Use tile samples as hot plates. Arrange hors d'oeuvres in a new paint tray. Put utensils and napkins in a new paint bucket.

Washington Did Not Sleep Here

At parties like this, you don't really need a lot of activities; holding a tour, telling the story of how it all came to be, and visiting will provide the entertainment.

Open houses are ideal situations to use name tags. Make yours from paint sample chips.

Play background music. You can choose light classical music or the music of ... sorry, have to say it ... the Carpenters.

Party Pitfall

Don't try to restrict your guests! That is, don't crowd them into your dining room or any other space too small to accommodate easy help-yourself food service. Leave that area for show and set up a makeshift feeding station in a locale that has room to move comfortably.

Don't Gild the Lily

If your home is newly built or remodeled, it is likely you will want your decor to stand out unobstructed. The addition of fresh flowers and low lighting (if in the evening) will be appropriate and provide ample ambience. Candles at night, if not in a position to get jostled, also would add an intimate tone to your housewarming.

Make posters of before photos and try to display them from the same angle they were shot for a before and after look.

Basically, incorporate your decorating tools (paint, swatches, samples, tiles) into your table design.

Chips and Tips

Give children smooth wood scraps to use as blocks, or pieces of fabric or paint swatches to make art projects with for their home or yours.

Classy Keepsakes

Besides your warmth send guests away with a home-decorating magazine, printed address labels or a potted plant.

Warm your new home with the love of family and friends, and you'll live there happily ever after.

The Least You Need to Know

➤ At an anniversary party, make sure to play the song the couple first danced to on their wedding night.

➤ The letters of the alphabet make the perfect plan for a graduation party.

➤ Decorate for a housewarming using all the leftover tools and supplies you used to get your house in shape.

Part 7

The Party's Ooooo-ver

When the last guest has left and the final candle has burned itself out, you probably wish you could just drop into bed yourself and call it a night. Unfortunately, your job has just begun. It is time to clean up and gather together the remnants of your party.

Chapter 25

Saying Good-Bye

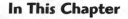

In This Chapter

➤ Casually and gracefully get your guests to leave

➤ Make the ride home easy for your guests

➤ Dealing with guests who drink too much

➤ Preparing for when the party just won't end

Guests are yawning, people are standing to stretch, the coffee cups have been drained, people are looking at their watches … the party's over. No matter how much fun it was or how successful, every party has to eventually end.

Know when to say when. However, when to say when does not mean that it's time to drop your veil of hospitality. In fact, this is probably when you have to turn on your charm the most. Saying good-night to your guests properly is just as important as how you welcome them, and in this chapter you'll learn how to send your guests home with style, making them beg for more.

Thaaaaat's All, Folks!

Once your party starts to show the unmistakable signs of being over—or preferably just before—stand and thank your guests warmly for coming. Something along the lines of, "It has been so much fun having you all here. We can't wait until we can have you over again," should just about do it.

If you're not comfortable doing that, try this. If the music has been playing all evening, turn it off. Don't refill anyone's drink or snack dish. Casually, but pointedly, pick up a couple of empty glasses and bring them into the kitchen. Unless your guests are very obtuse, they'll get the hint.

Should you need to be a little more pointed about ending the party, you might try to say, "You know, we'd love to have this go on all night, but we have to get the kids off to practice (or whatever seems appropriate) first thing in the morning, so I'm afraid we're going to have to call it a night."

Festive Facts

One couple gave a party that was so successful, their guests simply didn't want to go home. When it got to the point that the host and hostess couldn't keep their eyes open, they told the three couples who were still there to stay and enjoy themselves but they were going to bed. The next morning, not only had the guests not left, they brought the host and hostess breakfast in bed. By midmorning, they did finally depart, but only after helping their hosts to clean up.

If any of your guests make a sincere offer to help you clean up after your party, accept it. You will find that the extra help you have after a big party is a pure luxury, considering the time you have already put into your event.

Here's Your Dish, What's the Hurry?

As it gets closer to the party's end, start getting potluck dishes ready for guests to retrieve. Most people will come into the kitchen to collect their dishes, so have them all set to go—washed and dried, or covered if they contain food.

As guests are leaving, do a quick tour of your home to find items that they may have forgotten. If you do find any stray personal items, such as jewelry, clothing, or gifts, and know whom they belong to, give them a quick call that night to set their minds at ease and let them know the family treasures are intact.

If any guests have brought tables, chairs, or any other large equipment, be sure to arrange for help carrying the items to their vehicles. If borrowed items will be picked up the next day, be sure to label them with the owner's name and set them in a designated spot, separated from other items to be collected. If all items are marked, they will not be mixed up and mistaken for their look-alikes.

Chips and Tips

Little blank tags with strings work well to label bottles at B.Y.O.B. parties and can be found in most office-supply stores. They're very inexpensive and can be easily removed. However, remind your guests that in most states it is against the law to carry opened liquor bottles in the passenger compartment of one's car so that they remember to put them into their trunks.

Send the Party Home with Them

Unless you are throwing another party the next night, why not send some of the left-over food home with your guests?

Set out portions of leftover food in inexpensive individual see-through take-out containers available at party goods stores or your favorite deli. Your guests will be free to select and collect them on their way out the door.

Some hosts hand them out at the same time they present their guests with a souvenir. It all becomes part of the take-home package. Finish the presentation by adding a gift card reading "Goodies to Go for a Great Guest."

Watch Their Step

If your guests have to move out of your cozy, warm house into freezing snow mounds, it is certainly not your fault. However, you can do something to continue your role of the perfect host. In the cold-weather zones, guests may arrive in clear weather and after a few hours, leave to find their cars covered with snow. If snow is expected, hire a teen to shovel your walkways for your guests' easy departure.

Chips and Tips

Only give guests foods that will survive the drive well, especially if there could be any delay in re-frigerating the food once it gets taken home. Use careful judgment about any dairy-based foods.

Likewise, if stairs and sidewalks are slippery and icy, be sure to pour salt on them to make them safe for walking. Accompany any guest who might have a particularly difficult time maneuvering on ice. Make sure these areas are well lit.

In anticipation of cold weather conditions, recruit young drivers to be your official car starters and window scrapers. A bonus of doing this is that it may help you avoid a scene should one of your guests overindulge and you need to collect his or her keys.

If departing guests will have to dodge raindrops instead, enlist neighbor kids to shelter guests with umbrellas as they walk to their cars.

Party Pitfall

Salt can be painful when it gets on the paws of dogs or other animals who like to go outside. If you do have a dog, you might want to use sand in place of salt.

Emergency Road Service

Now and then, especially in unpleasant weather, a guest will have some car trouble. If you expect a crowd for your party, the odds are someone will experience one of these dilemmas, so have jumper cables, extra gasoline, phone numbers of all-night service stations, and a tire jack and pump handy.

Show Me the Way to Go Home ...

As a conscientious host, you will have taken certain precautions regarding overimbibing by any of your party guests. The problem might be decreasing due to strict DUI laws, but there is always the chance that someone will slip over the line without really trying.

Festive Facts

It only takes one 4-ounce glass of wine, one shot of alcohol, or one glass of beer more than once an hour to put most people over the legally intoxicated limit. In most states, the penalty is a fine, loss of one's driver's license, required "dummy driving" classes, and possibly community service or jail time.

To avoid liquor liability, here are some safety tips:

➤ Stay sober yourself so you can better judge your guests' sobriety score.

➤ Collect keys and coats from arriving guests and return them only to sober drivers at party's end.

➤ Encourage guests to carpool and observe the drinking, if any, of designated drivers.

➤ Never serve alcohol to anyone under age 21.

➤ Cut off the bar at a certain hour.

Okay! You have taken all the suggested precautions, done your duty as a discerning host, but a guest or two insists that they are fine and can drive. In general, if someone adamantly denies having had too much to drink, they probably have had too much to drink! Be prepared to drive them home, call a cab, or put them up for the night. That's why collecting car keys at the beginning of the evening is so important when serving alcohol.

As a last resort, your home may be turned into one! Before any festive function at your home, make a few preparations to turn your home into an impromptu bed-and-breakfast inn.

If you have guest accommodations, get ready with fresh bed linens, towels, new toothbrushes, travel-size deodorant, and open heat or air-conditioning vents. At the least, have pillows, sheets, and blankets on hand to make up a comfy resting place for sofa sleepers.

Providing these necessities will put you into the four-star B&B registry, for sure.

All of this extended hospitality will definitely put you in the Hosts' Hall of Honor as the "Host That Did the Most" to assure your guests' utmost comfort and enjoyment.

Chips and Tips

As a public service, a number of taxi companies around the country have adopted a program where they will take drunk drivers home for free. Check if there is such a program in your area.

Chips and Tips

Notify anyone who might be waiting for your delayed guest's arrival, such as parents, family members, roommates, or significant others, so they do not worry. This small gesture will mean that someone gets a good night's rest—even if it's not you.

Last-Minute Party Proofing

Police the party area, put away leftover foods, treat stains to prevent permanent damage, organize the kitchen, and, finally, shut down the house. Before you turn off the lights, though, take time to do the following:

➤ If smoking has been allowed in your home, walk through every room, empty the contents of ashtrays and wastebaskets into a garbage bag, take it outside, and douse it with water. This removes the possibility of someone having thrown a lit cigarette into the trash, where it may be slowly smoldering.

➤ Be sure all candles are completely snuffed out.

➤ Check your thermostat to be sure a guest has not adjusted it out of your home's comfort level.

➤ Dump all beverage glasses, so they won't provide refreshment for pets or early rising toddlers.

Festive Facts

A typical Midwestern snowstorm stopped the world and turned a group of guests at a small T.G.I.F. party into Weather Weekend Warriors at the host's home. While stranded until Monday morning, they made a game of survival that included cupboard and refrigerator raiding, setting sleeping schedules, fun and games guidance, shower scheduling, and group-therapy sessions to deal with cabin fever. After 60 hours of total togetherness, they came out smiling, still friends, and shouted "T.G.I.M.!"

Give Me a Ring

When you do head to bed, do not turn off your ringer in case there is yet another emergency that needs to be dealt with.

By this chapter, you have determined that your job of party host is indeed a big one, if you do it correctly. It won't be so hard, if you keep in mind the basic guidelines given in this book.

The Least You Need to Know

➤ Picking up is a graceful way to end the party.

➤ Supply guests with goody bags of leftovers.

➤ Make the trip from home to car safe for your guests.

➤ Be prepared for weather and automobile emergencies.

➤ Be tough on overimbibers.

Chapter 26

No Rest for the Weary ... Just Yet

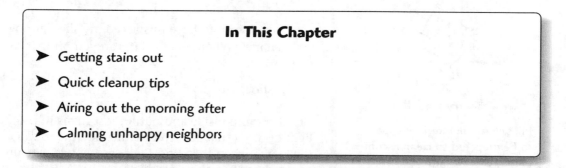

In This Chapter

➤ Getting stains out

➤ Quick cleanup tips

➤ Airing out the morning after

➤ Calming unhappy neighbors

Probably the last thing you want to do after you've said goodnight to the last guest and locked the doors is clean up. However, doing at least some of the work now will save you extra hours of work tomorrow trying to deal with the results of your not cleaning sooner.

Come on. If everyone pitches in, it'll be clean in no time, and this chapter will give you some of the quickest tips for making cleanup a breeze.

Out, Out, Damned Spot

Most stains can be cleaned if you handle them *immediately*. Keep commercial spot removers available to quickly tackle spills. Time is often of the essence in keeping a spot from becoming a stain. Here are just a few suggestions to help you get your favorite furnishings to look spotless again in no time:

➤ Blot, do not rub.

➤ Work from the outside of the spot in.

Chips and Tips

Do not use anything other than a white cloth or paper towel to remove stains. Some of the solutions may cause the dye in the cloth or towel to transfer to the stained area and compound your problem.

Party Pitfall

Ink will run before it disappears, so be prepared to clean it completely or wait until you can. Never put cleaning solution directly on an ink spot. Put it on a white cloth and blot.

➤ Do not overmoisten an area.

➤ For upholstery, check your care labels. If necessary, call in a professional as soon as possible.

➤ Machine-washable fabric: Pretreat with stain remover or liquid detergent. Wash in the warmest water suggested for your fabric.

A Silver Earring, a Sweater, and a Shoe?

Sometimes after a party you feel like you've been sent on a treasure hunt. Do these conversations sound familiar?

"Um, if you find a silver earring, it's mine."

"Okay."

"Hey, I seem to have misplaced my shoe during charades. When you find it, can you bring it to work?"

"A shoe? Ooookay."

Check around inside and out for lost items in the light of day. (That also gives someone time to call off the search when they find their earring had actually snagged itself on their sweater.)

They're Animals!

If you think you don't want to wake up to see the mess the morning after a party, think about your neighbors!

Make it a point to clean up any debris left outside your home or apartment before going to bed. Pick up empty bottles, cans, or glasses, and sweep away (and properly dispose of) cigarette butts.

You might want to hose down your patio or around the outside of your house to get rid of sticky residue or the makings of a buffet for bugs, and make sure any leftover food has been properly disposed of. You don't want to feed the neighborhood strays.

Sweep or vacuum all crumbs in your home as well. It's amazing how fast a trail of ants or roaches can smell food and start their own party.

Back by Popular Demand

One of the reasons you shouldn't mind going all out to cook for your party is that you have probably cooked enough to give yourself several other meals.

Leftovers are the leaping-off point for a number of incarnations of the same meal. However, the first thing you have to make sure of, before you do anything else, is that the food is safe to eat. If it has been sitting out at room temperature for two hours (starting from the time you took it out of the oven or removed it from the refrigerator) or more, throw it out.

There are whole cookbooks devoted to leftovers. When you plan your party menu, think about what you would like to do with the remainders.

Chips and Tips

Do not flush cigarette butts down your toilet. It can cause plumbing problems. However, do dispose of your butts in a jar filled partially with water to make sure you don't cause any fires. Since cigarette butts absorb water, be sure to have enough fluid to cover all the cigarettes.

Dealing with Dirty Dishes

Admittedly, no one wants to start rolling up their sleeves and diving into a huge pile of dirty dishes the minute a party ends. In most cases, the dishes can probably wait to be done in the morning. However, to avoid leftovers turning into cement or becoming a bug banquet, scrape the plates and rinse them. Either put them into a dishpan full of hot water, or put them into your dishwasher and set it to "Rinse and Hold."

Silverware should not be soaked. The minerals in your water can pit your silver or silver plating. Clean the silverware quickly, rinse thoroughly, and dry immediately. Rubber has been known to turn silverware dark, so don't let the silverware sit in your dish drain.

Chips and Tips

Even foods that have been sitting on ice or over heat are suspect. While it will lengthen the food's freshness, it's not the same as being in an oven or refrigerator. Remember, when in doubt, toss it out!

Taking Stock

One of the more mundane things you'll do in the aftermath of your party is to take inventory. It's amazing how many of your things "get lost" after a party ... and we're not talking about what your friends have left behind.

Festive Facts

Jessica was throwing her annual Christmas party at home, a gathering of 15–20 of her closest friends. The next day, during cleanup, she noticed that her toilet paper holder was missing. After searching the bathroom, all garbage bags, and even the hallway outside the bathroom, she determined it was gone. Years later she still wonders if someone could have taken off with her toilet paper holder.

That's why you will want to have an inventory of the items used before the party so you have something to compare your counts to after the fact. It only takes a few minutes, but those few minutes can save you big bucks.

Thirty Pieces of Silver

Before you throw out your trash, count your silverware. That's right, count the number of knives, forks, and spoons you are washing against the number you put out.

That means that you should set up an inventory sheet as you are setting up the party. It doesn't have to be fancy. Just keep track of everything you put out so you will know whether or not something accidentally landed in the garbage or the trash disposal.

Chips and Tips

Any dishes that contain starchy foods or eggs should be soaked in cold water. Hot water will only cause food to cook and harden more.

Rental Realities

It doesn't happen often, especially when you are working with a reputable rental company, but occasionally the number of itms you rented are not what is delivered. Usually your paperwork represents the order, not the delivery.

Count and inspect what you get. You may not have time to do it while the items are delivered (these people usually are working on a tight schedule), but take an immediate count and inspection when they leave. If there is a discrepancy or something is damaged, call the rental company immediately and notify them so they can adjust your paperwork. That means within the hour of receipt or you might be charged damages.

Try to get your delivery the day before your party instead of that day to allow time to obtain replacements. Also, be sure to check with the rental company to find out how they want their items prepared for return.

After the party, put all the rental items in one place and do a final inventory and inspection before they are returned.

Locking the Liquor Cabinet

If you were smart enough to find a liquor store that took unopened returns, match what you have against what you purchased.

In addition to what you are getting credit for, you also want to check your stock to see what liquors and mixers were consumed. This will help you to determine what you will need to restock for future parties.

Keep a pad by the bar. This will allow you to jot down the name of your guests' drinks so you'll know what to keep on hand in the future.

The Clean Team

When all else fails and you just don't want to deal with it, you can hire professionals to come in and put your house back in order. Some hosts say that this cleaning expense is just as important to the budget as food or entertainment.

As with hiring any type of vendor, get recommendations and be sure they're insured for any damage they may cause.

Party Pitfall

Diet drinks have a relatively short shelf life. Do not stock more diet soda than you can consume in, at most, a three-month period.

Festive Facts

One savvy hostess doesn't get her house deep cleaned until after a party. She says that with the right lighting and decor, guests don't notice her slightly soiled carpets and that her sofas need cleaning. However, after she has thrown one of her elaborate parties, a blind man can see the spots. When she calls in the professionals to clean her home, she gets to enjoy the freshly cleaned rug and sofas longer. When they start to get dirty months later, that's when she plans her next party.

The Morning After

Now that you've had a good night's rest, aren't you glad you did a lot of the chores last night? In addition to saving yourself a lot of work, you also can now find the coffee pot. Even more important is what you won't find this morning ... bugs.

Let's Clear the Air

It's amazing how quickly your home can take on the fragrance of a brewery. Imagine how your house would smell if you hadn't dumped the alcohol and taken out the trash last night.

Air conditioning or not, open your windows and give your house a nice shot of fresh air.

After all remaining stains have been treated, dust your carpets and upholstery with baking soda, leave it for a half hour, and then vacuum, or apply a commercial product designed to eliminate odors.

Festive Facts

Make sure your air-conditioning filters are clean so that your system can work optimally.

Thanks, Neighbor!

This thank you is best delivered in person and attached to something. If you have made noise, added traffic to the area, or did anything else that might have affected your neighbors, it's a good and proper idea to thank them.

If you have an extra dessert, bring it over. Were there bouquets of flowers that are still fresh and beautiful? Share them with your neighbor.

Whatever grumbling may have taken place the night before will end when your neighbor finds you standing in front of them with a warm smile and a big present.

The Least You Need to Know

➤ Do some cleanup before you go to bed to avoid unnecessary problems in the morning.

➤ Dispose of leftovers if you're not certain of their freshness.

➤ Tackle spots before they become stains.

➤ Return any rentals or lost items as soon as possible.

Chapter 27

Making Memories

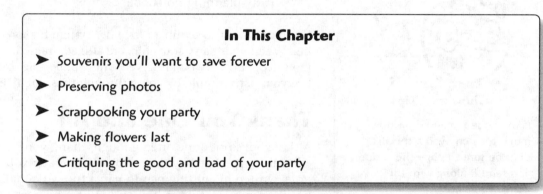

In This Chapter

➤ Souvenirs you'll want to save forever

➤ Preserving photos

➤ Scrapbooking your party

➤ Making flowers last

➤ Critiquing the good and bad of your party

You have taken care of all of the final details of your party; everything is returned, put away, or discarded. As you look around, there is little to remind you of the festivity. Events are divided into three main parts: the anticipation, the event itself, and the memory of it. Each of these stages is important to the total enjoyment of the event. The memory could easily fade away if not for some creativity and effort on your part.

In this chapter, you'll learn how to make those special memories from your party come to life. You'll learn how to make souvenirs that your guests will cherish, scrapbook, and preserve those fabulous pictures.

Souvenirs to Save

It would be a real shame if you did not have documentation of the party beginning at the moment the idea was sparked to this last memorable effort. Hopefully you have saved all the pieces of the party puzzle so the final picture will be complete. To create this trip down memory lane, collect samples of all the souvenir items, printed pieces, and photos from the party:

➤ Invitations, RSVP cards, name tags, and place cards

➤ Greeting cards

➤ Party documents including menus, recipes, and party tips

➤ Guest book

➤ Press clippings or announcements

➤ Photos

➤ Paperware such as napkins, coasters, goody bags

➤ Ribbons, confetti, streamers, small labels, or signs

➤ Game sheets

➤ Gift wrap

➤ Party-planning notebook

You might want to set up a file-folder system for sorting. When your party souvenirs are affixed, framed, mounted, or otherwise preserved, you will be able to relive your party simply by going through these archives.

Thank You One and All

Although it's not done often enough, thank-you notes are truly appreciated by the recipients. A thank-you note, written by putting pen to paper (no, an e-mail is not the same), is still the best and most proper way to express your thanks.

How Thoughtful

Before discarding any garbage or paper, check your trash for gift cards. It is important that each card is matched with the correct gift or marked as to what the present was so you'll be able to write an appropriate thank-you note.

If guests bring gifts that do not have a card, keep a pad handy to make note of them so they can be acknowledged later. A simple note like "flowers—Chuck and Connie" or "red wine—Barry and Luann" will save you a lot of aggravation. That is particularly true when you remember that John and Linda had a gift when they walked in, but you can't remember what it was.

The thank-you note doesn't have to be elaborate, but it should be sincere and specific. You want to thank your friends not only for their presents, but their presence as well. Use the following as a guideline:

Dear Laura and Don,

We just wanted to thank you so much for the terrific coffee-table book on fads. It surely has brought back a lot of memories. We hope you know that as much as we will delight in your gift, we enjoyed having you share our anniversary more. Thanks for being such great friends.

Warmly,

Mary and Jeff

As soon as possible, process film taken at the party and send a photo of your guest along with the thank-you note.

A photo taken of the guest of honor opening the gift is also a very personal addition to the giver's thank-you note.

Remember, even friends who did not bring a present deserve a warm thank-you note to acknowledge how much you appreciated the gift of their company.

Chips and Tips

If you are a habitual host, you may want to include a photo from a past party in which the invitee appears with your party invitation. Your friend will be reminded of the fun he has had at your parties and will be more eager to attend your next.

Good Job!

If you had a vendor—caterer, florist, entertainer, event planner—who did an outstanding job, tell them. Do it in writing. These letters are often used with their promotional materials, as referrals, or sometimes when applying for their industry awards. When sending the note, be sure to check on the correct spelling of contact names and be specific regarding whom you are thanking at the company.

When you take the time to say "good job," you can be assured that the rewards will come. Suddenly you may become a V.I.P. (Very Important Person) with them. They're likely to say to their employees when you shop there again, "Take care of Ms. Stearn, she's one of our best customers."

It only takes a moment to write a sincere note of appreciation.

Dear Bob and Kelly:

Just wanted to take a quick minute to say how happy we were with everything you sent over for our party last night. Everyone was so impressed with the designs that "hit just the right note" to tie into my musical theme. You know you'll be hearing from us soon.

Thanks again.

Best regards,

Pat and Jerry Mangino

I Was So Proud

You know we often remember to thank friends and strangers, but how often do we give thanks to our family? Everyone pitched in to make the evening a success. Shouldn't you let them know how special it was for you? Drop each of your helpers an individual note.

Dear Celia,

Your dad and I just wanted you to know how proud we were of you last night. You handled taking care of your chores with the "Love Boat" party so well. We couldn't have asked for a better "first mate!" Thanks again, honey.

We love you,

Mom and Dad

Can you just imagine how that will increase your child's esteem to get a note like that? It also will help the next time you want an assistant. Everyone benefits from being recognized and appreciated—even your kids.

Focus on Photos

A professional photographer will usually get your party proofs back in a short time, but due to the cost, you probably plan to send copies only to the honored guests as a special memento.

If you are the chief photographer, have extra copies made as souvenirs for guests or your scrapbook.

There will always be invited guests who are unable to attend, and who will love to receive photos as a consolation. Depending upon the relationship, these photos can be sent loose in an envelope, collected in an album, or framed as a collage.

Valued Video Visions

Watching a video of the event is not only fun for those who did not attend the party, but it will delight you, too. So often the hosts miss out on party happenings while they are busy attending to their guests. With a video documentation you can catch up on activities and video *ops* that were going on while you were elsewhere.

Once you have your rough video, computer programs can aid you with editing, adding titles, special effects, and music to complete it. Try to duplicate the videos for your special guests.

Scrapbooking Your Party Memories

You don't have to be an artist to preserve your party photos and mementos with *scrapbooking* methods, but it will look as though you are one. Hundreds of supplies, materials, and instructions for this photo phenomenon are available in craft, party, stationery, and department stores. There are even specialty shops and Web sites that sell a full line of scrapbooking goods.

Classes in scrapbooking are given in many retail outlets as well as in community education programs. There are even direct-sales companies that conduct home parties that include a demonstration, hands-on instructions, and the sale of scrapbooking supplies. Lettering applied with a calligraphy pen or special gel-roller pens in dot-connecting style, rub-on letters, or computer fonts can be part of the total design.

Create scrapbooks for each member of the family. As they get older and move off, they'll especially cherish the time you took to document their life.

Chips and Tips

Sending thank-you notes to kids is a great way for them to learn the importance of thanking people and the thrill you can get from being appreciated.

Chips and Tips

If you are more of a "shutterbad" than a shutterbug, you will be wise to ask a guest or two who are more skilled to share some of their good snaps.

Shindig Sayings

Photo and video **ops,** or opportunities, are those "Kodak Moments" when once-in-a-lifetime situations or occurrences take place.

Shindig Sayings

Scrapbooking is a technique used to artistically affix photographs on acid-free paper pages. Once glued in place, the fancy photos are enhanced with a variety of trimmings and clarified with captions, names, and dates written in special inks. The most important part of this concept is that all materials should be acid free, protecting photos from discoloration and deterioration.

Party Pitfall

Be extremely careful when working with priceless photos, as they can be so easily damaged. Make color copies instead. These can be cut, and if you make a mistake, you can simply have another color copy made.

Once you get into archiving old family photos, you can add to the historic value and supplement your projects with information about the period when the photos were taken. Consult history books, the Internet, or interview elderly relatives or others who would be familiar with the events chronicled. They will not only enjoy the attention, but will give you additional personal recollections. These "I was there" accounts will greatly add to the value you and your ancestors will put on these documents in the years to come.

You can print out titles and captions on your computer, but your handwriting, even if not pretty, will become a charming and personal part of these pages.

Why not take a crash course in scrapbooking before the next party you give or attend?

Other Photo Finishes

There are other very meaningful ways to preserve photo memories, ones that are more readily displayed. You need not have dozens of framed photos standing around your home, tacked to your bulletin board, or held on your refrigerator with a novelty magnet. Try some of the following ideas for preserving photos, from a party or otherwise:

➤ Arrange photos in a flip album in order of occurrence at the party, adding captions.

➤ Party photos can be attractively arranged under a glass table top. Add confetti, streamers, the invitation, and any other mementos that will complete the party picture.

➤ Cut and decoratively arrange party photos as if for a scrapbooking page, glue to a painted wooden or plastic serving tray, and cover with a decoupage finisher, like Mod Podge. Add a coat of lacquer for durability.

Extra, Extra Party News

Your party photos could head up the feature story on a hard-copy newsletter. Put out a publication reporting the party highlights in article form. Let your guests (and those who couldn't make it) read all about it! With a desktop-publishing program and a little know-how, you can produce a newsletter that could win the Party Pulitzer. Remember to preserve a copy of your newsletter in your acid-free scrapbook.

The same newsletter that looks so great in an instant copy version will be just as attractive when it arrives in the e-mail boxes of your Internet invitees. As quick as a click or keystroke, the text and graphics go flying out, reaching their destination in seconds.

How about putting your party on the Web? At no cost, you can create a Web site that recounts each facet of your gem of a gala. By simply posting your e-mail newsletter as a Web page and adding a photo album, you can star your guests at their party best. When you create your festivity finale in cyber-space, it can either be accessed by your guests with a password, or the party animals of the Web world can surf in and sign your guestbook.

Memories Medley

You've written thank-you notes, scrapbooked your party photos, and edited videotapes, so now it's time to utilize some other methods of preserving mementos of your grand gala.

You have an invitation, so beautiful or clever that it must be enjoyed beyond today, the impressive congratulatory telegram from the President, napkins in the shape of a jukebox—all too dear to discard or destroy. But how, other than in a strong box, can you save these treasured things?

You can artfully arrange and frame these three-dimensional pieces of memorabilia in a glass-covered shadowbox. You can include photos in the design to tell the story in more detail. Add small decorative items, party favors, gift cards, and even special recipes served at the party. All these things can be stored and displayed in the shadowbox.

When you are satisfied with the look of your celebration collection, the box can be hung on a wall,

Party Pitfall

Magnetic albums can seriously damage your photos. It is wise to attempt to carefully remount these treasures on acid-free pages.

Party Pitfall

A beautiful memento like a collage tray should not be used for actual serving, or the photos may be damaged by spills and cleaning. If given as a gift, gently remind the recipient of this.

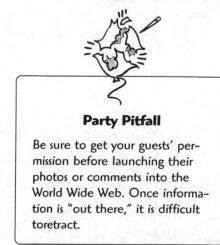

Party Pitfall

Be sure to get your guests' permission before launching their photos or comments into the World Wide Web. Once information is "out there," it is difficult to retract.

stood up on a shelf or laid on a table to serve as an everlasting reminder of an unforgettable party.

Forever Flowers

Did you have the most incredible floral centerpieces or buffet table arrangement? You can add this flower preservation idea to your memory medley.

Craft stores sell silica gel crystals, a fresh flower preserver. Just by placing your party petals into this compound you can remove the moisture and retain the original color and texture for many years.

Another alternative is to take the flowers and hang them in a dark, arid space and leave them for several weeks to create dried flowers.

There are companies that will freeze-dry your arrangements as well. Although the results are spectacular, it is a fairly expensive process and is usually reserved for flowers like bouquets or corsages that mark landmark events.

Party-Planning Critique

If you have produced your party with a planning notebook, journal, or software program, you have the perfect tool for analyzing the entire event process, including a critique of each phase. These records will prove invaluable in your future party plans.

The memories you've created will last not only your lifetime, but they will be used by others to sneak a glimpse into your existence. So party and remember them well.

Chips and Tips

A shadowbox can be purchased at craft stores or any place that sells picture frames.

Chips and Tips

You can grow a big surprise for your guest of honor. Save a few roses from the garden-fresh arrangement used at her party and propagate a cutting (check with a gardening expert or on the Internet for how-to). In a few months you can present her with small rose bushes loaded with sentiment.

The Least You Need To Know

➤ Save all your party mementos.

➤ Be generous with your thank-you notes.

➤ Share your photos and videos with friends and family.

➤ Scrapbooking is the best way to preserve photos.

➤ Journal and critique your party.

Party-Planning Worksheets

We've talked about a number of worksheets throughout the book, forms that will make it easier for you to plan your bash. Here you'll not only find two different budget sheets, one for a basic party and one for a major party, but you'll find a party-planning worksheet and a vendor sheet.

Use them wisely and well when planning your party.

Budget Breakout for a Basic Bash

	VENDOR	PHONE	DATE	STYLE/COLOR	COST	NOTES
Printed Pieces						
Invitations:						
Printing					$	
Special Envelope or packaging					$	
Addressing (calligraphy)					$	
Postage					$	
SUBTOTAL					$	
Seating cards, name tags:						
Hand crafted					$	
Purchased					$	
Lettering					$	
Napkins					$	
SUBTOTAL					$	
Food						
Do-it-yourself					$	
Server					$	
Caterer					$	
Cake					$	
SUBTOTAL					$	
Beverage						
Do-it-yourself (liquor, soda & supplies)					$	
Bartender Service (server plus supplies)					$	
SUBTOTAL					$	

	VENDOR	PHONE	DATE	STYLE/COLOR	COST	NOTES
Rental Items						
Linens					$	
Tables, chairs					$	
Dishes, glasses, serving dishes, flatware					$	
Lights, candles holders					$	
Photo and Video equipment					$	
SUBTOTAL					$	
Party Goods						
Paper and Plastic serving					$	
Table Covers					$	
Napkins, Place Mats					$	
SUBTOTAL					$	
Decor						
Room Decorations:						
Balloons					$	
Banners, Signs					$	
Props, effects					$	
Lights					$	
SUBTOTAL					$	
Table Decorations:						
Flowers					$	
Candles					$	
Centerpieces					$	
Napkin Holders					$	
SUBTOTAL					$	

continues

251

Budget Breakout for a Basic Bash   (continued)

	VENDOR	PHONE	DATE	STYLE/COLOR	COST	NOTES
Entertainment						
Band					$	
DJ					$	
Music (soloists, chamber groups, etc.)					$	
Specialty (clowns, face painters, etc.)					$	
SUBTOTAL					$	
Favors, Prizes and Gifts						
Imprinted					$	
Novelty					$	
Hand Crafted					$	
Gifts					$	
SUBTOTAL					$	
Other						
Party Planner					$	
Set up and tear down					$	
Servers					$	
Valet					$	
Photographer					$	
Videographer					$	
Costume or Special Dress					$	
Yard Spray					$	
Outdoor Restrooms					$	
SUBTOTAL						

	VENDOR	PHONE	DATE	STYLE/COLOR	COST	NOTES
For Weekend Events						
Transportation					$	
Welcome baskets/ bags in hotel rooms					$	
					$	
SUBTOTAL						
GRAND TOTAL					$	

Budget & Breakdown for a Blowout Bash

Event Name: _____   **Event Date:** _____

	VENDOR	PHONE	DATE	STYLE/COLOR	COST	NOTES
Imprinted Goods						
Save the Date Card						
Copy and Art Submitted						
View Proof						
Pick-Up						
Mail						
Invitations						
Envelopes						
Reply Card						
Reply Envelope						
Maps						
Copy and Art Submitted						
View Proof						
Pick-Up						
Calligraphy						
Pick-Up						
Mail						
Menu Cards						
Name Tags						
Other						

	VENDOR	PHONE	DATE	STYLE/COLOR	COST	NOTES
Specialty Items						
Mementos						
Napkins						
Glassware						
Other						
Other						
Rentals						
Chairs						
Tables						
Chair Covers						
Tablecloths						
Napkins						
Dishes						
Glasses						
Flatware						
Chafing Dishes						
Serving Bowls						
Serving Pieces						
Candle Holders						
Cooking Equipment						
Coffee Urn						
Bars						
Beverage Serving Pieces						
Other						
Other						

continues

255

Budget & Breakdown for a Blowout Bash (continued)

	VENDOR	PHONE	DATE	STYLE/ COLOR	COST	NOTES
Tents						
A/C						
Heat						
Flooring						
Permits						
Other						
Food						
Do-it-yourself						
Hors D'oeuvres						
Appetizer						
Main Course						
Dessert						
Caterer						
Hors D'oeuvres						
Appetizer						
Main Course						
Dessert						
Beverage						
Soft Drinks & Mixers						
Liquor						
Garnishes						
Staff						
Servers						
Bartenders						

	VENDOR	PHONE	DATE	STYLE/COLOR	COST	NOTES
Staff						
Uniforms/Costumes						
Entertainment						
Band						
# of Musicians						
Continuous Breaks						
Attire						
DJ(s)						
Dancers						
M.C.						
Attire						
Specialty Acts						
Attire						
Other						
Other						
Copywriting						
Specialty songs, poems, etc.						
Tech. & Operations						
Sound						
Lighting						
Special Effects						
Generators						
Audio/Visual						
Sanitary Facilities						
Technicians						

continues

Budget & Breakdown for a Blowout Bash   (continued)

	VENDOR	PHONE	DATE	STYLE/ COLOR	COST	NOTES
Tech. & Operations						
Cell Phones						
Beepers						
Walkie Talkies						
Decor						
Balloons						
Flowers						
Props						
Plants						
Runners						
Draping						
Signs/Banners						
Other						
Other						
Maintenance						
Set-Up/ Tear Down Crew						Arrive: Depart:
Cleaning Crew						Arrive: Depart:
Landscape						Arrive: Depart:
Pest Control						
Trash Bins						

	VENDOR	PHONE	DATE	STYLE/COLOR	COST	NOTES
Transportaion						
Cars						
Limos						
Buses						
Cabs						
Airplane						
Train						
Valet						
Other						
Photography						
Portrait						Arrive: Depart:
Informal						Arrive: Depart:
Disposable Cameras						Arrive: Depart:
Videography						
Event Planner						
Gifts						
Accommodations						# of Rooms
Amenities Baskets						Amt.
Goodies Baskets						Amt.
Other						

Party-Plan-at-a-Glance Worksheet

Occasion: _____

Date _____ Time _____

# of Guests _____ (Are these friends, family or other?)

_____

Hosts: _____

Guest(s) of Honor: _____

Special Date _____ (actual date of anniversary, birthday, etc. if different)

Location (if other than home): _____

_____

Theme or Motif: _____

Invitation Ideas: _____

_____

Food Ideas: _____

_____

Beverage Ideas: _____

_____

Rental equipment needed: _____

_____

_____

Activities and game ideas: _____

_____

_____

_____

Entertainment or talent needed: _____

_____

_____

Favors/gifts needed and ideas: _____

_____

_____

Photography/Videography: _____

Room Decorations: _____

_____

_____

Table Decorations: _____

_____

Special Details (place cards, name tags, napkin holders):

_____

_____

Servers or Helpers: _____

_____

Special Preparations: _____

_____

At-a-Glance Vendor Contact Sheet

Make copies of this sheet to record contact information for all vendors used for your party. Place sheets in your planning notebook or carry them with you for quick reference. In addition, create a separate planning worksheet for each vendor. Use pencil or erasable ink.

Company _____ **Service** _____

Contact _____ Title _____ Phone _____

Address _____ City _____ State ___ Zip _____

Cell # _____ Emergency # _____ Fax # _____

E-Mail _____ Web site _____

Comments, Hours, etc.: _____

_____

Company _____ **Service** _____

Contact _____ Title _____ Phone _____

Address _____ City _____ ST ___ Zip _____

Cell # _____ Emergency # _____ Fax # _____

E-Mail _____ Web site _____

Comments, Hours, etc.: _____

_____

Company _____ **Service** _____

Contact _____ Title _____ Phone _____

Address _____ City _____ ST ___ Zip _____

Cell # _____ Emergency # _____ Fax # _____

E-Mail _____ Web site _____

Comments, Hours, etc.: _____

_____

Company _____ **Service** _____

Contact _____ Title _____ Phone _____

Address _____ City _____ ST ___ Zip _____

Cell # _____ Emergency # _____ Fax # _____

E-Mail _____ Web site _____

Comments, Hours, etc.: _____

_____

Party–Planning Product and Service Resources

Hit of the Party Reference Materials and Web Sites

The following resources will be helpful to you in planning your next party. If you have a problem finding a party resource, contact the authors by phone, fax, e-mail, or regular mail for free and prompt assistance.

> **Phyllis Cambria and Patty Sachs**
> **Party Plans Plus**
> 208-439-1595(phone and fax)
> www.partyplansplus.com (Web site)
> partyinfo@partyplansplus.com (e-mail)
> P.O. Box 8146, Fort Lauderdale, FL 33310-8146

On our Web site you will find custom party plans, the most complete list of party resources, publications, videos, products, tapes, and party planning links. You'll also be able to sign up for our free newsletter. Here's few titles you'll find in our bookshop: *Pick A Party: The Big Book of Themes and Occasions*, *Pick A Party Cookbook*, and *Don't Wait—Celebrate!* by Patty Sachs and *Fun and Frugal Party Plans,* by Phyllis Cambria.

Advanced Graphics   Life-size cardboard stand-up figures of celebrities—and custom orders of your own celebrity. Phone 510-432-2262 or fax 510-432-9259.

Design-A-Foam   More than 250 polystyrene shapes available. Great for centerpieces and props. Check out the Web site at www.design-a-foam.com, or call 770-698-9060.

First Impressions   Unusual mailing containers, tubes, and envelopes. Call 612-424-9508 for a catalog.

Gamblers General Store   Hundreds of items for casino-style events. Phone 1-800-322-2447 or fax 702-366-0329.

Glow-Year Glasses   The hottest item for New Year's, graduation, or even wedding parties. Glow-in-the-dark plastic eyeglasses announcing the year, (the center 00s are the lenses) available with imprinting from Brainstorm Novelties 206-985-0737.

GreatEntertaining   For hundreds of theme party goods for all occasions at www.GreatEntertaining.com.

Greetings from the President!   To receive greetings for special occasions such as births, milestone birthdays, or anniversaries write: The White House Greetings Office OEOB, Room 39, Washington, D.C. 20502, Contact: Director Reminder Service.

Kid Stuff   They're not just for kids. Super selection of bags and boxes and toys for theme parties. Call 1-800-677-4712, or on the Web at www.kidstuffnet.com.

Panache Party Rentals   For exquisite linens, call 1-800-307-2789, or visit the Web site at www.linenswithpanache.com. Ships worldwide.

Rick's Movie Graphics   Hundreds of posters and publicity photos from movies and recording industry that are perfect for vintage or current theme-party decor. Call Rick at 1-800-252-0425.

Panic Button by Memory Makers   Here's the "Panic Button" everyone talks about pushing. It can be easily attached to any computer keyboard. Ideal for favor or promotional giveaway. Call 360-734-9506 Web site is www.panicbuttons.com.

Party Table Tops Video   Theme and holiday table decor. Step-by-step instructions for linens, tableware, centerpieces, lighting and candle effects, place cards and party favors both hand-crafted and improvised call (612) 392-4544 or http://buy.at/tabletops.

Rhode Island Novelty   Almost limitless assortment of toys, games, and novelty items Web site at www.rinovelty.com or call 1-800-528-5599.

SongSendsations   Custom songs and parodies written, recorded on cassette, and sent with a framed song sheet. Listen at http://listen.at/songsendsations. Phone/Fax 815-846-7460.

Sounds Abound On All Hallow's Eve   A masterful mix of evil audio. Great for parties, campfires, role-playing events, and other events. Check it out at doglake.com.

Theme Parties in a Box   Hundreds of theme party goods delivered in a box to your door (www.1800partyconsultant.com/1625).

Theme Party Web Sites

www.americanmusicclassics.com   This site will help you build your own CDs of hit songs for a very reasonable fee.

www.ampop.com   AMC's American Pop for your trivia-game questions and answers.

www.hisurf.com   Give your guests their Hawaiian names—a great name-tag idea. Also lots of resources for your luau.

holidays.net   A complete and neat site for every holiday's party plan.

Wine Selection

You should always choose a wine according to your own tastes. However, if you are looking for suggestions on the most recommended wines, here is your list:

Beef	Red Wine: Cabernet, Merlot, Pinot Noir
Canapes/Appetizers	White Wine: Chablis, Chardonnay, Chenin Blanc, Dry Riesling, Sauvignon Blanc, White Riesling, White Zinfandel; Champagne
Cheese, mild	White Wine: Chablis, Chardonnay, Chenin Blanc, Dry Riesling, Sauvignon Blanc, White Riesling; Blush Wine: White Zinfandel; Champagne
Cheese, strong	Red Wine: Beaujolais, Cabernet, Merlot, Pinot Noir, Zinfandel; White Wine: Dry Riesling, Sauvignon Blanc
Dessert, heavy	Red Wine: Port; White Wine: White Riesling
Dessert, light	White Wine: Chardonnay, Chenin Blanc, Sauvignon Blanc; Blush Wine: White Zinfandel; Champagne
Lamb	Red Wine: Cabernet, Merlot, Pinot Noir
Pasta w/red sauce	Red Wine: Beaujolais, Cabernet, Chianti, Merlot, Pinot Noir, Zinfandel
Pasta w/white sauce	White Wine: Chablis, Chardonnay, Chenin Blanc, Dry Riesling, White Riesling
Pork	White Wine: Chablis, Chardonnay, Chenin Blanc, Dry Riesling, White Riesling; Blush: White Zinfandel
Poultry	White Wine: Chablis, Chardonnay, Chenin Blanc, Dry Riesling, Sauvignon Blanc, White Riesling; Blush Wine: White Zinfandel

Seafood	White Wine: Chablis, Chardonnay, Chenin Blanc, Dry Riesling, White Riesling; Blush Wine: White Zinfandel
Veal	White Wine: Chablis, Chardonnay, Chenin Blanc, Dry Riesling, Sauvignon Blanc, White Riesling; Blush Wine: White Zinfandel

Calendar of U.S. Holidays

Holiday	Date
New Year's Day	January 1
Three Kings' Day (Christian observance)	January 6
Elvis Presley's Birthday	January 8
Winnie the Pooh Day	January 18
Martin Luther King Jr. Day (observed)	Third Monday in January
Groundhog Day	February 2
Lincoln's Birthday	February 12
Academy Award Nomination Announcements	Second Tuesday of February
Valentine's Day	February 14
Chinese New Year	Second new moon after winter solstice
National Earmuff Day	March 13
President's Day (observed)	Third Monday in February
Fat Tuesday/Mardi Gras	Tuesday before Ash Wednesday
Ash Wednesday	46 days prior to Easter
Washington's Birthday	February 22
Ides of March	March 15
St. Patrick's Day	March 17
First Day of Spring	On or near March 21
Palm Sunday (Christian observance)	One week before Easter

continues

continued

Holiday	Date
April Fools Day	April 1
Daylight Savings Time Begins	First Sunday in April
National Barbership Quartet Day	April 11
Take Our Daughters To Work Day	Fourth Tuesday of April
Passover (Jewish observance)	According to Jewish calendar
Good Friday (Christian observance)	Friday prior to Easter
Easter Sunday (Christian observance)	First Sunday after first full moon after Vernal Equinox
Earth Day	April 22
Secretaries' Day	Wednesday in the last full week of April
May Day	May 1
Cinco de Mayo	May 5
Mother's Day	Second Sunday in May
Mr. Rogers (Neighborhood) Day	May 22
Memorial Day	Last Monday in May
Tonga Emancipation Day	June 4
Flag Day	June 14
Father's Day	Third Sunday in June
First Day of Summer	On or near June 21
Independence Day	July 4
National Blueberry Muffin Day	July 11
Bastille Day	July 14
Friendship Day	First Sunday of August
Don't Wait—Celebrate Week	Second full week of August
Labor Day	First Monday in September
Grandparents Day	First Sunday after Labor Day
National Pet Memorial Day	Second Sunday of September
First Day of Fall	On or near September 21
Rosh Hashanah	According to Jewish calendar
Yom Kippur	According to Jewish calendar
Good Neighbor Day	Fourth Sunday of September
Columbus Day (observed)	Second Monday of October
Bosses Day	October 16
Mother-in-Laws Day	October 23
National Dessert Day	Second Thursday of October

Holiday	Date
Daylight Savings Time Ends	Last Sunday of October
Halloween	October 31
All Saints' Day	November 1
Sadie Hawkins Day	First Saturday of November
Election Day	First Tuesday after first Monday in November during even numbered years
Veteran's Day	November 11
Ramadan America	Depends on the sighting of the moon in North
Thanksgiving	Fourth Thursday in November
AIDS Awareness Day	December 1
Hanukkah (Jewish Observance)	According to Jewish calendar
Underdog Day	Third Friday of December
Christmas	December 25
Kwaanza (African-American observance)	December 26–January 1
New Year's Eve	December 31

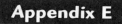

Glossary

a cappella   To sing without instrumental accompaniment.

alfresco   Taking place in the open air. It usually refers to dining outside.

angel hair   Spun white fiberglass that is draped on the tree like tinsel. It was used to give the tree a soft glow.

aphrodisiac   Anything that arouses sexual desire. Foods like oysters, chocolate, and asparagus are considered aphrodisiacs.

bangers and Mash   Sausage and mashed potatoes, delicious for breakfast, lunch, or dinner.

barbie   The Australian term for barbecue.

beluga caviar   Caviar taken from beluga sturgeon that swim in the Caspian Sea. The sturgeon has large eggs about the size of pearls that come in shades from gray to black.

benvenuto   "Welcome" in Italian.

blinis   Small buckwheat pancakes usually served with sour cream and smoked salmon or caviar.

boilermaker   A drink made by dropping a shot glass of bourbon into a mug of beer and immediately gulping it down.

brainstorm   To discuss ideas openly and spontaneously, being careful not to tell any one person that their idea is wrong or dumb.

B.Y.O.B.   Bring Your Own Bottle is a potable potluck concept where each guest brings his drink of choice, alcoholic or nonalcoholic.

canapés   Small pieces of bread or crackers that are covered with a tasty topping like cheese, meat, fish, or vegetables. The toppings can be slices or mixed into a spread.

Cantonese   The mildest and most common kind of Chinese food. It tends to be more colorful, less spicy, and is usually stir-fried.

challah   A traditional Jewish bread, airy and rich with eggs.

charger   A large, round platter that is put under a dinner plate as decoration.

chicken marsala   Chicken cutlets in marsala wine sauce.

collage   An artistic composition consisting of materials such as cloth, photos, or paper pasted on a surface. Picture frames that hold several small photos are also called collages.

compote   Fruit that has been cooked or stewed in syrup.

cornucopia   A goat's horn depicted as overflowing with fruit, flowers, and corn, signifying prosperity and abundance. Today, basket-weave, ceramic, or clay cornucopias are filled and used in table decor.

craft services   The services provided by caterers on film sets.

crepe   The French word for "pancake."

crostini   "Little toasts" in Italian. These thin slices of Italian bread are brushed with olive oil and toasted.

crudité   Raw vegetable pieces that are used as appetizers and often served with a dip.

Dark Knight   Another name for Batman.

family style   All the serving dishes are placed on the table and guests are expected to help themselves.

flambé   Flaming, or a flaming dessert.

flan   A Spanish baked custard coated in caramel. It is also known as *crème caramel* in France and *crema caramella* in Italy.

fondue   Taken from the French word *fonder*, which means "melt." There are three basic types of fondue. One is a hot melted cheese-and-wine combination into which guests dip bread. The second is hot oil in which bite-sized pieces of meat are dipped and cooked. The last type is a heated chocolate sauce that makes the perfect dip for fruit or cake.

goalposts   Used in football, this marker looks like the letter *H* with the crossbar raised about a quarter of the way down from the top instead of in the middle.

hala-kahikis   "Pineapples" in Hawaiian.

haute cuisine   Using the finest ingredients, prepared to perfection. Often the dishes are complicated and rich.

hero sandwich   A sandwich made with French or Italian bread, cold cuts or salads, and toppings (lettuce, tomato, onions, peppers, olives, etc.).

hospitality staffing services   An employment service that screens a waiter and guarantees a certain level of expertise.

idea meeting   A brainstorming session.

Karamu   The feast that is held to celebrate Kwanzaa.

karaoke   "Empty orchestra." This popular entertainment concept originated in Asia. The guests sing to the recorded background music, reading the words as they scan across a video screen.

kasha varnishkes   Roasted buckwheat grouts with bow-tie noodles and chicken stock.

kikombe cha Umoja   The unity cup used during Kwanzaa to toast ancestors.

kugel   Baked pudding with raisins, nuts, and sweet spices.

liqueurs   A variety of sweet alcoholic beverages usually made from fruits, nuts, spices, flowers, or essential oils.

liquid smoke   Used as an additive in barbecue dishes; gives off a taste similar to cooking with an open flame.

loukoumades   Fried honey puffs.

madelaines   Small sponge cakes shaped like shells and dusted with powdered sugar.

Mandarin   A Chinese cuisine that is wheat-based (as opposed to rice-based), consisting of dumplings, baked and steamed breads, and noodles. Mandarin-style meals usually include vegetable dishes, soups, tofu (soybean curd), and fish. The food is mild in taste.

Mazao   Fruits and vegetables served during Kwaanza.

Mkeka   The straw mat upon which all ceremonial objects are placed during the Kwanzaa ceremony.

Muhindi   An ear of corn used during Kwanzaa to represent the offspring (children) of the stalk (father of the house).

Murphy's Law   Whenever something can go wrong, it will go wrong.

nouvelle cuisine   "New cooking" in French. This movement, which started in the 1970s, took meals away from the heavy sauces and rich foods toward smaller, lighter, and fresher dishes.

on-site caterer   One that works only at a hotel, banquet hall, restaurant, or private club.

on-site manager   Someone who will show up on the day of your event to coordinate and oversee everything from the setup to the teardown and cleanup.

open or hosted bar   Guests are not expected to pay for any of the drinks available at the bar. An open bar can last the duration of the night, or for a set time period.

ops   Photo or video opportunities are those "Kodak Moments" when once-in-a-lifetime situations or occurrences take place.

party pool   Cohosting a celebration by planning it with another friend or relative means that you share in the guest list, the work, and the expenses.

pasta e fagioli   Kidney bean and macaroni soup.

phone chain   You call one guest and ask her to call one or two others whose names and numbers you supply.

pole lamps   were popular in the '50s and '60s. They consisted of a pole that extended from the ceiling to the floor with three or more lamps on it that could be adjusted to shine in different directions.

portafogli di vitello con porcini   Breaded veal cutlets stuffed with porcini mushrooms.

potato latkes   Potato pancakes made with grated potatoes, eggs, onions, matzo meal, and spices.

prosciutto   Italian for "ham."

raffia   A twinelike string made from the fiber of palm trees.

raincheck   Given when a catalog item or an item on sale is not available. That means when the stock has been replenished, you will automatically be sent the item.

RSVP   *Repondez, s'il vous plait* in French, or "please respond" in English.

scrapbooking   A technique used to artistically affix photographs on acidfree paper pages. Once glued in place, the fancy photos are enhanced with a variety of trimmings and clarified with captions, names, and dates written in special inks.

self-mailer   An invitation printed on heavy stock and folded either in half or in thirds, affixed with a seal, addressed, stamped, and mailed.

shooter   A drink made in a shot glass. The recipient drinks the liquor in one gulp, sometimes washing it down with lime or lemon.

skimmer   A flat straw hat.

smorgasbord   A Scandinavian buffet offering a variety of hot and cold foods.

sommelier   The steward or servant in charge of wines.

Spanish moss Dense greenish-gray strands of plant matter which usually attaches itself to tree trunks and branches by wiry roots.

S.W.A.P. A team who shows up at your party ready to work.

Szechwan A Chinese cuisine that is liberal in the use of garlic, scallions, and chilies. Consequently, it's the spiciest Chinese food available. Chicken, pork, river fish, and shellfish are all popular items.

tie-dye A method of producing irregularly colored fabrics by tying the fabric with string before placing it in the die.

top shelf or **call brand** A liquor that is more expensive than a bar brand and usually asked for by brand name.

trattoria An outdoor Italian restaurant.

uplights A light that resembles a wide tube, or a can with the light bulb inserted at the bottom so that it can shine up.

videographer A photographer who uses moving pictures to tell a story.

V.I.P. Very Important Person.

wahines "Women" in Hawaiian.

wallflowers People who are so shy that they remain on the sidelines at parties and dances and resemble wallpaper flowers.

white elephant A gift that is usually a joke gift, or something the giver may have received in the past and doesn't want or need.

Index

THE COMPLETE IDIOT'S GUIDE TO

Arts & Sciences | Business & Personal Finance | Computers & the Internet | Family & Home | Hobbies & Crafts | Language Reference | Health & Fitness | Personal Enrichment | Sports & Recreation | Teens

IDIOTSGUIDES.COM
Introducing a new and different Web site

Millions of people love to learn through *The Complete Idiot's Guide*® books. Discover the same pleasure online in **idiotsguides.com**–part of The Learning Network.

Idiotsguides.com is a new and different Web site, where you can:

* Explore and download more than 150 fascinating and useful mini-guides—FREE! Print out or send to a friend.

* Share your own knowledge and experience as a mini-guide contributor.

* Join discussions with authors and exchange ideas with other lifelong learners.

* Read sample chapters from a vast library of *Complete Idiot's Guide*® books.

* Find out how to become an author.

* Check out upcoming book promotions and author signings.

* Purchase books through your favorite online retailer.

Learning for Fun. Learning for Life.

IDIOTSGUIDES.COM • LEARNINGNETWORK.COM